PRESERVED LOCOMOTIVES
OF BRITISH RAILWAYS

TWENTY-FIRST EDITION

Ian Beardsley

Published by Platform 5 Publishing Ltd,
52 Broadfield Road, Sheffield, S8 0XJ, England.

Printed in England by The Amadeus Press, Cleckheaton, West Yorkshire.

ISBN 978 1 915984 26 5

© 2024 Platform 5 Publishing Ltd, All rights reserved. No part of this publication may be reproduced or transmitted in any form or by any means electronic, mechanical, photocopying, recording or otherwise, without prior permission of the publisher.

▲ 4900 Class 4-6-0 4930 HAGLEY HALL crosses Oldbury Viaduct with the Severn Valley Railway's 15.40 Bridgnorth–Kidderminster Town on 15 April 2023. *Peter Foster*

CONTENTS

Foreword to the Twenty-First Edition 4
Introduction 4
1. **Steam Locomotives** 6
    1.1. Great Western Railway & Absorbed Companies' Steam Locomotives 7
    1.2. Southern Railway & Constituent Companies' Steam Locomotives 20
    1.3. London Midland & Scottish Railway & Constituent Companies' Steam Locomotives 32
    1.4. London & North Eastern Railway & Constituent Companies' Steam Locomotives 48
    1.5. British Railways Standard Steam Locomotives 62
    1.6. War Department Steam Locomotives 67
    1.7. United States Army Transportation Corps Steam Locomotives 71
    1.8. New Build Steam Locomotives 72
    1.9. Replica Steam Locomotives 77
2. **Diesel Locomotives** 81
    2.1. London Midland & Scottish Railway Diesel Locomotives 82
    2.2. Southern Railway Diesel Locomotives 84
    2.3. British Railways Diesel Locomotives 84
    2.4. Experimental Diesel Locomotives 112
    2.5. Civil Engineers' Diesel Locomotives 113
    2.6. New Build Diesel Locomotives 114
    2.7. Replica Diesel Locomotives 114
3. **Electric Locomotives** 115
    3.1. Pre-Grouping Design Electric Locomotives 115
    3.2. Pre-Grouping Design Battery-Electric Locomotive 116
    3.3. LNER Design Electric Locomotives 116
    3.4. British Railways Electric Locomotives 117
4. **Gas Turbine Vehicles** 122
5. **Multiple Unit Vehicles** 124
    5.1. Steam Rail Motor 125
    5.2. Petrol Electric Railcar 125
    5.3. SR Petrol Railcar 125
    5.4. GWR Diesel Railcars 127
    5.5. British Railways Diesel Multiple Units 127
    5.6. Southern Railway Electric Multiple Units 147
    5.7. Pullman Car Company Electric Multiple Units 149
    5.8. LMS & Constituent Companies' Electric Multiple Units 150
    5.9. LNER & Constituent Companies' Electric Multiple Units 151
    5.10. British Railways & Post Privatisation Electric Multiple Units 152
    5.11. Eurostar Units 166
6. **Grimsby & Immingham Light Railway Tramway Cars** 167
Appendix I. List of Locations 168
Appendix II. Abbreviations Used 173
Appendix III. Weights & Measurements 173
Appendix IV. DMU, DEMU and EMU Type Codes 174
Appendix V. Private Manufacturer Codes 175

Front Cover Photograph: On 16 April 2022, Class O2 0-4-4T W24 CALBOURNE approaches Ashey with the Isle of Wight Steam Railway's 11.58 Smallbrook Junction–Wootton service. **Nick Gilliam**

Back Cover Photograph (top): 50035 Ark Royal poses beneath the signal gantry on the approach to the Severn Valley Railway's Kidderminster Town terminus on 26 September 2023. **Tom McAtee**

Back Cover Photograph (bottom): Derby Lightweight DMBS 79900 pulls away from Quorn with the Great Central Railway's 15.32 Rothley–Loughborough Central on 22 April 2023. **Tom McAtee**

FOREWORD TO THE TWENTY-FIRST EDITION

Welcome to the 21st edition of the Platform 5 guide to preserved standard and broad gauge locomotives of British Railways.

Almost two years have elapsed since publication of the previous edition of this book, and those two years have seen many movements of preserved locomotives and multiple unit vehicles between locations. They have also seen more diesel and electric locomotives and multiple unit vehicles move into preservation, including the first examples of Classes 91, 313, 315 and 321. As with previous editions of this book, it should be noted that for some diesel and electric locomotives and multiple unit vehicles that are currently considered to be "preserved", this status is not irreversible. At least several locomotives that have appeared in previous editions are no longer included, having been either returned to commercial operation or scrapped.

It is the intention that all surviving steam, diesel and electric locomotives and multiple unit vehicles that once belonged to, were operated in revenue-earning service by or were built to the designs of British Railways, its predecessors or its successors will be listed either in this book or the Platform 5 "Narrow Gauge Steam Locomotives of Britain & Ireland" book if classed as "preserved", or otherwise in the annual Platform 5 "British Railways Pocket Book No. 1: Locomotives" or "British Railways Locomotives & Coaching Stock" bound volume. There is inevitably some overlap between this book and the last two titles, particularly with "heritage" diesel and electric locomotives that continue to see use on the main line, such as Deltic D9000 "Royal Scots Grey" and electric locomotive E3137/86259 "Les Ross/Peter Pan", and some multiple unit vehicles that are now in industrial service, which can be found in all three. Similarly, ambiguity surrounding the status of some locomotives and multiple unit vehicles associated with Locomotive Services has led to them being listed in all three of these books in the past. Following an objective review, we have decided that only those that are truly "preserved" or are unlikely to return to the main line during the currency of this book will now be included here.

Finally, one of the most common queries we receive concerns former BR diesel locomotives that are not listed in this book. Please be aware that some former industrial locomotives carry "fake" numbers and are not actually ex-BR. Such locomotives can be found in publications that deal with former industrial locomotives. As a general rule, if a "preserved" locomotive carrying a BR number cannot be found in this book, it is likely to be an impostor!

ACKNOWLEDGEMENTS & CONTACT DETAILS

Thanks are extended to all those individuals and railways who have assisted in the updating of this book. In particular, the author would like to thank readers who have contacted us with amendments to the 20th edition. As always, the author is not infallible and would very much welcome notification of any corrections or updates to this book of which readers have first-hand knowledge.

Please send comments or amendments to the Platform 5 address on the title page or by e-mail to updates@platform5.com (telephone 0114 255 2625).

The book is updated to information received by March 2024.

Ian Beardsley

UPDATES

Updates to this book are published in Platform 5's monthly magazine, **Today's Railways UK**, which is the only magazine to carry official Platform 5 stock changes. **Today's Railways UK** is available from good newsagents or on a direct subscription (see the inside front cover of this book).

INTRODUCTION

This book contains details of all preserved standard (4' 8½") and broad (7' 0¼") gauge locomotives and multiple unit vehicles that have been in the ownership of, built to the designs of, or operated under the jurisdiction of, the British Railways Board, its constituents or its descendants, in revenue earning service or on the main line. Locomotives solely used in workshops and depots are excluded, as are those solely built for export. Apart from the odd exception, only locomotives or multiple unit vehicles that are no longer in the ownership of descendants of the British Railways Board or commercial railway companies are included.

Also included are War Department "Austerity" steam locomotives and those steam locomotives built for the United States Army Transportation Corps that are currently resident in Great Britain. Many of these saw use on Great Britain's main line railways, particularly during World War II.

GENERAL NOTES

This book has been divided into several main categories, namely steam locomotives, diesel locomotives, electric locomotives, gas turbine vehicles, multiple unit vehicles and trams. Further details applicable to each category are given in the introductory paragraph of each section.

Notes regarding technical details of the various locomotives and multiple unit vehicles can be found in the introductory paragraphs for each section. A few details are, however, consistent for each section, these being:

NUMBERS

All numbers carried by the locomotives and multiple unit vehicles included are shown, except in the case of any temporary identity changes for filming or similar events and numbers carried when in industrial use, unless they are still carried. Details are also given of the current identity if it has not been carried previously. For each section, numbers are given in chronological order wherever possible, or other logical order if more appropriate. Where a logical order is used, please refer to the introductory paragraphs of each section for further details.

NAMES AND CLASS NAMES

Unofficial class names and names bestowed after preservation are shown in inverted commas. Names bestowed after preservation are only shown if carried at the time of publication or immediately prior to the commencement of an ongoing overhaul, however. Official names are shown without inverted commas and irrespective of whether they are still carried. If more than one official name has been carried, then the most recent is shown, with those previously carried given as a footnote/s. If, however, an earlier official name is carried at the time of publication then this is shown and details of other official names carried are given as a footnote/s. Where different names are (or have previously been) carried on either side of a locomotive, this is indicated with a forward slash.

LOCATIONS

The location where the locomotive or multiple unit vehicle is normally to be found is given. Fuller details of locations in Great Britain, including OS grid references, are provided in Appendix I. List of Locations. It is not uncommon for locomotives and multiple unit vehicles to visit other locations for operation or display, however. Where such visits are of a medium- or long-term nature, the locomotive or multiple unit vehicle is shown at the host location, with a footnote giving its home location. In particular, a number of Class 08 shunters belonging to preservation groups can spend long periods on hire to main line operators. Locomotives and multiple unit vehicles also often spend varying periods away for mechanical attention. Where this is of a long-term nature, the location where this attention is taking place is shown as a footnote.

A small number of steam locomotives are permitted to work trains on the national rail network. Such locomotives invariably spend long periods away from their home bases undertaking such duties.

(N) denotes a locomotive or multiple unit vehicle that forms part of the National Collection; a group of historically important items that have been saved as a representation of the nation's railway heritage. The National Collection is maintained under the direction of the National Railway Museum and most items are usually to be found at the museum's York headquarters or at the Shildon outpost. National Collection items can sometimes be found in use or on display at other locations.

GAUGE

All locomotives and multiple unit vehicles are standard gauge (4' 8½") unless stated otherwise.

BUILD DETAILS

For each locomotive, the builder, works number (if any) and year of build are given. Private builder codes can be found in Appendix V.

1. STEAM LOCOMOTIVES

GENERAL

Almost from the birth of the railways until the 1960s, steam was the principal form of propulsion, its rapid decline in the 1960s being the impulse for much of the preservation movement. Generally, steam locomotives are arranged in numerical order of the British Railways number, except for very old locomotives that did not receive numbers in the series pertaining at nationalisation in 1948, which are listed at the end of each pre-nationalisation company section.

WHEEL ARRANGEMENT

The Whyte notation is used to describe steam locomotives and diesel shunting locomotives with coupled driving wheels. Where their wheels are connected via coupling rods, the number of leading wheels are given, followed by the number of driving wheels and then the trailing wheels, with each of these numbers being separated by a dash. Suffixes are used to denote tank locomotives as follows: T – side tank, PT – pannier tank, ST – saddle tank, WT – well tank. For example, a 2-6-2T would be a tank locomotive with two leading wheels, six driving wheels and two trailing wheels. A VB suffix is used to denote a locomotive with a vertical boiler, while a G is used for geared locomotives. Where a locomotive's wheels are connected by means other than coupling rods, w is used to indicate the number of powered axles. For example, a 4wVBGT would be a vertical-boilered geared tank locomotive with four powered axles.

DIMENSIONS

These are given in imperial units for steam locomotives as follows:

Boiler pressure   In pounds force per square inch (lbf/sq in).

Cylinders   Cylinder dimensions. The diameter is given first, followed by the stroke. (I) indicates two inside cylinders, (O) two outside cylinders, (V) two vertical cylinders, (3) three cylinders (two outside and one inside) and (4) four cylinders (two outside and two inside).

Wheel diameters   These are given from front to back, ie leading, driving, trailing.

Weights   These are given in full working order.

TRACTIVE EFFORT

This is given at 85% boiler pressure to the nearest 10 lbf for steam locomotives. Phillipson's formula has been used to calculate these as follows:

TE = $(0.85d^2snp)/2w$

where   TE = tractive effort in pounds force;
         d = cylinder diameter (inches);
         s = piston stroke (inches);
         n = number of cylinders;
         p = maximum boiler pressure (lb/sq in);
         w = new driving wheel diameter (inches).

BRAKES

Steam locomotives are assumed to have train vacuum brakes unless otherwise stated.

VALVE GEAR

Unless stated otherwise, valve gear on steam locomotives is assumed to be inside the locomotive, except Walschaerts and Caprotti gears, which are assumed to be outside. Exceptions are LMS-design 5MT 4-6-0 44767 with outside Stephenson valve gear, LNER (ex-GER) N7 0-6-2T 69621 with inside cylinders and Walschaerts valve gear, and various 4-cylinder GWR 4-6-0s with inside Walschaerts valve gear and rocking shafts for the outside cylinders.

GWR

1.1. GREAT WESTERN RAILWAY AND ABSORBED COMPANIES' STEAM LOCOMOTIVES

GENERAL

The GWR was the only one of the Big Four companies that existed at the time of the grouping, when a number of other smaller companies were absorbed. These were virtually all in Wales and included the Cambrian Railways, Cardiff Railway, Rhymney Railway and Taff Vale Railway. Prior to 1923, the GWR had also absorbed smaller concerns at various dates.

NUMBERING & CLASSIFICATION SYSTEM

The locomotives of the absorbed companies were given the lower numbers and GWR classes the higher numbers. Instead of arranging classes in blocks, the GWR adopted a system whereby the second digit remained constant within a class, eg the 0-6-2Ts numbered 5600–99 continued with 6600–99. Sometimes, earlier numbers were filled in, eg 5101–99 continued with 4100–99. Classes were always denoted by the number of the first member of the class to be built, which was not always the lowest number in the series. GWR locomotives were not renumbered by BR on nationalisation.

The listing here is presented in locomotive number order rather than class number, except that locomotives of the same class are listed together. Locomotives with no GWR number are listed at the end, whilst the surviving broad gauge locomotive is listed at the beginning.

POWER CLASSIFICATION & ROUTE RESTRICTION SYSTEM

The GWR adopted a power classification letter code system, which ranged from A to E in ascending order of power. Certain small locomotives that were below group A were said to be unclassified and the "Kings" were classed as "special", being higher than "E". BR power classifications are also shown in brackets in this section.

The power classification letter was shown on the cabside on a coloured spot showing the route restriction. In ascending order of restriction these were as follows: Yellow, Blue, Red, Double Red. Where no restriction is specified, locomotives were unrestricted.

▶ An example of a Great Western route restriction spot (the red spot) and power classification ("D") on 4073 Class 4-6-0 5080 DEFIANT. **Ian Beardsley**

1.1.1. BROAD GAUGE LOCOMOTIVE

The fledgling Great Western Railway was laid to a gauge of 7' 0¼", as directed by engineer Isambard Kingdom Brunel. A number of other companies in the South-West and South Wales also adopted this gauge. However, in 1846 the Parliament's Gauge Commission recommended that 4' 8½" gauge be used as standard in the future, and by 1892 all broad gauge lines had been converted to standard gauge.

SOUTH DEVON RAILWAY — 0-4-0VBWT
Built: 1868.
Wheel Diameter: 3' 0".   **Cylinders:** 9" x 12" (V).

GWR	SDR		
2180	151 TINY	South Devon Railway (N)	Sara 1868

1.1.2. STANDARD GAUGE LOCOMOTIVES

No. 12 — 4wVBGT
Built: 1926. Returned to manufacturer after three months' service.
Boiler Pressure: 275 lbf/sq in.   **Weight:** 20 tons.
Wheel Diameter: 2' 6".   **Cylinders:** 6" x 9" (I).
Valve Gear: Rotary cam.   **Tractive Effort:** 7200 lbf.

GWR		
12	Cholsey & Wallingford Railway	S 6515/1926

TAFF VALE RAILWAY CLASS O2 — 0-6-2T
Built: 1899. 9 built. Survivor sold by GWR 1929.
Boiler Pressure: 160 lbf/sq in.   **Weight:** 61.5 tons.
Wheel Diameters: 4' 6½", 3' 1".   **Cylinders:** 17½" x 26" (I).
Valve Gear: Stephenson. Slide valves.   **Tractive Effort:** 19870 lbf.
Power Classification: B.   **Restriction:** Blue.

GWR	TVR		
426	85	Keighley & Worth Valley Railway	NR 5408/1899

TAFF VALE RAILWAY CLASS O1 — 0-6-2T
Built: 1894–97. 14 built. Survivor sold by GWR 1927.
Boiler Pressure: 150 lbf /sq in.   **Weight:** 56.4 tons.
Wheel Diameters: 4' 6½", 3' 8¾".   **Cylinders:** 17½" x 26" (I).
Valve Gear: Stephenson. Slide valves.   **Tractive Effort:** 18630 lbf.
Power Classification: A.   **Restriction:** Yellow.

GWR	TVR	WD		
450	28	205–70205 GORDON	Gwili Railway (N)	Cardiff West Yard 306/1897

PORT TALBOT RAILWAY — 0-6-0ST

Built: 1900/01. 6 built. Survivor sold by GWR 1934.
Boiler Pressure: 160 lbf/sq in.
Wheel Diameter: 4' 0½".
Valve Gear: Stephenson. Slide valves.
Power Classification: A.
Weight: 44 tons.
Cylinders: 16" x 24" (I).
Tractive Effort: 17 230 lbf.
Restriction: Yellow.

GWR	PTR		
813	26	Severn Valley Railway	HC 555/1901

POWLESLAND & MASON — 0-4-0ST

Built: 1903–06. Survivor sold by GWR 1928 for industrial use.
Boiler Pressure: 140 lbf/sq in.
Wheel Diameter: 3' 6".
Valve Gear: Stephenson. Slide valves.
Weight: 24.85 tons.
Cylinders: 14" x 20" (O).
Tractive Effort: 11 110 lbf.

GWR	P&M		
921	6	Mountsorrel & Rothley Community Heritage Centre	BE 314/1906

CARDIFF RAILWAY — 0-4-0ST

Built: 1898. 2 built. Rebuilt Tyndall Street Works 1916.
Boiler Pressure: 160 lbf/sq in.
Wheel Diameter: 3' 2½".
Valve Gear: Hawthorn-Kitson.
Weight: 25.5 tons.
Cylinders: 14" x 21" (O).
Tractive Effort: 14 540 lbf.

GWR	CARR		
1338	5	Didcot Railway Centre	K 3799/1898

ALEXANDRA DOCKS & RAILWAY COMPANY — 0-4-0ST

Built: 1897. Rebuilt Swindon 1903. Sold by GWR 1932 for industrial use.
Boiler Pressure: 160 lbf/sq in.
Wheel Diameter: 3' 0".
Valve Gear: Stephenson. Slide valves.
Weight: 22.5 tons.
Cylinders: 14" x 20" (O).
Tractive Effort: 11 110 lbf.

GWR	AD		
1340 TROJAN	TROJAN	Didcot Railway Centre	AE 1386/1897

1361 CLASS — 0-6-0ST

Built: 1910. Churchward design for dock shunting. 5 built (1361–65).
Boiler Pressure: 150 lbf/sq in.
Wheel Diameter: 3' 8".
Valve Gear: Allan.
Power Classification: Unclassified (0F).
Weight: 35.2 tons.
Cylinders: 16" x 20" (O).
Tractive Effort: 14 840 lbf.

1363	Didcot Railway Centre	Swindon 2377/1910

1366 CLASS — 0-6-0PT

Built: 1934. Collett design for dock shunting. Used to work Weymouth Quay boat trains. 6 built (1366–71).
Boiler Pressure: 165 lbf/sq in.
Wheel Diameter: 3' 8".
Valve Gear: Stephenson. Slide valves.
Power Classification: Unclassified (1F).
Weight: 35.75 tons.
Cylinders: 16" x 20" (O).
Tractive Effort: 16 320 lbf.

1369	South Devon Railway	Swindon 1934

NORTH PEMBROKESHIRE & FISHGUARD RAILWAY 0-6-0ST

Built: 1878. Absorbed by GWR 1898. Sold to Gwendraeth Valley Railway in 1910. Absorbed by GWR again in 1923 but sold in March of that year to Kidwelly Tinplate Company.
Boiler Pressure: 140 lbf/sq in.
Wheel Diameter: 4' 0".
Valve Gear: Stephenson. Slide valves.
Weight: 30.95 tons.
Cylinders: 16" x 22" (I).
Tractive Effort: 13960 lbf.

GWR	GVR	NP&FR		
1378	2	MARGARET	Scolton Manor Park	FW 410/1878

1500 CLASS 0-6-0PT

Built: 1949. Hawksworth design. 10 built (1500–09).
Boiler Pressure: 200 lbf/sq in.
Wheel Diameter: 4' 7½".
Valve Gear: Walschaerts. Piston valves.
Power Classification: C (4F).
Weight: 58.2 tons.
Cylinders: 17½" x 24" (O).
Tractive Effort: 22510 lbf.
Restriction: Red.

1501	Severn Valley Railway	Swindon 1949

1600 CLASS 0-6-0PT

Built: 1949–55. Hawksworth design. 70 built (1600–69).
Boiler Pressure: 165 lbf/sq in.
Wheel Diameter: 4' 1½".
Valve Gear: Stephenson. Slide valves.
Power Classification: A (2F).
Weight: 41.6 tons.
Cylinders: 16½" x 24" (I).
Tractive Effort: 18510 lbf.
Restriction: Uncoloured.

1638	Kent & East Sussex Railway	Swindon 1951

1638 is currently under overhaul at Leaky Finders, Hele, Exeter.

2301 CLASS DEAN GOODS 0-6-0

Built: 1883–99. Dean design. 280 built (2301–2580).
Boiler Pressure: 180 lbf/sq in superheated.
Wheel Diameter: 5' 2".
Cylinders: 17½" x 24" (I).
Tractive Effort: 18 140 lbf.
Power Classification: A (2MT).
Weight–Loco: 37 tons.
      –Tender: 36.75 tons.
Valve Gear: Stephenson. Slide valves.
Restriction: Uncoloured.

2516	STEAM – Museum of the Great Western Railway (N)	Swindon 1557/1897

2800 CLASS 2-8-0

Built: 1903–19. Churchward design for heavy freight. 84 built (2800–83).
Boiler Pressure: 225 lbf/sq in superheated.
Wheel Diameters: 3' 2", 4' 7½".
Cylinders: 18½" x 30" (O).
Tractive Effort: 35380 lbf.
Power Classification: E (8F).
Weight–Loco: 75.5 tons.
      –Tender: 43.15 tons.
Valve Gear: Stephenson. Piston valves.
Restriction: Blue.

2807	Gloucestershire Warwickshire Railway	Swindon 2102/1905
2818	STEAM – Museum of the Great Western Railway	Swindon 2122/1905
2857	Severn Valley Railway	Swindon 2763/1918
2859	Cambi UK, Radnor Park Industrial Estate, Congleton	Swindon 2765/1918
2873	Dartmouth Steam Railway	Swindon 2779/1918
2874	Gloucestershire Warwickshire Railway	Swindon 2780/1918

▲ Alexandra Docks & Railway Company 0-4-0ST 1340 TROJAN is seen resting in-between duties at Didcot Railway Centre on 26 August 2023. **Peter Foster**

▼ During a visit to the East Somerset Railway, 5700 Class 0-6-0PT L92 runs around its train at Mendip Vale on 8 May 2022. **Ian Beardsley**

2884 CLASS — 2-8-0

Built: 1938–42. Collett development of 2800 Class with side window cabs. 81 built (2884–99, 3800–64).
Boiler Pressure: 225 lbf/sq in superheated.
Wheel Diameters: 3′ 2″, 4′ 7½″.
Cylinders: 18½″ x 30″ (O).
Tractive Effort: 35 380 lbf.
Power Classification: E (8F).
Weight–Loco: 76.25 tons.
 –Tender: 43.15 tons.
Valve Gear: Stephenson. Piston valves.
Restriction: Blue.

2885	Tyseley Locomotive Works	Swindon 1938
3802	Llangollen & Corwen Railway	Swindon 1938
3803	Dartmouth Steam Railway	Swindon 1939
3814	Northern Steam Engineering, Stockton	Swindon 1940
3822	Didcot Railway Centre	Swindon 1940
3845	Honeybourne Airfield Industrial Estate	Swindon 1942
3850	Gloucestershire Warwickshire Railway	Swindon 1942
3855	East Lancashire Railway	Swindon 1942
3862	Northampton & Lamport Railway	Swindon 1942

2251 CLASS — 0-6-0

Built: 1930–48. Collett design. 120 built (2251–99, 2200–50, 3200–19).
Boiler Pressure: 200 lbf/sq in superheated.
Wheel Diameter: 5′ 2″.
Cylinders: 17½″ x 24″ (I).
Tractive Effort: 20 150 lbf.
Power Classification: B (3MT).
Weight–Loco: 43.4 tons.
 –Tender: 36.75 tons.
Valve Gear: Stephenson. Slide valves.
Restriction: Yellow.

3205	South Devon Railway	Swindon 1946

3200 CLASS "DUKEDOG" — 4-4-0

Built: Rebuilt 1936–39 by Collett using the frames of "Bulldogs" and the boilers of "Dukes". 30 built (9000–29).
Boiler Pressure: 180 lbf/sq in
Wheel Diameters: 3′ 8″, 5′ 8″.
Cylinders: 18″ x 26″ (I).
Tractive Effort: 18 950 lbf.
Power Classification: B.
Weight–Loco: 49 tons.
 –Tender: 40 tons.
Valve Gear: Stephenson. Piston valves.
Restriction: Yellow.

3217–9017	"EARL OF BERKELEY"	Vale of Rheidol Railway	Swindon 1938

On loan from the Bluebell Railway.

3700 CLASS CITY — 4-4-0

Built: 1903. Churchward design. Reputed to be the first loco to achieve 100 mph hauling a Plymouth–Paddington "Ocean Mails" special in 1904. 20 built (3400–09/3433–42).
Boiler Pressure: 200 lbf/sq in superheated.
Wheel Diameters: 3′ 2″, 6′ 8½″.
Cylinders: 18″ x 26″ (I).
Tractive Effort: 17 800 lbf.
Weight–Loco: 55.3 tons.
 –Tender: 36.75 tons.
Valve Gear: Stephenson. Piston valves.

BR	GWR		
3440	3717	CITY OF TRURO	STEAM – Museum of the Great Western Railway (N) Swindon 2000/1903

5700 CLASS   0-6-0PT

Built: 1929–49. Collett design. The standard GWR shunter. 863 built (5700–99, 6700–79, 7700–99, 8700–99, 3700–99, 3600–99, 4600–99, 9600–82, 9700–9799). Six of the preserved examples saw use with London Transport following withdrawal by British Railways.
Boiler Pressure: 200 lbf/sq in.   **Weight:** 47.5 tons (§ 49 tons).
Wheel Diameter: 4' 7½".   **Cylinders:** 17½" x 24" (I).
Valve Gear: Stephenson. Slide valves.   **Tractive Effort:** 22 510 lbf.
Power Classification: C (4F).   **Restriction:** Blue (Yellow from 1950).

GWR	LTE		
3650§		Didcot Railway Centre	Swindon 1939
3738§		Didcot Railway Centre	Swindon 1937
4612§		Bodmin Railway	Swindon 1942
5764	L95	Severn Valley Railway	Swindon 1929
5775	L89	Keighley & Worth Valley Railway	Swindon 1929
5786	L92	South Devon Railway	Swindon 1930
7714		Severn Valley Railway	KS 4449/1930
7715	L99	Buckinghamshire Railway Centre	KS 4450/1930
7752	L94	Tyseley Locomotive Works	NBL 24040/1930
7754		Llangollen & Corwen Railway	NBL 24042/1930
7760	L90	Sonic Rail Services, Burnham-on-Crouch	NBL 24048/1930
9600§		Tyseley Locomotive Works	Swindon 1945
9629§		Pontypool & Blaenavon Railway	Swindon 1946
9642§		RSS, Rye Farm, Wishaw	Swindon 1946
9681§		Dean Forest Railway	Swindon 1949
9682§		Dean Forest Railway	Swindon 1949

9642 is currently under overhaul at the Flour Mill Workshop, Bream.

4000 CLASS   STAR   4-6-0

Built: 1906–23. Churchward design for express passenger trains. 73 built (4000–72).
Boiler Pressure: 225 lbf/sq in superheated.   **Weight–Loco:** 75.6 tons.
Wheel Diameters: 3' 2", 6' 8½".   –**Tender:** 40 tons.
Cylinders: 15" x 26" (4).   **Tractive Effort:** 27 800 lbf.
Valve Gear: Inside Walschaerts. Rocking levers for outside valves. Piston valves.
Power Classification: D (5P).   **Restriction:** Red.

4003	LODE STAR	National Railway Museum, York (N)	Swindon 2231/1907

4073 CLASS   CASTLE   4-6-0

Built: 1923–50. Collett development of Star Class. 166 built (4073–99, 5000–5099, 7000–37). In addition, one Pacific (111) and five Stars (4000/09/16/32/37) were rebuilt as Castles.
Boiler Pressure: 225 lbf/sq in superheated.   **Weight–Loco:** 79.85 tons.
Wheel Diameters: 3' 2", 6' 8½".   –**Tender:** 46.7 tons.
Cylinders: 16" x 26" (4).   **Tractive Effort:** 31 630 lbf.
Valve Gear: Inside Walschaerts. Rocking levers for outside valves. Piston valves.
Power Classification: D (7P).   **Restriction:** Red.

d   Rebuilt with double chimney.   x   Dual (air/vacuum) brakes.

4073	CAERPHILLY CASTLE	STEAM – Museum of the Great Western Railway (N)	Swindon 1923
4079	PENDENNIS CASTLE	Didcot Railway Centre	Swindon 1924
5029 x	NUNNEY CASTLE	LNWR Heritage, Crewe	Swindon 1934
5043 d	EARL OF MOUNT EDGCUMBE	Tyseley Locomotive Works	Swindon 1936
5051	DRYSLLWYN CASTLE	Didcot Railway Centre	Swindon 1936
5080	DEFIANT	Tyseley Locomotive Works	Swindon 1939
7027	THORNBURY CASTLE	Tyseley Locomotive Works	Swindon 1949
7029 d	CLUN CASTLE	Tyseley Locomotive Works	Swindon 1950

5043 was named BARBURY CASTLE to 09/37.
5051 was named EARL BATHURST from 08/37.
5080 was named OGMORE CASTLE to 01/41.

5101 CLASS — 2-6-2T

Built: 1929–49. Collett development of Churchward 3100 Class. 140 built (5101–10, 5150–99, 4100–79).
Boiler Pressure: 200 lbf/sq in superheated.
Wheel Diameters: 3' 2", 5' 8", 3' 8".
Valve Gear: Stephenson. Piston valves.
Power Classification: D (4MT).
Weight: 78.45 tons.
Cylinders: 18" x 30" (O).
Tractive Effort: 24300 lbf.
Restriction: Yellow.

Number	Location	Builder/Year
4110	East Somerset Railway	Swindon 1936
4121	Tyseley Locomotive Works	Swindon 1937
4141	Epping Ongar Railway	Swindon 1946
4144	Didcot Railway Centre	Swindon 1946
4150	Severn Valley Railway	Swindon 1947
4160	South Devon Railway	Swindon 1948
5164	Tyseley Locomotive Works	Swindon 1930
5199	Battlefield Line	Swindon 1934

4110 is on loan from the Dartmouth Steam Railway.
In addition, 5193 has been rebuilt by the West Somerset Railway as a small-boilered version of a 4300 Class 2-6-0 tender locomotive, numbered 9351. See New Build Steam Locomotives section.

4200 CLASS — 2-8-0T

Built: 1910–23. Churchward design. 105 built (4201–99, 4200, 5200–04).
Boiler Pressure: 200 lbf/sq in superheated.
Wheel Diameters: 3' 2", 4' 7½".
Valve Gear: Stephenson. Piston valves.
Power Classification: E (7F).
Weight: 81.6 tons.
Cylinders: 18½" x 30" (O).
Tractive Effort: 31450 lbf.
Restriction: Red.

Number	Name	Location	Builder/Year
4247		Dartmouth Steam Railway	Swindon 2637/1916
4248		STEAM – Museum of the Great Western Railway	Swindon 2638/1916
4253		Kent & East Sussex Railway	Swindon 2643/1917
4270		Locomotive Storage, Margate	Swindon 2850/1919
4277	"HERCULES"	North Norfolk Railway	Swindon 2857/1920

4247 is currently under overhaul at the East Somerset Railway.
4277 is on loan from the Dartmouth Steam Railway.

4500 CLASS — 2-6-2T

Built: 1906–24. Churchward design. (§ Built 1927–29. Collett development with larger tanks). 175 built (4500–99, 5500–74).
Boiler Pressure: 200 lbf/sq in superheated.
Wheel Diameters: 3' 2", 4' 7½", 3' 2".
Valve Gear: Stephenson. Piston valves.
Power Classification: C (4MT).
Weight: 57.9 tons (§ 61 tons).
Cylinders: 17" x 24" (O).
Tractive Effort: 21250 lbf.
Restriction: Yellow.

x Dual (air/vacuum) brakes.

Number	Name	Location	Builder/Year
4555		Chinnor & Princes Risborough Railway	Swindon 1924
4561		West Somerset Railway	Swindon 1924
4566		Severn Valley Railway	Swindon 1924
4588§		Tyseley Locomotive Works	Swindon 1927
5521§ x	L150	Epping Ongar Railway	Swindon 1927
5526§		South Devon Railway	Swindon 1928
5532§		Llangollen & Corwen Railway	Swindon 1928
5538§		Flour Mill Workshop, Bream	Swindon 1928
5539§		Barry Tourist Railway	Swindon 1928
5541§		Dean Forest Railway	Swindon 1928
5542§		South Devon Railway	Swindon 1928
5552§		Bodmin Railway	Swindon 1928
5553§		Bodmin Railway	Swindon 1928
5572§		Didcot Railway Centre	Swindon 1929

4555 is on loan from the Dartmouth Steam Railway.
5521 is on loan from the Flour Mill Worksop, Bream.
5553 is on loan from Peak Rail.

▲ 4073 Class 4-6-0 7029 CLUN CASTLE passes Batheaston with the 08.19 Solihull–Bristol, the outward leg of Vintage Trains' "Merchant Venturer" railtour, on 6 December 2022. **Glen Batten**

▼ 4500 Class 2-6-2T 4555 climbs away from Goodrington with the Dartmouth Steam Railway's 11.15 Paignton–Kingswear on 11 May 2023. **Glen Batten**

1400 CLASS   0-4-2T

Built: 1932–36. Collett design. Push & Pull fitted. Locomotives renumbered in 1946. 75 built (1400–74).
Boiler Pressure: 165 lbf/sq in.
Wheel Diameters: 5′ 2″, 3′ 8″.
Valve Gear: Stephenson. Slide valves.
Power Classification: Unclassified (1P).
Weight: 41.3 tons.
Cylinders: 16″ x 24″ (I).
Tractive Effort: 13 900 lbf.

1932 No.	1946 No.		
4820	1420	South Devon Railway	Swindon 1933
4842	1442	Tiverton Museum	Swindon 1935
4850	1450	Severn Valley Railway	Swindon 1935
4866	1466	Didcot Railway Centre	Swindon 1936

4850-1450 is currently under overhaul at the Flour Mill Workshop, Bream.
4866-1466 is currently under overhaul at the West Somerset Railway.

4900 CLASS   HALL   4-6-0

Built: 1928–43. Collett development of Churchward Saint Class. 259 in class. (4900 rebuilt from Saint) 4901-99, 5900-99, 6900-58 built as Halls.
Boiler Pressure: 225 lbf/sq in superheated.
Wheel Diameters: 3′ 2″, 6′ 0″.
Cylinders: 18½″ x 30″ (O).
Tractive Effort: 27 270 lbf.
Power Classification: D (5MT).
Weight–Loco: 75 tons.
         –Tender: 46.7 tons.
Valve Gear: Stephenson. Piston valves.
Restriction: Red.

4920	DUMBLETON HALL	Warner Brothers Studio Tour, Toshimaen, Tokyo, Japan	Swindon 1929
4930	HAGLEY HALL	Severn Valley Railway	Swindon 1929
4936	KINLET HALL	West Somerset Railway	Swindon 1929
4953	PITCHFORD HALL	Epping Ongar Railway	Swindon 1929
4965	ROOD ASHTON HALL	Tyseley Locomotive Works	Swindon 1930
4979	WOOTTON HALL	Ribble Steam Railway	Swindon 1930
5900	HINDERTON HALL	Didcot Railway Centre	Swindon 1931
5952	COGAN HALL	Tyseley Locomotive Works	Swindon 1935
5967	BICKMARSH HALL	Northampton & Lamport Railway	Swindon 1937
5972	OLTON HALL	Warner Brothers Studio Tour, Leavesden	Swindon 1937

4920 currently carries the identity 5972 "HOGWARTS CASTLE".
4965 previously carried the identity 4983 ALBERT HALL.
5972 currently carries the name "HOGWARTS CASTLE", as used in the "Harry Potter" films.

4936 is currently under overhaul at Tyseley Locomotive Works.
5972 is on loan from West Coast Railway Company, Carnforth.

5205 CLASS   2-8-0T

Built: 1923–25/1940. Collett development of 4200 class. 60 built (5205–64).
Boiler Pressure: 200 lbf/sq in superheated.
Wheel Diameters: 3′ 2″, 4′ 7½″.
Valve Gear: Stephenson. Piston valves.
Power Classification: E (8F).
Weight: 82.1 tons.
Cylinders: 19″ x 30″ (O).
Tractive Effort: 33 170 lbf.
Restriction: Red.

5224		Peak Rail	Swindon 1925
5227		Didcot Railway Centre	Swindon 1924
5239	"GOLIATH"	Dartmouth Steam Railway	Swindon 1924

5600 CLASS — 0-6-2T

Built: 1924–28. Collett design. 200 built (5600–99, 6600–99).
Boiler Pressure: 200 lbf/sq in superheated. **Weight:** 68 tons.
Wheel Diameters: 4′ 7½″, 3′ 8″. **Cylinders:** 18″ x 26″ (I).
Valve Gear: Stephenson. Piston valves. **Tractive Effort:** 25 800 lbf.
Power Classification: D (5MT). **Restriction:** Red.

5619	Telford Steam Railway	Swindon 1925
5637	Swindon & Cricklade Railway	Swindon 1925
5643	Ribble Steam Railway	Swindon 1925
5668	Kent & East Sussex Railway	Swindon 1926
6619	Kent & East Sussex Railway	Swindon 1928
6634	Peak Rail	Swindon 1928
6686	NL Engineering (North West), Blackrod	AW 974/1928
6695	Swindon & Cricklade Railway	AW 983/1928
6697	Didcot Railway Centre	AW 985/1928

6000 CLASS KING — 4-6-0

Built: 1927–30. Collett design. 30 built (6000–29).
Boiler Pressure: 250 lbf/sq in superheated. **Weight–Loco:** 89 tons.
Wheel Diameters: 3′ 0″, 6′ 6″. **–Tender:** 46.7 tons.
Cylinders: 16¼″ x 28″ (4). **Tractive Effort:** 40 290 lbf.
Valve Gear: Inside Walschaerts. Piston valves. Rocking levers for outside valves.
Power Classification: Special (8P). **Restriction:** Double Red.

x   Dual (air/vacuum) brakes.

6000	KING GEORGE V	STEAM – Museum of the Great Western Railway (N)	Swindon 1927
6023	KING EDWARD II	Didcot Railway Centre	Swindon 1930
6024 x	KING EDWARD I	LNWR Heritage, Crewe	Swindon 1930

▲ During the Gloucestershire Warwickshire Railway's Cotswold Festival of Steam on 14 May 2023, 7800 Class 4-6-0 7820 DINMORE MANOR hauls a short freight train past Didbrook. **Martyn Tattam**

6100 CLASS 2-6-2T

Built: 1931–35. Collett development of 5101 Class. 70 built (6100–69).
Boiler Pressure: 225 lbf/sq in superheated. **Weight**: 78.45 tons.
Wheel Diameters: 3' 2", 5' 8", 3' 8". **Cylinders**: 18" x 30" (O).
Valve Gear: Stephenson. Piston valves. **Tractive Effort**: 27 340 lbf.
Power Classification: D (5MT). **Restriction**: Blue.

6106	Didcot Railway Centre	Swindon 1931

6400 CLASS 0-6-0PT

Built: 1932–37. Collett design. Push & Pull fitted. 40 built (6400–39).
Boiler Pressure: 165 lbf/sq in. **Weight**: 45.6 tons.
Wheel Diameter: 4' 7½". **Cylinders**: 16½" x 24" (I).
Valve Gear: Stephenson. Slide valves. **Tractive Effort**: 16 510 lbf.
Power Classification: A (2P). **Restriction**: Yellow.

6412	South Devon Railway	Swindon 1934
6430	Gwili Railway	Swindon 1937
6435	Bodmin Railway	Swindon 1937

6430 is on loan from the South Devon Railway.

6959 CLASS   MODIFIED HALL   4-6-0

Built: 1944–49. Hawksworth development of Hall Class. 71 built (6959–99, 7900–29).
Boiler Pressure: 225 lbf/sq in superheated. **Weight–Loco**: 75.8 tons.
Wheel Diameters: 3' 2", 6' 0".   —**Tender**: 47.3 tons.
Cylinders: 18½" x 30" (O). **Valve Gear**: Stephenson. Piston valves.
Tractive Effort: 27 270 lbf. **Restriction**: Red.
Power Classification: D (5MT).

6960	RAVENINGHAM HALL	Locomotive Storage, Margate	Swindon 1944
6984	OWSDEN HALL	Buckinghamshire Railway Centre	Swindon 1948
6989	WIGHTWICK HALL	Bluebell Railway	Swindon 1948
6990	WITHERSLACK HALL	Great Central Railway	Swindon 1948
6998	BURTON AGNES HALL	Didcot Railway Centre	Swindon 1949
7903	FOREMARKE HALL	Gloucestershire Warwickshire Railway	Swindon 1949

6989 is on loan from the Buckinghamshire Railway Centre.

7200 CLASS 2-8-2T

Built: 1934–50. Collett rebuilds of 4200 and 5205 Class 2-8-0Ts. 54 built (7200–53).
Boiler Pressure: 200 lbf/sq in superheated. **Weight**: 92.6 tons.
Wheel Diameters: 3' 2", 4' 7½", 3' 8". **Cylinders**: 19" x 30" (O).
Valve Gear: Stephenson. Piston valves. **Tractive Effort**: 33 170 lbf.
Power Classification: E (8F). **Restriction**: Blue.

7200	(rebuilt from 5275)	Buckinghamshire Railway Centre	Swindon 1930 reb 1934
7202	(rebuilt from 5277)	Didcot Railway Centre	Swindon 1930 reb 1934
7229	(rebuilt from 5264)	East Lancashire Railway	Swindon 1926 reb 1935

7800 CLASS   MANOR   4-6-0

Built: 1938–50. Collett design for secondary main lines. 30 built (7800–29).
Boiler Pressure: 225 lbf/sq in superheated. **Weight–Loco**: 68.9 tons.
Wheel Diameters: 3' 0", 5' 8".   —**Tender**: 40 tons.
Cylinders: 18" x 30" (O). **Valve Gear**: Stephenson. Piston valves.
Tractive Effort: 27 340 lbf. **Restriction**: Blue.
Power Classification: D (5MT).

7802	BRADLEY MANOR	Severn Valley Railway	Swindon 1938
7808	COOKHAM MANOR	Didcot Railway Centre	Swindon 1938

7812	ERLESTOKE MANOR	Severn Valley Railway	Swindon 1939
7819	HINTON MANOR	Severn Valley Railway	Swindon 1939
7820	DINMORE MANOR	Gloucestershire Warwickshire Railway	Swindon 1950
7821	DITCHEAT MANOR	Designer Outlet Swindon	Swindon 1950
7822	FOXCOTE MANOR	Tyseley Locomotive Works	Swindon 1950
7827	LYDHAM MANOR	Dartmouth Steam Railway	Swindon 1950
7828	ODNEY MANOR	West Somerset Railway	Swindon 1950

7802 is currently under overhaul at Tyseley Locomotive Works.
7821 is on loan from the West Somerset Railway.

4300 CLASS   2-6-0

Built: 1911–32. Churchward design. 342 built (4300–99, 5300–99, renumbered from 8300–99 between 1944 and 1948), 6300–99, 7300–21, 7322–41 (renumbered from 9300–19 between 1956 and 1959).
Boiler Pressure: 200 lbf/sq in superheated. **Weight–Loco:** 62 tons.
Wheel Diameters: 3′ 2″, 5′ 8″.   –**Tender:** 40 tons.
Cylinders: 18½″ x 30″ (O). **Valve Gear:** Stephenson. Piston valves.
Tractive Effort: 25670 lbf. **Restriction:** Blue.
Power Classification: D (4MT).

8322–5322	Didcot Railway Centre	Swindon 1917
9303–7325	Severn Valley Railway	Swindon 1932

In addition, 5101 Class 2-6-0 5193 has been rebuilt by the West Somerset Railway as an outwardly similar 9351 Class 2-6-0 tender locomotive, numbered 9351. See New Build Steam Locomotives section.

9400 CLASS   0-6-0PT

Built: 1947–56. Hawksworth design. 210 built (9400–99, 8400–99, 3400–09).
Boiler Pressure: 200 lbf/sq in (* superheated). **Weight:** 55.35 tons.
Wheel Diameter: 4′ 7½″. **Cylinders:** 17½″ x 24″ (I).
Valve Gear: Stephenson. Slide valves. **Tractive Effort:** 22510 lbf.
Power Classification: C (4F). **Restriction:** Red.

9400*	STEAM – Museum of the Great Western Railway (N)	Swindon 1947
9466	West Somerset Railway	RSH 7617/1952

BURRY PORT & GWENDRAETH VALLEY RAILWAY   0-6-0ST

Built: 1900. **Weight:** 29 tons.
Wheel Diameter: 3′ 6″. **Cylinders:** 14″ x 20″(O)

This locomotive was supplied new to the BPGVR and was sold into industrial service in 1914.

2	PONTYBEREM	Flour Mill Workshop	AE 1421/1900

SANDY & POTTON RAILWAY   0-4-0WT

Built: 1857. The Sandy & Potton Railway became part of the LNWR and the loco worked on the Cromford & High Peak Railway from 1863–78. The loco was sold to the Wantage Tramway in 1878.
Boiler Pressure: 120 lbf/sq in. **Weight:** 15 tons.
Wheel Diameter: 3′ 0″. **Cylinders:** 9″ x 12″ (O).
Tractive Effort: 5510 lbf.

SPR	LNWR	WT		
SHANNON	1863	5	Didcot Railway Centre (N)	GE 1857

SOUTHERN

1.2. SOUTHERN RAILWAY AND CONSTITUENT COMPANIES' STEAM LOCOMOTIVES

GENERAL

The Southern Railway (SR) was an amalgamation of the London, Brighton & South Coast Railway (LBSCR), London & South Western Railway (LSWR) and South Eastern & Chatham Railway (SECR), the last of which was formed in 1898 through the amalgamation of the South Eastern Railway (SER) and London, Chatham & Dover Railway (LCDR).

NUMBERING SYSTEM

In 1924, after the formation of the SR the previous year, all locomotives (including new builds) were given a prefix letter to denote the works that maintained them as follows:

A   Ashford Works. All former SECR locomotives plus some D1, L1 and U1 Class locomotives.
B   Brighton Works. All former LBSCR locomotives plus some D1 Class locomotives.
E   Eastleigh Works. All former LSWR locomotives plus LN, V and Z Class locomotives.

In 1931, the prefixes were abandoned and a new numbering system was introduced. Locomotives that had been given an "E" prefix kept their earlier number (those that had numbers starting with a "0" had 3000 added to their number, however). Locomotives that had been given an "A" prefix had 1000 added to their number, and locomotives that had been given a "B" prefix had 2000 added to their number. Eg A27 became 1027, B636 became 2636 and E0298 became 3298.

In 1941, Bulleid introduced yet another numbering system, based on the UIC classification system, for his new locomotives. This consisted of two numbers, representing the number of leading and trailing axles respectively, followed by a letter denoting the number of the driving axles and then the locomotive serial number. The first MN 4-6-2 was therefore 21C1, and the first Q1 0-6-0 was C1.

In 1948, British Railways added 30000 to the number of most ex-SR locomotives. The 3xxx (formerly 0xxx) series were totally renumbered, though, while the Q1s became 33xxx, the MNs 35xxx and the WCs and BBs 34xxx. Isle of Wight locomotives had their own number series, denoted by a "W" prefix. This indicated that they were maintained at Ryde Works and was carried until the end of steam on the island.

In the section that follows, locomotives are listed generally in order of BR numbers, except that locomotives of the same class are listed together. Four old locomotives, which were withdrawn before nationalisation, are listed at the end of the section.

CLASSIFICATION SYSTEM

The LBSCR originally classified locomotive classes by a letter, which denoted their use. A further development was to add a number, to identify different classes of similar use. A rebuild was signified by an "X" suffix. In its latter years, new classes of different wheel arrangement were given different letters. The SECR gave each class a letter. A number after the letter signified either a new class which was a modification of the original or a rebuild. The SR perpetuated this system. The LSWR had an odd system based on the works order number for the first locomotive of the class to be built. These went A1, B1......Z1, A2......Z2, A3......etc and did not only apply to locomotives. Locomotives bought from outside contractors were classified by the first number to be delivered, eg "0298 Class".

CLASS O2   0-4-4T

Built: 1889–95. Adams LSWR design. 60 built.
Boiler Pressure: 160 lbf/sq in.   **Weight:** 48.4 tons.
Wheel Diameters: 4′ 10″, 3′ 1″.   **Cylinders:** 17″ x 24″ (I).
Valve Gear: Stephenson. Slide valves.   **Tractive Effort:** 17 235 lbf.
BR Power Classification: 1P.

Air braked.

BR	SR	LSWR		
W24	E209–W24	209 CALBOURNE	Isle of Wight Steam Railway	Nine Elms 341/1891

CLASS M7   0-4-4T

Built: 1897–1911. Drummond LSWR design. 105 built.
Boiler Pressure: 175 lbf/sq in.   **Weight:** 60.15 tons.
Wheel Diameters: 5′ 7″, 3′ 7″.   **Cylinders:** 18½″ x 26″ (I).
Valve Gear: Stephenson. Slide valves.   **Tractive Effort:** 19 760 lbf.
BR Power Classification: 2P.

30053 was Push & Pull fitted and air braked.

BR	SR	LSWR		
30053	E53–53	53	Swanage Railway	Nine Elms 1905
30245	E245–245	245	National Railway Museum, York (N)	Nine Elms 501/1897

CLASS USATC S100   0-6-0T

Built: 1942–43 by Vulcan Works, Wilkes-Barre, PA, USA for US Army Transportation Corps. 93 built (a further 289 were built by other builders). 15 were sold to SR in 1947 of which 14 became 61–74.
Boiler Pressure: 210 lbf/sq in.   **Weight:** 46.5 tons.
Wheel Diameter: 4′ 6″.   **Cylinders:** 16½″ x 24″ (O).
Valve Gear: Walschaerts. Piston valves.   **Tractive Effort:** 21 600 lbf.
BR Power Classification: 3F.

BR	SR	USATC	Present		
30064	64	1959		Southall Depot	VIW 4432/1943
30065	65	1968		Kent & East Sussex Railway	VIW 4441/1943
30070	70	1960	WD 300	Kent & East Sussex Railway	VIW 4433/1943
30072	72	1973		East Lancashire Railway	VIW 4446/1943

30065 was also numbered DS237 and named MAUNSELL.
30070 was also numbered DS238 from 1963 and named WAINWRIGHT. It currently carries the name "MAJOR GENERAL FRANK. S. ROSS."

CLASS B4   0-4-0T

Built: 1891–1909. Adams LSWR design for dock shunting. 25 built.
Boiler Pressure: 140 lbf/sq in.   **Weight:** 33.45 tons.
Wheel Diameter: 3′ 9¾″.   **Cylinders:** 16″ x 22″ (O).
Valve Gear: Stephenson. Slide valves.   **Tractive Effort:** 14 650 lbf.
BR Power Classification: 1F.

BR	SR			
30096	E96–96	NORMANDY	Bluebell Railway	Nine Elms 396/1893
30102	E102–102	GRANVILLE	Bressingham Steam Museum	Nine Elms 406/1893

CLASS T9 — 4-4-0

Built: 1889–1924. Drummond LSWR express passenger design. 66 built.
Boiler Pressure: 175 lbf/sq in superheated. **Weight–Loco:** 51.8 tons.
Wheel Diameters: 3′ 7″, 6′ 7″. **–Tender:** 44.85 tons.
Cylinders: 19″ x 26″ (I). **Valve Gear:** Stephenson. Slide valves.
Tractive Effort: 17 670 lbf. **BR Power Classification:** 3P.

BR	SR	LSWR		
30120	E120–120	120	Swanage Railway (N)	Nine Elms 572/1899

CLASS S15 (URIE) — 4-6-0

Built: 1920–21. Urie LSWR design. 20 built (30496–515).
Boiler Pressure: 180 lbf/sq in superheated. **Weight–Loco:** 79.8 tons.
Wheel Diameters: 3′ 7″, 5′ 7″. **–Tender:** 57.8 tons.
Cylinders: 21″ x 28″ (O). **Valve Gear:** Walschaerts. Piston valves.
Tractive Effort: 28 200 lbf. **BR Power Classification:** 6F.

BR	SR	LSWR		
30499	E499–499	499	Mid Hants Railway	Eastleigh 1920
30506	E506–506	506	Mid Hants Railway	Eastleigh 1920

CLASS Q — 0-6-0

Built: 1938–39. Maunsell SR design. 20 built (30530–549).
Boiler Pressure: 200 lbf/sq in superheated. **Weight–Loco:** 49.5 tons.
Wheel Diameter: 5′ 1″. **–Tender:** 40.5 tons.
Cylinders: 19″ x 26″ (I). **Valve Gear:** Stephenson. Piston valves.
Tractive Effort: 26 160 lbf. **BR Power Classification:** 4F.

BR	SR		
30541	541	Bluebell Railway	Eastleigh 1939

30541 is currently under overhaul at Leaky Finders, Hele, Exeter.

0415 CLASS — 4-4-2T

Built: 1882–85. Adams LSWR design. 72 built.
Boiler Pressure: 160 lbf/sq in. **Weight:** 55.25 tons.
Wheel Diameters: 3′ 0″, 5′ 7″, 3′ 0″. **Cylinders:** 17½″ x 24″ (O).
Valve Gear: Stephenson. Slide valves. **Tractive Effort:** 14 920 lbf.
BR Power Classification: 1P.

BR	SR	EKR	LSWR		
30583	3488	5	0488–488	Bluebell Railway	N 3209/1885

0298 CLASS — 2-4-0WT

Built: 1863–75. WG Beattie LSWR design. Last used on the Wenfordbridge branch in Cornwall. 85 built. Survivors reboilered in 1921.
Boiler Pressure: 160 lbf/sq in. **Weight:** 35.75 (§ 36.3) tons.
Wheel Diameters: 3′ 7¾″, 5′ 7″. **Cylinders:** 16½″ x 22″ (O).
Valve Gear: Allan. **Tractive Effort:** 12 160 lbf.
BR Power Classification: 0P.

BR	SR	LSWR		
30585§	E0314–3314	0314	Buckinghamshire Railway Centre	BP 1414/1874 reb Elh 1921
30587	E0298–3298	0298	Bodmin Railway (N)	BP 1412/1874 reb Elh 1921

▲ Class Q 0-6-0 30541 leads a short goods train into Horsted Keynes during the Bluebell Railway's Giants of Steam gala on 15 October 2022. **Phil Barnes**

▼ Maunsell Class S15 4-6-0 825 approaches Goathland summit as it passes Moorgates with the North Yorkshire Moors Railway's 12.35 Whitby–Pickering service on 27 March 2023. **Paul Biggs**

CLASS N15   KING ARTHUR   4-6-0

Built: 1925–27. Maunsell SR development of Urie LSWR design. 54 built (30448–457, 30763–806).
Boiler Pressure: 200 lbf/sq in superheated.   **Weight–Loco:** 80.7 tons.
Wheel Diameters: 3′ 7″, 6′ 7″.   **–Tender:** 57.5 tons.
Cylinders: 20½″ x 28″ (O).   **Valve Gear:** Walschaerts. Piston valves.
Tractive Effort: 25 320 lbf.   **BR Power Classification:** 5P.

BR	SR			
30777	E777–777	SIR LAMIEL	Great Central Railway (N)	NBL 23223/1925

CLASS S15 (MAUNSELL)   4-6-0

Built: 1927–36. Maunsell SR development of Urie LSWR design. 25 built (30823–847).
Boiler Pressure: 200 lbf/sq in superheated.   **Weight–Loco:** 80.7 (* 79.25) tons.
Wheel Diameters: 3′ 7″, 5′ 7″.   **–Tender:** 56.4 tons.
Cylinders: 20½″ x 28″ (O).   **Valve Gear:** Walschaerts. Piston valves.
Tractive Effort: 29 860 lbf.   **BR Power Classification:** 6F.

BR	SR			
30825	E825–825		North Yorkshire Moors Railway	Eastleigh 1927
30828	E828–828	"HARRY A FRITH"	Mid Hants Railway	Eastleigh 1927
30830	E830–830		North Yorkshire Moors Railway	Eastleigh 1927
30847*	847		Bluebell Railway	Eastleigh 1936

30825 has been restored using a substantial number of components from 30841.

CLASS LN   LORD NELSON   4-6-0

Built: 1926–29. Maunsell SR design. 16 built (30850–65).
Boiler Pressure: 220 lbf/sq in superheated.   **Weight–Loco:** 83.5 tons.
Wheel Diameters: 3′ 1″, 6′ 7″.   **–Tender:** 57.95 tons.
Cylinders: 16½″ x 26″ (4).   **Valve Gear:** Walschaerts. Piston valves.
Tractive Effort: 33 510 lbf.   **BR Power Classification:** 7P.

BR	SR			
30850	E850–850	LORD NELSON	Mid Hants Railway (N)	Eastleigh 1926

CLASS V   SCHOOLS   4-4-0

Built: 1930–35. Maunsell SR design. 40 built (30900–39).
Boiler Pressure: 220 lbf/sq in superheated.   **Weight–Loco:** 67.1 tons.
Wheel Diameters: 3′ 1″, 6′ 7″.   **–Tender:** 42.4 tons.
Cylinders: 16½″ x 26″ (3).   **Valve Gear:** Walschaerts. Piston valves.
Tractive Effort: 25 130 lbf.   **BR Power Classification:** 5P.

BR	SR			
30925	925	CHELTENHAM	Mid Hants Railway (N)	Eastleigh 1934
30926	926	REPTON	North Yorkshire Moors Railway	Eastleigh 1934
30928	928	STOWE	Bluebell Railway	Eastleigh 1934

928–30928 is currently under overhaul at the Buckinghamshire Railway Centre.

CLASS P   0-6-0T

Built: 1909–10. Wainwright SECR design. 8 built.
Boiler Pressure: 160 lbf/sq in.   **Weight:** 28.5 tons.
Wheel Diameter: 3′ 9″.   **Cylinders:** 12″ x 18″ (I).
Valve Gear: Stephenson. Slide valves.   **Tractive Effort:** 7830 lbf.
BR Power Classification: 0F.

BR	SR	SECR		
31027	A27–1027	27		Bluebell Railway	Ashford 1910
31178	A178–1178	178		Locomotive Storage, Margate	Ashford 1910
31323	A323–1323	323	"BLUEBELL"	Bluebell Railway	Ashford 1910

31556	556–A556–1556	753–5753		Kent & East Sussex Railway	Ashford 1909

178–A178–1178–31178 is on loan from the Bluebell Railway.

CLASS O1   0-6-0

Built: 1903–15. Wainwright SECR design. 66 built. 59 were rebuilt out of 122 "O" class.
Boiler Pressure: 150 lbf/sq in.   **Weight–Loco:** 41.05 tons.
Wheel Diameter: 5′ 1″.   **–Tender:** 28.20 tons.
Cylinders: 18″ x 26″ (I).   **Valve Gear:** Stephenson. Slide valves.
Tractive Effort: 17610 lbf.   **BR Power Classification:** 1F.

BR	SR	SECR		
31065	A65–1065	65	Bluebell Railway	Ashford 1896 reb 1908

CLASS H   0-4-4T

Built: 1904–15. Wainwright SECR design. 66 built.
Boiler Pressure: 160 lbf/sq in.   **Weight:** 54.4 tons.
Wheel Diameters: 5′ 6″, 3′ 7″.   **Cylinders:** 18″ x 26″ (I).
Valve Gear: Stephenson. Slide valves.   **Tractive Effort:** 17360 lbf.
BR Power Classification: 1P.

Push & Pull fitted. Dual (air/vacuum) brakes.

BR	SR	SECR		
31263	A263–1263	263	Bluebell Railway	Ashford 1905

CLASS C   0-6-0

Built: 1900–08. Wainwright SECR design. 109 built.
Boiler Pressure: 160 lbf/sq in.   **Weight–Loco:** 43.8 tons.
Wheel Diameter: 5′ 2″.   **–Tender:** 38.25 tons.
Cylinders: 18½″ x 26″ (I).   **Valve Gear:** Stephenson. Slide valves.
Tractive Effort: 19520 lbf.   **BR Power Classification:** 2F.

BR	SR	SECR		
31592–DS239	A592–1592	592	Bluebell Railway	Longhedge 1902

CLASS U   2-6-0

Built: 1928–31. Maunsell SR design. 50 built (31610–639, 31790–809). 31790–809 were converted from Class K (River Class) 2-6-4Ts.
Boiler Pressure: 200 lbf/sq in superheated.   **Weight–Loco:** 61.9 (* 62.55) tons.
Wheel Diameters: 3′ 1″, 6′ 0″.   **–Tender:** 42.4 tons.
Cylinders: 19″ x 28″ (O).   **Valve Gear:** Walschaerts. Piston valves.
Tractive Effort: 23870 lbf.   **BR Power Classification:** 4MT.

*   Formerly Class K 2-6-4T A806 RIVER TORRIDGE built Ashford 1926.

BR	SR		
31618	A618–1618	Bluebell Railway	Brighton 1928
31625	A625–1625	Swanage Railway	Ashford 1929
31638	A638–1638	Bluebell Railway	Ashford 1931
31806*	A806–1806	Swanage Railway	Brighton 1928

CLASS D   4-4-0

Built: 1901–07. Wainwright SECR design. 51 built.
Boiler Pressure: 175 lbf/sq in.   **Weight–Loco:** 50 tons.
Wheel Diameters: 3′ 7″, 6′ 8″.   **–Tender:** 39.1 tons.
Cylinders: 19¼″ x 26″ (I).   **Valve Gear:** Stephenson. Slide valves.
Tractive Effort: 17910 lbf.   **BR Power Classification:** 1P.

BR	SR	SECR		
31737	A737–1737	737	National Railway Museum, York (N)	Ashford 1901

▲ One of several locomotives from the national collection on loan to the Mid Hants Railway, Class V 4-4-0 30925 CHELTENHAM passes Wanders Curve on 2 June 2022. **Martyn Tattam**

▼ During a visit to the Spa Valley, South Eastern & Chatham Railway Class O1 0-6-0 65 stands at Eridge on 17 June 2023 prior to departing with the 16.15 to Tunbridge Wells West. **Phil Barnes**

CLASS N • 2-6-0

Built: 1917–34. Maunsell SECR design. Some built by SR. 80 built (31810–875, 31400–414).
Boiler Pressure: 200 lbf/sq in. **Weight–Loco:** 59.4 tons.
Wheel Diameters: 3' 1", 5' 6". **–Tender:** 39.25 tons.
Cylinders: 19" x 28" (O). **Valve Gear:** Walschaerts. Piston valves.
Tractive Effort: 26040 lbf. **BR Power Classification:** 4MT.

BR	SR		
31874	A874–1874	Swanage Railway	Woolwich Arsenal 1925

CLASS E4 • 0-6-2T

Built: 1897–1903. R Billinton LBSCR design. 75 built.
Boiler Pressure: 160 lbf/sq in. **Weight:** 56.75 tons.
Wheel Diameters: 5' 0", 4' 0". **Cylinders:** 18" x 26" (I).
Valve Gear: Stephenson. Slide valves. **Tractive Effort:** 19090 lbf.
BR Power Classification: 2MT.

BR	SR	LBSCR			
32473	B473–2473	473	BIRCH GROVE	Bluebell Railway	Brighton 1898

CLASSES A1 & A1X   "TERRIER"   0-6-0T

Built: 1872–80 as Class A1*. Stroudley LBSCR design. Most rebuilt to A1X from 1911. 50 built.
Boiler Pressure: 150 lbf/sq in. **Weight:** 28.25 tons.
Wheel Diameter: 4' 0". **Cylinders:** 14" († 13", * 12") x 20" (I).
Valve Gear: Stephenson. Slide valves. **Tractive Effort:** 10410 lbf († 8890 lbf, * 7650 lbf).
BR Power Classification: 0P.

a   Air brakes   x   Dual (air/vacuum) brakes.

BR	SR	LBSCR			
32636 x†	B636–2636	72	FENCHURCH	Bluebell Railway	Brighton 1872
32640 a	W11–2640	40	NEWPORT	Isle of Wight Steam Railway	Brighton 1878
32646 x	W2–W8	46–646	FRESHWATER	Isle of Wight Steam Railway	Brighton 1876
32650 x*	B650–W9	50–650	WHITECHAPEL	Spa Valley Railway	Brighton 1876
DS680 a*	A751–680S	54–654	WADDON	Exporail, The Canadian Railway Museum, Montreal, Canada	Brighton 1875
32655	B655–2655	55–655	STEPNEY	Bluebell Railway	Brighton 1875
32662 x*	B662–2662	62–662	MARTELLO	Bressingham Steam Museum	Brighton 1875
32670		70	POPLAR	Kent & East Sussex Railway	Brighton 1872
32678 x	B678–W4–W14–2678	78–678	KNOWLE	Kent & East Sussex Railway	Brighton 1880
–	a 380S	82–682	BOXHILL	National Railway Museum, York (N)	Brighton 1880

32640   was Isle of Wight Central Railway No. 11 and has also been named BRIGHTON.
32646   was Freshwater Yarmouth and Newport Railway No. 2. It was later sold to the LSWR and became 734. It has also been named NEWINGTON.
32650   became 515S and later DS515 (departmental) under BR. It was named FISHBOURNE when on the Isle of Wight. It is now named "SUTTON".
32670   was originally Kent & East Sussex Railway No. 3. It has also been named BODIAM.
DS680   was sold to the SECR and became its No. 751.
32678   was named BEMBRIDGE when on the Isle of Wight.

CLASS Q1 • 0-6-0

Built: 1942. Bulleid SR "Austerity" design. Bulleid Firth Brown driving wheels. 40 built (33001–40).
Boiler Pressure: 230 lbf/sq in superheated. **Weight–Loco:** 51.25 tons.
Wheel Diameter: 5' 1". **–Tender:** 38 tons.
Cylinders: 19" x 26" (I). **Valve Gear:** Stephenson. Slide valves.
Tractive Effort: 30080 lbf. **BR Power Classification:** 5F.

BR	SR		
33001	C1	National Railway Museum, York (N)	Brighton 1942

CLASSES WC & BB   WEST COUNTRY and BATTLE OF BRITAIN   4-6-2

Built: 1945–51. Bulleid SR design with "air-smoothed" casing and Bulleid Firth Brown driving wheels. 110 built (34001–110). All preserved examples built at Brighton except 34101 (Eastleigh).
Boiler Pressure: 250 lbf/sq in superheated.   **Weight–Loco:** 86 (* 91.65) tons.
Wheel Diameters: 3' 1", 6' 2", 3' 1"   **–Tender:** 42.7, 47.9 or 47.75 tons.
Cylinders: 16$^{3}/_{8}$" x 24" (3).   **Tractive Effort:** 27 720 lbf.
Valve Gear: Bulleid chain driven (* Walschaerts. Piston valves).
BR Power Classification: 6MT as built. Reclassified 7P5F from 1953. Rebuilt locomotives reclassified 7P6F.

*   Rebuilt at Eastleigh by Jarvis 1957–61 (including the removal of the air-smoothed casing).
x   Dual (air/vacuum) brakes.

BR	SR			
34007	21C107	WADEBRIDGE	Mid Hants Railway	1945
34010*	21C110	SIDMOUTH	Hope Farm, Sellindge	1945 reb 1959
34016*	21C116	BODMIN	West Coast Railway Company, Carnforth	1945 reb 1959
34023	21C123	BLACKMORE VALE	Bluebell Railway	1946
34027* x	21C127	TAW VALLEY	Severn Valley Railway	1946 reb 1957
34028*	21C128	EDDYSTONE	Swanage Railway	1946 reb 1958
34039*	21C139	BOSCASTLE	Great Central Railway	1946 reb 1959
34046* x	21C146	BRAUNTON	LNWR Heritage, Crewe	1946 reb 1959
34051	21C151	WINSTON CHURCHILL	National Railway Museum, Shildon (N)	1946
34053*	21C153	SIR KEITH PARK	Spa Valley Railway	1947 reb 1958
34058*	21C158	SIR FREDERICK PILE	Hope Farm, Sellindge	1947 reb 1960
34059*	21C159	SIR ARCHIBALD SINCLAIR	Bluebell Railway	1947 reb 1960
34067 x	21C167	TANGMERE	West Coast Railway Company, Carnforth	1947
34070	21C170	MANSTON	Mid Hants Railway	1947
34072		257 SQUADRON	Spa Valley Railway	1948
34073		249 SQUADRON	West Coast Railway Company, Carnforth	1948
34081		92 SQUADRON	Nene Valley Railway	1948
34092		CITY OF WELLS	East Lancashire Railway	1949
34101*		HARTLAND	North Yorkshire Moors Railway	1950 reb 1960
34105		SWANAGE	Mid Hants Railway	1950

34023 was named BLACKMOOR VALE to 04/50.
34092 was named WELLS to 03/50.

34007 is currently under overhaul at Riley & Son (Electromec), Heywood.
34053 is currently under overhaul at the Swanage Railway.

CLASS MN   MERCHANT NAVY   4-6-2

Built: 1941–49. Bulleid SR design with air-smoothed casing and similar features to "WC" and "BB". All rebuilt 1956–59 by Jarvis to more conventional appearance. 30 built (35001–30). All locomotives built (and rebuilt) at Eastleigh.
Boiler Pressure: 250 lbf/sq in superheated.   **Weight–Loco:** 97.9 tons.
Wheel Diameters: 3' 1", 6' 2", 3' 7".   **–Tender:** 47.8 tons.
Cylinders: 18" x 24" (3).   **Valve Gear:** Walschaerts. Piston valves.
Tractive Effort: 33 490 lbf.   **BR Power Classification:** 8P.

x   Dual (air/vacuum) brakes.   §   Sectioned.

BR	SR			
35005	21C5	CANADIAN PACIFIC	Mid Hants Railway	1941 reb 1959
35006	21C6	PENINSULAR & ORIENTAL S.N. CO.	Gloucestershire Warwickshire Railway	1941 reb 1959
35009	21C9	SHAW SAVILL	Riley & Son (Electromec), Heywood	1942 reb 1957
35010	21C10	BLUE STAR	Colne Valley Railway	1942 reb 1957
35011	21C11	GENERAL STEAM NAVIGATION	Swindon & Cricklade Railway	1944 reb 1959
35018	21C18	BRITISH INDIA LINE	West Coast Railway Company, Carnforth	1945 reb 1956
35022		HOLLAND-AMERICA LINE	LNWR Heritage, Crewe	1948 reb 1956
35025		BROCKLEBANK LINE	Hope Farm, Sellindge	1948 reb 1956
35027		PORT LINE	LNWR Heritage, Crewe	1948 reb 1957

▲ On 6 October 2023, during a visit to the Mid Hants, London, Brighton & South Coast Railway Class A1 0-6-0T 72 FENCHURCH leaves Alresford with a shuttle service to Ropley. **Nick Gilliam**

▼ Rebuilt West Country Class 4-6-2 34028 EDDYSTONE accelerates away from Corfe Castle on 25 June 2022 with one of the Swanage Railway's service to Norden. **Martyn Tattam**

▲ Rebuilt Merchant Navy Class 4-6-2 35018 BRITISH INDIA LINE climbs Wilpshire bank with the 15.25 Carlisle–Lancaster leg of "The Dalesman" railtour on 14 June 2022. **Tom McAtee**

▼ Newly restored London South Western Railway Class T3 4-4-0 563 approaches Herston Halt with the Swanage Railway's first train of the day on 6 January 2024. **Stephen Ginn**

35028 x	CLAN LINE		Stewarts Lane Depot, London		1948 reb 1959
35029 §	ELLERMAN LINES		National Railway Museum, York (N)		1949 reb 1959

35005 is currently under overhaul at Arlington Fleet Services, Eastleigh Works.
35011 is being restored to its original air-smoothed condition.
35022 and 35027 are currently dismantled.

CLASS E1   0-6-0T

Built: 1874–83. Stroudley LBSCR design. 80 built.
Boiler Pressure: 160 lbf/sq in.   **Weight:** 44.15 tons.
Wheel Diameter: 4′ 6″.   **Cylinders:** 17″ x 24″ (I).
Valve Gear: Stephenson. Slide valves.   **Tractive Effort:** 17 470 lbf.

SR	LBSCR	Present			
B110	110	W2	"YARMOUTH"	Isle of Wight Steam Railway	Brighton 1877

B110 was originally named BURGUNDY.

CLASS B1   "GLADSTONE"   0-4-2

Built: 1882–91. Stroudley LBSCR design. 49 built.
Boiler Pressure: 150 lbf/sq in.   **Weight–Loco:** 38.7 tons.
Wheel Diameters: 6′ 6″, 4′ 6″.   **–Tender:** 29.35 tons.
Cylinders: 18¼″ x 26″ (I).   **Valve Gear:** Stephenson. Slide valves.
Tractive Effort: 14 160 lbf.

Air brakes.

SR	LBSCR			
B618	214–618	GLADSTONE	National Railway Museum, York (N)	Brighton 1882

CLASS T3   4-4-0

Built: 1882–93. Adams LSWR design. 20 built.
Boiler Pressure: 175 lbf/sq in.   **Weight–Loco:** 48.55 tons.
Wheel Diameters: 3′ 7″, 6′ 7″.   **–Tender:** 33.2 tons
Cylinders: 19″ x 26″ (O).   **Tractive Effort:** 17 670 lbf.
Valve Gear: Stephenson. Slide valves.

SR	LSWR		
E563–563	563	Swanage Railway	Nine Elms 380/1893

CANTERBURY & WHITSTABLE RAILWAY   0-4-0

Built: 1830. Robert Stephenson & Company design.
Boiler Pressure: 40 lbf/sq in.   **Weight–Loco:** 6.25 tons
Wheel Diameter: 4′ 0″.   **–Tender:**
Cylinders: 10½″ x 18″ (O).   **Tractive Effort:** 2680 lbf.

INVICTA	Whitstable Community Museum & Gallery	RS 24/1830

1.3. LONDON MIDLAND & SCOTTISH RAILWAY & CONSTITUENT COMPANIES' STEAM LOCOMOTIVES

GENERAL

The LMS was formed in 1923 by the amalgamation of the Midland Railway (MR), London & North Western Railway (LNWR), Caledonian Railway (CR), Glasgow & South Western Railway (GSWR) and Highland Railway (HR), plus a few smaller railways. Prior to this, the North London Railway (NLR) and Lancashire & Yorkshire Railway (L&Y) had been absorbed by the LNWR and the London, Tilbury & Southend Railway (LTSR) had been absorbed by the MR.

NUMBERING SYSTEM

Originally, number series were allocated to divisions as follows:

1– 4999	Midland Division (Midland and North Staffordshire Railway).
5000– 9999	Western Division "A" (LNWR).
10000–13999	Western Division "B" (L&Y).
14000–17999	Northern Division (Scottish railways).

From 1934 onwards, all LMS standard locomotives and new builds were numbered in the range 1–9999, and any locomotives that would have had their numbers duplicated had 20000 added to their original number.

At nationalisation, 40000 was added to all LMS numbers except the locomotives that were renumbered in the 2xxxx series, which were further renumbered, generally in the 58xxx series. In the following section, locomotives are listed in order of BR number or in the position of the BR number they would have carried had they lasted into BR days, except for very old locomotives that are listed at the end of the section.

CLASSIFICATION SYSTEM

LMS locomotives did not generally have unique class designations but were referred to by their power classification, which varied from 0 to 8 followed by the letters "P" for a passenger locomotive and "F" for a freight locomotive. BR adopted the LMS system and used the description "MT" to denote mixed traffic locomotives. The power classifications are generally shown in the class headings.

MIDLAND 115 CLASS (1P)   "SPINNER"   4-2-2

Built: 1896–99. Johnson design. 15 built (670–684).
Boiler Pressure: 170 lbf/sq in.   **Weight–Loco:** 43.95 tons.
Wheel Diameters: 3' 10", 7' 9", 4' 4½".   **–Tender:** 21.55 tons.
Cylinders: 19" x 26" (I).   **Valve Gear:** Stephenson. Slide valves.
Tractive Effort: 15 280 lbf.

LMS	MR		
673	118–673	National Railway Museum, York (N)	Derby 1897

CLASS 4P   COMPOUND   4-4-0

Built: 1902–03. Johnson Midland design. Rebuilt by Deeley 1914–19 to a similar design to the Deeley compounds, which were built 1905–09. A further similar batch was built by the LMS in 1924–32. 240 built (41000–199, 40900–939).
Boiler Pressure: 200 lbf/sq in superheated.   **Weight–Loco:** 61.7 tons.
Wheel Diameters: 3' 6½", 7' 0".   **–Tender:** 45.9 tons.
Cylinders: One high pressure. 19" x 26" (I).   **Tractive Effort:** 23 205 lbf.
          Two low pressure. 21" x 26" (O).
Valve Gear: Stephenson. Slide valves on low-pressure cylinders, piston valves on high-pressure cylinder.

BR	LMS	MR		
41000	1000	1000 (2631 pre-1907)	Barrow Hill Roundhouse (N)	Derby 1902 reb 1914

CLASS 2MT   2-6-2T

Built: 1946–52. Ivatt LMS design. 130 built (41200–329).
Boiler Pressure: 200 lbf/sq in superheated.   **Weight:** 65.2 (* 63.25) tons.
Wheel Diameters: 3' 0", 5' 0", 3' 0".   **Cylinders:** 16½" (* 16") x 24" (O).
Valve Gear: Walschaerts. Piston valves.   **Tractive Effort:** 18 510 (* 17 410) lbf.

x Dual (air/vacuum) brakes.

41241*	Keighley & Worth Valley Railway	Crewe 1949
41298 x	Isle of Wight Steam Railway	Crewe 1951
41312	Mid Hants Railway	Crewe 1952
41313 x	Isle of Wight Steam Railway	Crewe 1952

CLASS 1F   0-6-0T

Built: 1878–99. Johnson Midland design. Rebuilt with Belpaire boiler 1926. 240 built (1660–1899).
Boiler Pressure: 150 lbf/sq in.   **Weight:** 45.45 tons.
Wheel Diameter: 4' 7".   **Cylinders:** 17" x 24" (I).
Valve Gear: Stephenson. Slide valves.   **Tractive Effort:** 16 080 lbf.

BR	LMS	MR		
41708	1708	1418–1708	Barrow Hill Roundhouse	Derby 1880

Currently under overhaul at Tyseley Locomotive Works.

LTSR 79 CLASS (3P)   4-4-2T

Built: 1909. Whitelegg LTSR design. 4 built.
Boiler Pressure: 170 lbf/sq in.   **Weight:** 69.35 tons.
Wheel Diameters: 3', 6", 6' 6", 3' 6".   **Cylinders:** 19" x 26" (O).
Valve Gear: Stephenson. Slide valves.   **Tractive Effort:** 17 390 lbf.

Dual (air/vacuum) brakes.

BR	LMS	MR	LTSR			
41966	2148	2177	80	THUNDERSLEY	Bressingham Steam Museum (N)	RS 3367/1909

▲ Class 2MT 2-6-2T 41298 nears its destination as it heads an Isle of Wight Steam Railway service from Smallbrook Junction to Wootton on 24 May 2023. **Anthony Hicks**

▼ Class 5MT 4-6-0 44871 approaches Arisaig with the 12.50 Fort William–Mallaig "Jacobite" service on 26 June 2023. **Anthony Hicks**

CLASS 4MT — 2-6-4T

Built: 1945–51. Fairburn modification of Stanier design (built 1936–43). This in turn was a development of a Fowler design (built 1927–34). 383 built (Stanier & Fairburn) (42050–299/425–494/537–699).
Boiler Pressure: 200 lbf/sq in superheated. **Weight:** 85.25 tons.
Wheel Diameters: 3′ 3½″, 5′ 9″, 3′ 3½″. **Cylinders:** 19¾″ x 26″ (O).
Valve Gear: Walschaerts. Piston valves. **Tractive Effort:** 24 670 lbf.

42073	Lakeside & Haverthwaite Railway	Brighton 1950
42085	Lakeside & Haverthwaite Railway	Brighton 1951

CLASS 4MT — 2-6-4T

Built: 1934. Stanier LMS 3-cylinder design for LTSR line. 37 built (42500–536).
Boiler Pressure: 200 lbf/sq in superheated. **Weight:** 92.5 tons.
Wheel Diameters: 3′ 3½″, 5′ 9″, 3′ 3½″. **Cylinders:** 16″ x 26″ (3).
Valve Gear: Walschaerts. Piston valves. **Tractive Effort:** 24 600 lbf.

BR	LMS		
42500	2500	East Lancashire Railway (N)	Derby 1934

CLASS 5MT — "CRAB" — 2-6-0

Built: 1926–32. Hughes LMS design. 245 built (42700–944).
Boiler Pressure: 180 lbf/sq in superheated. **Weight–Loco:** 66 tons.
Wheel Diameters: 3′ 6½″, 5′ 6″. **–Tender:** 42.2 (* 41.5) tons.
Cylinders: 21″ x 26″ (O). **Valve Gear:** Walschaerts. Piston valves.
Tractive Effort: 26 580 lbf.

BR	LMS		
42700	13000–2700	National Railway Museum, York (N)	Horwich 1926
42765*	13065–2765	East Lancashire Railway	Crewe 5757/1927
42859	13159–2859	East Lancashire Railway	Crewe 5981/1930

13159–2859–42859 is incomplete and dismantled.

CLASS 5MT — 2-6-0

Built: 1933–34. Stanier LMS design. 40 built (42945–984).
Boiler Pressure: 225 lbf/sq in superheated. **Weight–Loco:** 69.1 tons.
Wheel Diameters: 3′ 3½″, 5′ 6″. **–Tender:** 42.2 tons.
Cylinders: 18″ x 28″ (O). **Valve Gear:** Walschaerts. Piston valves.
Tractive Effort: 26 290 lbf.

BR	LMS		
42968	13268–2968	Severn Valley Railway	Crewe 1934

CLASS 4MT — 2-6-0

Built: 1947–52. Ivatt design. 162 built (43000–161).
Boiler Pressure: 225 lbf/sq in superheated. **Weight–Loco:** 59.1 tons.
Wheel Diameters: 3′ 0″, 5′ 3″. **–Tender:** 40.3 tons.
Cylinders: 17½″ x 26″ (O). **Valve Gear:** Walschaerts. Piston valves.
Tractive Effort: 24 170 lbf.

43106	Severn Valley Railway	Darlington 2148/1951

CLASS 4F — 0-6-0

Built: 1911–41. Fowler Midland "Big Goods" design. Locomotives from 44027 onwards were LMS design with tenders with solid coal guards (Midland tenders had coal rails). The preserved Midland locomotive was given an LMS tender by BR. 772 built (43835–44606).
Boiler Pressure: 175 lbf/sq in superheated. **Weight–Loco:** 48.75 tons.
Wheel Diameter: 5' 3". –**Tender:** 41.2 tons
Cylinders: 20" x 26" (I). **Valve Gear:** Stephenson. Piston valves.
Tractive Effort: 24560 lbf.

BR	LMS	MR		
43924	3924	3924	Keighley & Worth Valley Railway	Derby 1920
44027	4027		Vale of Berkeley Railway, Sharpness (N)	Derby 1924
44123	4123		Avon Valley Railway	Crewe 5658/1925
44422	4422		Churnet Valley Railway	Derby 1927

CLASS 5MT — "BLACK 5" — 4-6-0

Built: 1934–51. Stanier design. 842 built (44658–45499).
Boiler Pressure: 225 lbf/sq in superheated. **Weight–Loco:** 72.1 (* 75.3) tons.
Wheel Diameters: 3' 3½", 6' 0". –**Tender:** 53.65 (* 53.8) tons.
Cylinders: 18½" x 28" (O). **Tractive Effort:** 25450 lbf.
Valve Gear: Walschaerts. Piston valves. 44767 has outside Stephenson with piston valves.

x Dual (air/vacuum) brakes.

BR	LMS			
44767 *	4767	"GEORGE STEPHENSON"	West Coast Railway Company, Carnforth	Crewe 1947
44806	4806		North Yorkshire Moors Railway	Derby 1944
44871 x	4871		Riley & Son (Electromec), Heywood	Crewe 1945
44901	4901		Private site, Malvern	Crewe 1945
44932	4932		West Coast Railway Company, Carnforth	Horwich 1945
45000	5000		National Railway Museum, Shildon (N)	Crewe 216/1935
45025	5025		Strathspey Railway	VF 4570/1934
45110	5110		West Coast Railway Company, Carnforth	VF 4653/1935
45163	5163		Colne Valley Railway	AW 1204/1935
45212 x	5212		Keighley & Worth Valley Railway	AW 1253/1935
45231 x	5231	"THE SHERWOOD FORESTER"	LNWR Heritage, Crewe	AW 1286/1936
45293	5293		Colne Valley Railway	AW 1348/1936
45305	5305	"ALDERMAN AE DRAPER"	Great Central Railway	AW 1360/1937
45337	5337		East Lancashire Railway	AW 1392/1937
45379	5379		Locomotive Storage, Margate	AW 1434/1937
45407 x	5407	"THE LANCASHIRE FUSILIER"	Riley & Son (Electromec), Heywood	AW 1462/1937
45428	5428	"ERIC TREACY"	North Yorkshire Moors Railway	AW 1483/1937
45491	5491		Great Central Railway	Derby 1943

5379–45379 is on loan from the Mid Hants Railway.

CLASS 6P (Formerly 5XP) — JUBILEE — 4-6-0

Built: 1934–36. Stanier taper boiler development of Patriot class. 191 built (45552–742).
Boiler Pressure: 225 lbf/sq in superheated. **Weight–Loco:** 79.55 tons.
Wheel Diameters: 3' 3½", 6' 9". –**Tender:** 53.65 tons.
Cylinders: 17" x 26" (3). **Valve Gear:** Walschaerts. Piston valves.
Tractive Effort: 26610 lbf.

* Fitted with double chimney.

BR	LMS			
45593	5593	KOLHAPUR	Tyseley Locomotive Works	NBL 24151/1934
45596 *	5596	BAHAMAS	Keighley & Worth Valley Railway	NBL 24154/1935
45690	5690	LEANDER	West Coast Railway Company, Carnforth	Crewe 288/1936
45699	5699	GALATEA	West Coast Railway Company, Carnforth	Crewe 297/1936

▲ Class 7P 4-6-0 46100 ROYAL SCOT heads south along the West Coast Main Line at Stableford on 3 August 2022 with a Saphos Trains charter from Carnforth to Stratford-upon-Avon. **Brad Joyce**

▼ Princess Coronation Class 4-6-2 6233 DUCHESS OF SUTHERLAND passes Egham with the outbound leg of a Victoria–Bristol Temple Meads railtour on 10 December 2022. **Jamie Squibbs**

CLASS 7P (Formerly 6P)   ROYAL SCOT   4-6-0

Built: 1927–30. Fowler parallel boiler design. All rebuilt 1943–55 with taper boilers and curved smoke deflectors. 71 built (46100–170).
Boiler Pressure: 250 lbf/sq in superheated.
Wheel Diameters: 3′ 3½″, 6′ 9″.
Cylinders: 18″ x 26″ (3).
Tractive Effort: 33 150 lbf.
Weight–Loco: 83 tons.
–Tender: 54.65 tons.
Valve Gear: Walschaerts. Piston valves.

x   Dual (air/vacuum) brakes.

BR	LMS			
46100 x	6100	ROYAL SCOT	LNWR Heritage, Crewe	Derby 1930 reb Crewe 1950
46115	6115	SCOTS GUARDSMAN	West Coast Railway Company, Carnforth	NBL 23610/1927 reb Crewe 1947

6100–46100 was built as 6152 THE KING'S DRAGOON GUARDSMAN but swapped identities permanently with 6100 ROYAL SCOT in 1933 for a tour of the USA.

CLASS 8P (Formerly 7P)   PRINCESS ROYAL   4-6-2

Built: 1933–35. Stanier design. 13 built (46200–212).
Boiler Pressure: 250 lbf/sq in superheated.
Wheel Diameters: 3′ 0″, 6′ 6″, 3′ 9″.
Cylinders: 16¼″ x 28″ (4).
Tractive Effort: 40 290 lbf.
Weight–Loco: 105.5 tons.
–Tender: 54.65 tons.
Valve Gear: Walschaerts. Piston valves.

x   Dual (air/vacuum) brakes.

BR	LMS			
46201 x	6201	PRINCESS ELIZABETH	West Coast Railway Company, Carnforth	Crewe 107/1933
46203	6203	PRINCESS MARGARET ROSE	Midland Railway-Butterley	Crewe 253/1935

▲ Class 3F "Jinty" 0-6-0T 47298 is pictured at Rawtenstall on the East Lancashire Railway on 4 June 2023.
Brian Dobbs

CLASS 8P (Formerly 7P)   PRINCESS CORONATION   4-6-2

Built: 1937–48. Stanier design. 24 of this class were built streamlined but had the casing removed later. Certain locomotives were built with single chimneys, but all finished up with double chimneys. The tenders were fitted with steam-driven coal pushers. 38 built (46220–257).
Boiler Pressure: 250 lbf/sq in superheated.   **Weight–Loco**: 105.25 tons.
Wheel Diameters: 3' 0", 6' 9", 3' 9".   **–Tender**: 56.35 tons.
Cylinders: 16½" x 28" (4).   **Valve Gear**: Walschaerts. Piston valves.
Tractive Effort: 40000 lbf.

[1] Built streamlined and with single chimney. Double chimney fitted 1943. Destreamlined 1947–2009.
[2] Never streamlined and built with single chimney. Double chimney fitted 1941. Dual (air/vacuum) brakes.
[3] Built streamlined and with double chimney. Destreamlined 1946.

BR	LMS			
46229[1]	6229	DUCHESS OF HAMILTON	National Railway Museum, York (N)	Crewe 1938
46233[2]	6233	DUCHESS OF SUTHERLAND	Midland Railway-Butterley	Crewe 1938
46235[3]	6235	CITY OF BIRMINGHAM	Thinktank Birmingham Science Museum	Crewe 1939

6229 carried the identity 6220 CORONATION whilst in the USA between 1938 and 1943.

CLASS 2MT   2-6-0

Built: 1946–53. Ivatt design. 128 built (46400–527).
Boiler Pressure: 200 lbf/sq in superheated.   **Weight–Loco**: 47.1 (* 48.45) tons.
Wheel Diameters: 3' 0", 5' 0".   **–Tender**: 37.15 tons.
Cylinders: 16" (* 16½") x 24" (O).   **Valve Gear**: Walschaerts. Piston valves.
Tractive Effort: 17410 (* 18510) lbf.

46428		East Lancashire Railway	Crewe 1948
46441		Lakeside & Haverthwaite Railway	Crewe 1950
46443		Severn Valley Railway	Crewe 1950
46447		East Somerset Railway	Crewe 1950
46464		Strathspey Railway	Crewe 1950
46512*	"E.V. COOPER ENGINEER"	Strathspey Railway	Swindon 1952
46521*		Great Central Railway	Swindon 1953

46521 is currently under overhaul at Tyseley Locomotive Works.

CLASS 3F   "JINTY"   0-6-0T

Built: 1924–31. Fowler LMS development of Midland design. 422 built (47260–47681).
Boiler Pressure: 160 lbf/sq in.   **Weight**: 49.5 tons.
Wheel Diameter: 4' 7".   **Cylinders**: 18" x 26" (I).
Valve Gear: Stephenson. Slide valves.   **Tractive Effort**: 20830 lbf.

BR	LMS		
47279	7119–7279	Keighley & Worth Valley Railway	VF 3736/1924
47298	7138–7298	East Lancashire Railway	HE 1463/1924
47324	16407–7324	East Lancashire Railway	NBL 23403/1926
47327	16410–7327	Midland Railway-Butterley	NBL 23406/1926
47357	16440–7357	Midland Railway-Butterley	NBL 23436/1926
47383	16466–7383	Severn Valley Railway	VF 3954/1926
47406	16489–7406	Great Central Railway	VF 3977/1926
47445	16528–7445	Midland Railway-Butterley	HE 1529/1927
47493	16576–7493	Spa Valley Railway	VF 4195/1928
47564	16647–7564	Midland Railway-Butterley	HE 1580/1928

47327 currently carries the identity SDJR 23.
47445 is currently under overhaul at Riley & Son (Electromec), Heywood.
47406 is currently under overhaul at Locomotive Maintenance Services, Loughborough.
47564 was latterly used as a stationary boiler numbered 2022. Currently dismantled.

CLASS 8F   2-8-0

Built: 1934–46. Stanier design. 331 built for LMS (8000–8225, 8301–8399, 8490–8495). A further 521 were built to Ministry of Supply (208), Railway Executive Committee (245) and LNER (68) orders. Many of these operated on Britain's railways, with 228 being shipped overseas during World War II. Post-war, many were taken into LMS/BR stock, including some returned from overseas.
Boiler Pressure: 225 lbf/sq in superheated.   **Weight–Loco:** 72.1 tons.
Wheel Diameters: 3′ 3½″, 4′ 8½″.   **–Tender:** 53.65 tons.
Cylinders: 18½″ x 28″ (O).   **Valve Gear:** Walschaerts. Piston valves.
Tractive Effort: 32 440 lbf.

§   Became Persian Railways 41.109.

BR	LMS	WD			
48151	8151		West Coast Railway Company, Carnforth	Crewe 1942
48173	8173		Churnet Valley Railway	Crewe 1943
48305	8305		Great Central Railway	Crewe 1943
48431	8431		Keighley & Worth Valley Railway	Swindon 1944
48624	8624		Great Central Railway	Ashford 1943
48773	8233	307–70307–500§	Severn Valley Railway	NBL 24607/1940

In addition, the following two locomotives were built to Ministry of Supply orders and have been repatriated to Great Britain:

*   Number allocated but never carried.

Dual (air/vacuum) brakes.

BR	LMS	WD	TCDD		
–	8274*	348	45160	Private site, Malvern	NBL 24648/1940
–	–	554	45170	Bo'ness & Kinneil Railway	NBL 24755/1942

▲ Lancashire & Yorkshire Railway Class 21 0-4-0ST 11243 leads a demonstration freight train around Chicken Curve on the Gloucestershire Warwickshire Railway on 14 May 2023. **Martyn Tattam**

LNWR CLASS G2 (7F) — 0-8-0

Built: 1921–22. Beames development of earlier Bowen-Cooke LNWR design. 60 built (49395–454). In addition, many earlier locos were rebuilt to similar condition.
Boiler Pressure: 175 lbf/sq in superheated.   **Weight–Loco**: 62 tons.
Wheel Diameter: 4' 5½".   **–Tender**: 40.75 tons.
Cylinders: 20½" x 24" (I).   **Valve Gear**: Joy. Piston valves.
Tractive Effort: 28 040 lbf.

BR	LMS	LNWR		
49395	9395	485	National Railway Museum, Shildon (N)	Crewe 5662/1921

L&Y CLASS 5 (2P) — 2-4-2T

Built: 1889–1909. Aspinall L&Y design. 309 built.
Boiler Pressure: 180 lbf/sq in.   **Weight**: 55.45 tons.
Wheel Diameters: 3' 7⅛", 5' 8", 3' 7⅛".   **Cylinders**: 18" x 26" (I).
Valve Gear: Joy. Slide valves.   **Tractive Effort**: 18 990 lbf.

BR	LMS	L&Y		
50621	10621	1008	National Railway Museum, York (N)	Horwich 1/1889

L&Y CLASS 21 (0F)   "PUG"   0-4-0ST

Built: 1891–1910. Aspinall L&Y design. 57 built.
Boiler Pressure: 160 lbf/sq in.   **Weight**: 21.25 tons.
Wheel Diameter: 3' 0¾".   **Cylinders**: 13" x 18" (O).
Valve Gear: Stephenson. Slide valves.   **Tractive Effort**: 11 370 lbf.

BR	LMS	L&Y		
51218	11218	68	Keighley & Worth Valley Railway	Horwich 811/1901
–	11243	19	East Lancashire Railway	Horwich 1097/1910

L&Y CLASS 23 (2F) — 0-6-0ST

Built: 1891–1900. Aspinall rebuild of Barton Wright L&Y 0-6-0. 230 rebuilt.
Boiler Pressure: 140 lbf/sq in.   **Weight**: 43.85 tons.
Wheel Diameter: 4' 6".   **Cylinders**: 17½" x 26" (I).
Valve Gear: Joy. Slide valves.   **Tractive Effort**: 17 590 lbf.

BR	LMS	L&Y		
–	11456	752	East Lancashire Railway	BP 1989/1881 reb Horwich 1896

Currently carries the number 51456, which it would have carried had it continued into BR service.

L&Y CLASS 25 (2F) — 0-6-0

Built: 1876–87. Barton Wright L&Y design. 280 built.
Boiler Pressure: 140 lbf/sq in.   **Weight–Loco**: 39.05 tons.
Wheel Diameter: 4' 6".   **–Tender**: 28.5 tons.
Cylinders: 17½" x 26" (I).   **Valve Gear**: Joy. Slide valves.
Tractive Effort: 17 590 lbf.

BR	LMS	L&Y		
52044	12044	957	Keighley & Worth Valley Railway	BP 2840/1887

L&Y CLASS 27 (3F) — 0-6-0

Built: 1889–1917. Aspinall L&Y design. 448 built.
Boiler Pressure: 180 lbf/sq in.   **Weight–Loco**: 44.3 tons.
Wheel Diameter: 5" 1".   **–Tender**: 26.1 tons.
Cylinders: 18" x 26" (I).   **Valve Gear**: Joy. Slide valves.
Tractive Effort: 21 170 lbf.

BR	LMS	L&Y		
52322	12322	1300	East Lancashire Railway	Horwich 420/1896

CLASS 7F — 2-8-0

Built: 1914–25. Fowler design for Somerset & Dorset Joint Railway (Midland and LSWR jointly owned). 11 built (53800–810).
Boiler Pressure: 190 lbf/sq in superheated.
Wheel Diameters: 3′ 3½″, 4′ 7½″.
Cylinders: 21″ x 28″ (O).
Tractive Effort: 35 950 lbf.
Weight–Loco: 64.75 tons.
     –Tender: 26.1 tons.
Valve Gear: Walschaerts. Piston valves.

BR	LMS	SDJR		
53808	9678–13808	88	Mid Hants Railway	RS 3894/1925
53809	9679–13809	89	North Norfolk Railway	RS 3895/1925

53809 is on long-term loan from the Midland Railway-Butterley.

CALEDONIAN RAILWAY (1P) — 4-2-2

Built: 1886. Drummond design. 1 built for the Edinburgh International Exhibition.
Boiler Pressure: 160 lbf/sq in.
Wheel Diameters: 3′ 6″, 7′ 0″, 4′ 6″.
Cylinders: 18″ x 26″ (I).
Tractive Effort: 13 640 lbf.
Weight–Loco: 41.35 tons.
     –Tender: 35.4 tons.
Valve Gear: Stephenson. Slide valves.

BR	LMS	CR		
–	14010	123	Glasgow Riverside Museum	N 3553/1886

CALEDONIAN RAILWAY 439 CLASS (2P) — 0-4-4T

Built: 1900–14. McIntosh design. 68 built.
Boiler Pressure: 160 lbf/sq in.
Wheel Diameters: 5′ 9″, 3′ 2″.
Valve Gear: Stephenson. Slide valves.
Weight: 53.95 tons.
Cylinders: 18″ x 26″ (I).
Tractive Effort: 16 600 lbf.

Dual (air/vacuum) brakes.

BR	LMS	CR		
55189	15189	419	Bo'ness & Kinneil Railway	St Rollox 1907

GSWR 322 CLASS (3F) — 0-6-0T

Built: 1917. Drummond design. 3 built.
Boiler Pressure: 160 lbf/sq in.
Wheel Diameter: 4′ 2″.
Valve Gear: Walschaerts. Piston valves.
Weight: 40 tons.
Cylinders: 17″ x 22″ (O).
Tractive Effort: 17 290 lbf.

BR	LMS	GSWR		
–	16379	9	Glasgow Riverside Museum	NBL 21521/1917

CALEDONIAN RAILWAY 812 CLASS (3F) — 0-6-0

Built: 1899–1900. McIntosh design. 96 built (57550–645).
Boiler Pressure: 160 lbf/sq in.
Wheel Diameter: 5′ 0″.
Cylinders: 18½″ x 26″ (I).
Tractive Effort: 20 170 lbf.
Weight–Loco: 45.7 tons.
     –Tender: 37.9 tons.
Valve Gear: Stephenson. Slide valves.

BR	LMS	CR		
57566	17566	828	Spa Valley Railway	St Rollox 1899

828–17566–57566 is on loan from the Strathspey Railway.

▲ Class 7F 2-8-0 53809 awaits departure from Sheringham, on the North Norfolk Railway, on 23 August 2023. **Alisdair Anderson**

▼ Whilst on loan to the Battlefield Line, Caledonian Railway 439 Class 0-4-4T 419 leads a train for Shenton away from Shackerstone on 17 April 2022. **Ian Beardsley**

▲ With Glasgow & South Western Railway 322 Class 0-6-0T 9 above, Highland Railway "Jones Goods" 4-6-0 103 stands at Glasgow's Riverside Museum on 9 June 2023. **Robert Pritchard**

▼ LNWR 2-2-2 3020 CORNWALL occupies part of the former Oxford Rewley Road station at the Buckinghamshire Railway Centre on 17 July 2022. **Ian Beardsley**

HIGHLAND RAILWAY (4F) "JONES GOODS" 4-6-0

Built: 1894. Jones design. 15 built.
Boiler Pressure: 175 lbf/sq in.
Wheel Diameters: 3' 3", 5' 3".
Cylinders: 20" x 26" (O).
Tractive Effort: 24560 lbf.

Weight–Loco: 56 tons.
       –Tender: 38.35 tons.
Valve Gear: Stephenson. Slide valves.

BR	LMS	HR		
–	17916	103	Glasgow Riverside Museum	SS 4022/1894

NORTH LONDON RAILWAY 75 CLASS (2F) 0-6-0T

Built: 1879–1905. Park design. 30 built.
Boiler Pressure: 160 lbf/sq in.
Wheel Diameter: 4' 4".
Valve Gear: Stephenson. Slide valves.

Weight: 45.55 tons.
Cylinders: 17" x 24" (O).
Tractive Effort: 18140 lbf.

BR	LMS	LNWR	NLR		
58850	7505–27505	2650	76–116	Bluebell Railway	Bow 181/1881

LNWR COAL TANK (2F) 0-6-2T

Built: 1881–97. Webb design. 300 built.
Boiler Pressure: 150 lbf/sq in.
Wheel Diameters: 4' 5½", 3' 9".
Valve Gear: Stephenson. Slide valves.

Weight: 43.75 tons.
Cylinders: 17" x 24" (I).
Tractive Effort: 16530 lbf.

BR	LMS	LNWR		
58926	7799	1054	Keighley & Worth Valley Railway	Crewe 2979/1888

MIDLAND 156 CLASS (1P) 2-4-0

Built: 1866–68. Kirtley design. 31 built.
Boiler Pressure: 140 lbf/sq in.
Wheel Diameters: 4' 3", 6' 3".
Cylinders: 18" x 24" (I).
Tractive Effort: 12340 lbf.

Weight–Loco: 41.25 tons.
       –Tender: 34.85 tons.
Valve Gear: Stephenson. Slide valves.

BR	LMS	MR		
–	2–20002	158–158A–2	Barrow Hill Roundhouse (N)	Derby 1866

NORTH STAFFS RAILWAY New L CLASS (3F) 0-6-2T

Built: 1903–23. Hookham design. 34 built.
Boiler Pressure: 175 lbf/sq in.
Wheel Diameters: 5' 0", 4' 0".
Valve Gear: Stephenson. Slide valves.

Weight: 64.95 tons.
Cylinders: 18½" x 26" (I).
Tractive Effort: 22060 lbf.

LMS	NSR		
2271	2	Foxfield Railway	Stoke 1923

Although built in 1923, this loco carried an NSR number as the NSR was not taken over by the LMS until 1 July 1923.

LNWR PRECEDENT (1P) 2-4-0

Built: 1874–82 (renewed 1887–1901). Webb design. 166 built.
Boiler Pressure: 150 lbf/sq in.
Wheel Diameters: 3' 9", 6' 9".
Cylinders: 17" x 24" (I).
Tractive Effort: 10920 lbf.

Weight–Loco: 35.6 tons.
       –Tender: 25 tons.
Valve Gear: Allan.

LMS	LNWR			
5031	790	HARDWICKE	National Railway Museum, Shildon (N)	Crewe 3286/1892

LNWR 2-2-2

Built: 1847. Trevithick design rebuilt by Ramsbottom in 1858.
Boiler Pressure: 140 lbf/sq in.   **Weight–Loco:** 29.9 tons.
Wheel Diameters: 3' 6", 8' 6", 3' 6".   **–Tender:** 25 tons.
Cylinders: 17¼" x 24" (O).   **Valve Gear:** Stephenson. Slide valves.
Tractive Effort: 8330 lbf.

LNWR
173–3020   CORNWALL   Buckinghamshire Railway Centre (N)   Crewe 35/1847

LNWR 0-4-0ST

Built: 1865. Ramsbottom design. Sold by LNWR 1919.
Boiler Pressure: 120 lbf/sq in.   **Weight:** 22.75 tons.
Wheel Diameter: 4' 0".   **Cylinders:** 14" x 20" (I).
Tractive Effort: 8330 lbf.

LNWR
1439–1985–3042   Ribble Steam Railway (N)   Crewe 842/1865

GRAND JUNCTION RAILWAY 2-2-2

Built: 1845. Trevithick design.
Boiler Pressure: 120 lbf/sq in.   **Weight–Loco:** 20.4 tons.
Wheel Diameters: 3' 6", 6' 0", 3' 6".   **–Tender:** 16.4 tons. (stored at the Science
Cylinders: 15" x 20" (O).   Museum Store, Wroughton, Wiltshire).
Tractive Effort: 6375 lbf.   **Valve Gear:** Allan.

LNWR   GJR
49   49–1868   COLUMBINE   Science Museum, London (N)   Crewe 25/1845

FURNESS RAILWAY 0-4-0

Built: 1846. 4 built.
Boiler Pressure: 110 lbf/sq in.   **Weight–Loco:** 20 tons.
Wheel Diameter: 4' 9".   **–Tender:** 13 tons.
Cylinders: 14" x 24" (I).   **Valve Gear:** Stephenson. Slide valves.
Tractive Effort: 7720 lbf.

3   COPPERNOB   National Railway Museum, York (N)   BCK 1846

FURNESS RAILWAY 0-4-0

Built: 1863 as 0-4-0. Sold in 1870 to Barrow Steelworks and numbered 7. Rebuilt 1915 as 0-4-0ST. Restored to original condition 1999.
Boiler Pressure: 120 lbf/sq in.   **Wheel Diameter:** 4'10".
Cylinders: 15½" x 24"(I).   **Tractive Effort:** 10 140 lbf.

20   Ribble Steam Railway   SS 1435/1863

FURNESS RAILWAY 0-4-0ST

Built: 1865 as 0-4-0. Sold in 1873 to Barrow Steelworks and numbered 17. Rebuilt 1921 as 0-4-0ST.
Boiler Pressure: 120 lbf/sq in.   **Wheel Diameter:** 4'3".
Cylinders: 15½" x 24"(I).   **Tractive Effort:** 11 532 lbf.

FR   Present
25   6   Ribble Steam Railway   SS 1585/1865

LIVERPOOL & MANCHESTER RAILWAY   0-2-2

Built: 1829 for the Rainhill trials.
Boiler Pressure: 50 lbf/sq in.   **Weight–Loco:** 4.25 tons.
Wheel Diameters: 4' 8½", 2' 6".   **–Tender:** 5.2 tons.
Cylinders: 8" x 17" (O).   **Tractive Effort:** 820 lbf.

| 1 | ROCKET | National Railway Museum, Shildon (N) | RS 1/1829 |

LIVERPOOL & MANCHESTER RAILWAY   0-4-0

Built: 1829 for the Rainhill trials.
Boiler Pressure: 50 lbf/sq in.   **Weight–Loco:** 4.25 tons.
Wheel Diameter: 4' 6".   **–Tender:** 5.2 tons.
Cylinders: 7" x 18" (O).   **Tractive Effort:** 690 lbf.

SANS PAREIL   National Railway Museum, Shildon (N)   Hack 1829

LIVERPOOL & MANCHESTER RAILWAY   0-4-2

Built: 1838–39. 4 built. The survivor was the star of the film "The Titfield Thunderbolt".
Boiler Pressure: 50 lbf/sq in.   **Weight–Loco:** 14.45 tons.
Wheel Diameters: 5' 0", 3' 3".   **–Tender:**
Cylinders: 14" x 24" (I).   **Tractive Effort:** 3330 lbf.

LNWR   *L&MR*
116   57   LION   Museum of Liverpool   TKL 1838

MERSEY RAILWAY   0-6-4T

Built: 1885. Withdrawn 1903 on electrification. 5 was sold to Shipley colliery in Derbyshire.
Boiler Pressure: 150 lbf/sq in.   **Weight:** 67.85 tons.
Wheel Diameters: 4' 7", 3' 0".   **Cylinders:** 21" x 26" (I).
Valve Gear: Stephenson. Slide valves.   **Tractive Effort:** 26 600 lbf.

| 1 | THE MAJOR | NSW Rail Museum, Thirlmere, Australia | BP 2601/1885 |
| 5 | CECIL RAIKES | Museum of Liverpool Store, Bootle | BP 2605/1885 |

HIGHLAND RAILWAY (DUKE OF SUTHERLAND)   0-4-4T

Built: 1895 for the Duke of Sutherland. Exported to Canada 1965, repatriated to Britain 2011.
Boiler Pressure: 150 lbf/sq in.   **Weight:** 25 tons.
Wheel Diameters: 4' 6", 2' 6".   **Cylinders:** 13" x 18" (I).
Valve Gear: Stephenson.   **Tractive Effort:** 7183 lbf.

–   DUNROBIN   Beamish: The Living Museum of the North   SS 4085/1895
Currently under overhaul at the Severn Valley Railway.

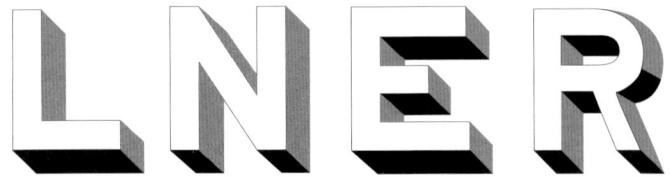

1.4. LONDON & NORTH EASTERN RAILWAY AND CONSTITUENT COMPANIES' STEAM LOCOMOTIVES

GENERAL

The LNER was formed in 1923 through the amalgamation of the Great Northern Railway (GNR), North Eastern Railway (NER), Great Eastern Railway (GER), Great Central Railway (GCR), North British Railway (NBR) and Great North of Scotland Railway (GNSR). Prior to this, the Hull & Barnsley Railway (H&B) had been absorbed by the NER in 1922.

NUMBERING SYSTEM

Initially, pre-grouping locomotive numbers were retained, but in September 1923 suffix letters started to be applied depending upon the works that repaired the locomotives. In 1924, locomotives were renumbered in blocks as follows: NER locomotives remained unaltered, GNR locomotives had 3000 added, GCR 5000, GNSR 6800, GER 7000 and NBR 9000. New locomotives filled in gaps between existing numbers. By 1943, the numbering of new locomotives had become so haphazard that it was decided to completely renumber locomotives so that locomotives of a particular class were all contained in the same block of numbers. This was carried out in 1946. On nationalisation in 1948, 60000 was added to LNER numbers.

In the following section, locomotives are listed in order of BR number or in the position of the BR number they would have carried if they had lasted into BR days, except for very old locomotives, which are listed at the end of the section.

CLASSIFICATION SYSTEM

The LNER gave each class a unique code consisting of a letter denoting the wheel arrangement and a number denoting the individual class within the wheel arrangement. Route availability (RA) was denoted by a number, the higher the number the more restricted the route availability.

CLASS A4 — 4-6-2

Built: 1935–38. Gresley streamlined design. MALLARD attained the world speed record for a steam locomotive of 126 mph in 1938 and is still unbeaten. 35 built (2509–12, 4462–69/82–4500/4900–03).
Boiler Pressure: 250 lbf/sq in superheated. **Weight–Loco:** 102.95 tons.
Wheel Diameters: 3′ 2″, 6′ 8″, 3′ 8″. **–Tender:** 64.15 tons.
Cylinders: 18½″ x 26″ (3). **Tractive Effort:** 35 450 lbf.
Valve Gear: Walschaerts with derived motion for inside cylinder. Piston valves.
BR Power Classification: 8P. **RA:** 9.

x Dual (air/vacuum) brakes.
* Restored with single chimney.

BR	LNER			
60007 x	4498–7	SIR NIGEL GRESLEY	LNWR Heritage, Crewe	Doncaster 1863/1937
60008	4496–8	DWIGHT D. EISENHOWER	National Railroad Museum, Green Bay, Wisconsin, USA	Doncaster 1861/1937
60009 x	4488–9	UNION OF SOUTH AFRICA	Balbuthie Farm, Kilconquhar	Doncaster 1853/1937
60010 *	4489–10	DOMINION OF CANADA	Exporail, The Canadian Railway Museum, Montreal, Canada	Doncaster 1854/1937
60019 x	4464–19	BITTERN	Locomotive Storage, Margate	Doncaster 1866/1937
60022	4468–22	MALLARD	National Railway Museum, York (N)	Doncaster 1870/1938

60008 was originally named GOLDEN SHUTTLE and 60010 was originally named WOODCOCK.

CLASS A3 — 4-6-2

Built: 1922–35. Gresley design. Built as Class A1 (later reclassified A10 after the Peppercorn A1s were being designed), but rebuilt to A3 in 1947. 79 built (60035–113). Fitted (1959) with Kylchap blastpipe, double chimney and (1961) German-style smoke deflectors. Restored to single chimney on preservation in 1963, but reverted to double chimney in 1993. The locomotive has also carried the number 4472 in preservation, a number it never carried as an A3, since it was renumbered 103 in 1946.
Boiler Pressure: 220 lbf/sq in superheated. **Weight–Loco:** 96.25 tons.
Wheel Diameters: 3′ 2″, 6′ 8″, 3′ 8″. **–Tender:** 62.4 tons.
Cylinders: 19″ x 26″ (3). **Tractive Effort:** 32 910 lbf.
Valve Gear: Walschaerts with derived motion for inside cylinder. Piston valves.
BR Power Classification: 7P. **RA:** 9.

Dual (air/vacuum) brakes.

BR	LNER			
60103	1472–4472–502–103	FLYING SCOTSMAN	National Railway Museum, York (N)	Doncaster 1564/1923

CLASS A2 — 4-6-2

Built: 1947–48. Peppercorn development of Thompson design. 15 built (60525–539).
Boiler Pressure: 250 lbf/sq in superheated. **Weight–Loco:** 101 tons.
Wheel Diameters: 3′ 2″, 6′ 2″, 3′ 8″. **–Tender:** 60.35 tons.
Cylinders: 19″ x 26″ (3). **Valve Gear:** Walschaerts. Piston valves.
Tractive Effort: 40 430 lbf. **BR Power Classification:** 8P.
RA: 9.

Dual (air/vacuum) brakes.

60532	BLUE PETER	LNWR Heritage, Crewe	Doncaster 2023/1948

▲ Class A4 4-6-2 60007 SIR NIGEL GRESLEY is seen shortly after crossing Broadsands Viaduct, on the Dartmouth Steam Railway, with a railtour to Kingswear on 3 June 2023. **David Hunt**

▼ On 23 June 2023, Class A3 4-6-2 60103 FLYING SCOTSMAN passes Prickwillow with the return leg of a Railway Touring Company railtour from King's Cross to Great Yarmouth. **Aubrey Evans**

CLASS V2　　　　　　　　　　　　　　　　　　　　　　　　　　2-6-2

Built: 1936–44. Gresley design for express passenger and freight. 184 built (60800–983).
Boiler Pressure: 220 lbf/sq in superheated. **Weight–Loco:** 93.1 tons.
Wheel Diameters: 3′ 2″, 6′ 2″, 3′ 8″. 　　　　　　　　　　　**–Tender:** 52 tons.
Cylinders: 18½″ x 26″ (3). 　　　　　　　**Tractive Effort:** 33 730 lbf.
Valve Gear: Walschaerts with derived motion for inside cylinder. Piston valves.
BR Power Classification: 6MT. 　　　　　**RA:** 9.

BR	LNER			
60800	4771–800	GREEN ARROW	Danum Gallery, Library & Museum, Doncaster (N)	Doncaster 1837/1936

CLASS B1　　　　　　　　　　　　　　　　　　　　　　　　　　4-6-0

Built: 1942–52. Thompson design. 410 built (61000–409).
Boiler Pressure: 225 lbf/sq in superheated. **Weight–Loco:** 71.15 tons.
Wheel Diameters: 3′ 2″, 6′ 2″. 　　　　　　　　　　　　　　　**–Tender:** 52 tons.
Cylinders: 20″ x 26″ (O). 　　　　　　　**Valve Gear:** Walschaerts. Piston valves.
Tractive Effort: 26 880 lbf. 　　　　　　**BR Power Classification:** 5MT.
RA: 5.

x　Dual (air/vacuum) brakes.

BR	LNER			
61264	1264		Great Central Railway (Nottingham)	NBL 26165/1947
61306 x		"MAYFLOWER"	LNWR Heritage, Crewe	NBL 26207/1948

The original MAYFLOWER was 61379. 61264 also carried DEPARTMENTAL LOCOMOTIVE No. 29.

CLASS B12　　　　　　　　　　　　　　　　　　　　　　　　　　4-6-0

Built: 1911–28. Holden GER Class S69. 81 built (1500–70, 8571–80). Survivor rebuilt to B12/3 1933.
Boiler Pressure: 180 lbf/sq in superheated. **Weight –Loco:** 69.5 tons.
Wheel Diameters: 3′ 3″, 6′ 6″. 　　　　　　　　　　　　　　　**–Tender:** 39.3 tons.
Cylinders: 20″ x 28″ (I). 　　　　　　　**Valve Gear:** Stephenson. Piston valves.
Tractive Effort: 21 970 lbf. 　　　　　　**BR Power Classification:** 4P.
RA: 5.

Dual (air/vacuum) brakes.

BR	LNER		
61572	8572–1572	North Norfolk Railway	BP 6488/1928

Currently under overhaul at Riley & Son (Electromec), Heywood.

CLASS K4　　　　　　　　　　　　　　　　　　　　　　　　　　2-6-0

Built: 1937–38. Gresley design for West Highland line. 6 built (61993–98).
Boiler Pressure: 200 lbf/sq in superheated. **Weight–Loco:** 68.4 tons.
Wheel Diameters: 3′ 2″, 5′ 2″. 　　　　　　　　　　　　　　　**–Tender:** 44.2 tons.
Cylinders: 18½″ x 26″ (3). 　　　　　　　**Tractive Effort:** 36 600 lbf.
Valve Gear: Walschaerts with derived motion for inside cylinder. Piston valves.
BR Power Classification: 5P6F. 　　　　**RA:** 6.

BR	LNER			
61994	3442–1994	THE GREAT MARQUESS	Balbuthie Farm, Kilconquhar	Darlington 1761/193

CLASS K1   2-6-0

Built: 1949–50. Peppercorn design. 70 built (62001–070).
Boiler Pressure: 225 lbf/sq in superheated.
Wheel Diameters: 3' 2", 5' 2".
Cylinders: 20" x 26" (O).
Tractive Effort: 32080 lbf.
RA: 6.
Weight–Loco: 66 tons.
    –Tender: 52.2 tons.
Valve Gear: Walschaerts. Piston valves.
BR Power Classification: 6MT.

BR				
62005		North Yorkshire Moors Railway		NBL 26609/1949

Currently under overhaul at West Coast Railway Company, Carnforth.

CLASS D40   4-4-0

Built: 1899–1921. Pickersgill GNSR Class F. 21 built.
Boiler Pressure: 165 lbf/sq in superheated.
Wheel Diameters: 3' 9½", 6' 1".
Cylinders: 18" x 26" (I).
Tractive Effort: 16180 lbf.
RA: 4.
Weight –Loco: 48.65 tons.
    –Tender: 37.4 tons.
Valve Gear: Stephenson. Slide valves.
BR Power Classification: 1P.

BR	LNER	GNSR			
62277	6849–2277	49	GORDON HIGHLANDER	Bo'ness & Kinneil Railway	NBL 22563/1920

CLASS D34   GLEN   4-4-0

Built: 1913–20. Reid NBR Class K. 32 built.
Boiler Pressure: 165 lbf/sq in superheated.
Wheel Diameters: 3' 6", 6' 0".
Cylinders: 20" x 26" (I).
Tractive Effort: 22100 lbf.
RA: 6.
Weight–Loco: 57.2 tons.
    –Tender: 46.65 tons.
Valve Gear: Stephenson. Piston valves.
BR Power Classification: 3P.

BR	LNER	NBR			
62469	9256–2469	256	GLEN DOUGLAS	Glasgow Riverside Museum	Cowlairs 1913

CLASS D11   IMPROVED DIRECTOR   4-4-0

Built: 1919–22. Robinson GCR Class 11F. 11 built (62660–670). 24 similar locos were built by the LNER.
Boiler Pressure: 180 lbf/sq in superheated.
Wheel Diameters: 3' 6", 6' 9".
Cylinders: 20" x 26" (I).
Tractive Effort: 19640 lbf.
RA: 6.
Weight–Loco: 61.15 tons.
    –Tender: 48.3 tons.
Valve Gear: Stephenson. Piston valves.
BR Power Classification: 3P.

BR	LNER	GCR			
62660	5506–2660	506	BUTLER HENDERSON	Barrow Hill Roundhouse (N)	Gorton 1919

CLASS D49/1   4-4-0

Built: 1927–29. Gresley design. 36 built (62700–735).
Boiler Pressure: 180 lbf/sq in superheated.
Wheel Diameters: 3' 1¼", 6' 8".
Cylinders: 17" x 26" (3).
Valve Gear: Walschaerts with derived motion for inside cylinder. Piston valves.
BR Power Classification: 4P.
Weight–Loco: 66 tons.
    –Tender: 52 tons.
Tractive Effort: 21560 lbf.
RA: 8.

BR	LNER			
62712	246–2712	MORAYSHIRE	Bo'ness & Kinneil Railway	Darlington 1391/1928

Currently under overhaul at Locomotive Maintenance Services, Loughborough.

▲ Class B1 4-6-0 61306 "MAYFLOWER" makes a spirited departure from Littlehampton whilst working a Steam Dreams Rail Co railtour to Eastleigh on 10 June 2023. **Paul Biggs**

▼ With the North Sea in the background, Class J15 0-6-0 564 climbs past the golf course at Sheringham on 9 October 2022 with the North Norfolk Railway's vintage train. **Robert Falconer**

CLASS E4 — 2-4-0

Built: 1891–1902. Holden GER Class T26. 100 built.
Boiler Pressure: 160 lbf/sq in.
Wheel Diameters: 4′ 0″, 5′ 8″.
Cylinders: 17½″ x 24″ (I).
Tractive Effort: 14 700 lbf.
RA: 2.
Weight–Loco: 40.3 tons.
 –Tender: 30.65 tons.
Valve Gear: Stephenson. Slide valves.
BR Power Classification: 1MT.

Air brakes.

BR	LNER	GER		
62785	7490–7802–2785	490	Bressingham Steam Museum (N)	Stratford 836/1894

CLASS C1 — 4-4-2

Built: 1902–10. Ivatt GNR Class C1. 94 built.
Boiler Pressure: 170 lbf/sq in.
Wheel Diameters: 3′ 8″, 6′ 8″, 3′ 8″.
Cylinders: 20″ x 24″ (O).
Tractive Effort: 17 340 lbf.
RA: 7.
Weight–Loco: 69.6 tons.
 –Tender: 43.1 tons.
Valve Gear: Stephenson. Slide valves.
BR Power Classification: 2P.

BR	LNER	GNR		
–	3251–2800	251	Danum Gallery, Library & Museum, Doncaster (N)	Doncaster 991/1902

CLASS Q6 — 0-8-0

Built: 1913–21. Raven NER Class T2. 120 built (63340–459).
Boiler Pressure: 180 lbf/sq in superheated.
Wheel Diameter: 4′ 7¼″.
Cylinders: 20″ x 26″ (O).
Tractive Effort: 28 800 lbf.
RA: 6.
Weight–Loco: 65.9 tons.
 –Tender: 44.1 tons.
Valve Gear: Stephenson. Piston valves.
BR Power Classification: 6F.

BR	LNER	NER		
63395	2238–3395	2238	North Yorkshire Moors Railway	Darlington 1918

CLASS Q7 — 0-8-0

Built: 1919–24. Raven NER Class T3. 15 built (63460–474).
Boiler Pressure: 180 lbf/sq in superheated.
Wheel Diameter: 4′ 7¼″.
Cylinders: 18½″ x 26″ (3).
Tractive Effort: 36 960 lbf.
RA: 7.
Weight–Loco: 71.6 tons.
 –Tender: 44.1 tons.
Valve Gear: Stephenson. Piston valves.
BR Power Classification: 8F.

BR	LNER	NER		
63460	901–3460	901	National Railway Museum, Shildon (N)	Darlington 1919

CLASS O4 — 2-8-0

Built: 1911–20. Robinson GCR Class 8K. 129 built. A further 521 were built following an order from the Railway Operating Department (ROD). These saw service on British and overseas railways during and after World War I. Some subsequently passed to British railway administrations whilst others were sold abroad.
Boiler Pressure: 180 lbf/sq in superheated.
Wheel Diameters: 3′ 6″, 4′ 8″.
Cylinders: 21″ x 26″ (O).
Tractive Effort: 31 330 lbf.
RA: 6.
Weight–Loco: 73.2 tons.
   –Tender: 48.3 tons.
Valve Gear: Stephenson. Piston valves.
BR Power Classification: 7F.

BR	LNER	GCR		
63601	5102–3509–3601	102	Great Central Railway (N)	Gorton 1911

ROD				
1984		Dorrigo Steam Railway & Museum, New South Wales, Australia		NBL 22042/1918
2003		Dorrigo Steam Railway & Museum, New South Wales, Australia		Gorton 1918
2004		Richmond Vale Railway Museum, Kurri-Kurri, NSW, Australia		Gorton 1918

CLASS J21 — 0-6-0

Built: 1886–95. Worsdell NER Class C. 201 built.
Boiler Pressure: 160 lbf/sq in superheated.
Wheel Diameter: 5′ 1¼″.
Cylinders: 19″ x 24″ (I).
Tractive Effort: 19 240 lbf.
RA: 3.
Weight–Loco: 43.75 tons.
   –Tender: 36.95 tons.
Valve Gear: Stephenson. Piston valves.
BR Power Classification: 2F.

BR	LNER	NER		
65033	876–5033	876	Stainmore Railway	Gateshead 1889

Currently under overhaul at Locomotive Maintenance Services, Loughborough.

CLASS J36 — 0-6-0

Built: 1888–1900. Holmes NBR Class C. 168 built.
Boiler Pressure: 165 lbf/sq in.
Wheel Diameter: 5′ 0″.
Cylinders: 18″ x 26″ (I).
Tractive Effort: 20 240 lbf.
RA: 3.
Weight–Loco: 41.95 tons.
   –Tender: 33.5 tons.
Valve Gear: Stephenson. Slide valves.
BR Power Classification: 2F.

BR	LNER	NBR			
65243	9673–5243	673	MAUDE	Bo'ness & Kinneil Railway	N 4392/1891

CLASS J15 — 0-6-0

Built: 1883–1913. Worsdell GER Class Y14. 189 built.
Boiler Pressure: 160 lbf/sq in.
Wheel Diameter: 4′ 11″.
Cylinders: 17½″ x 24″ (I).
Tractive Effort: 16 940 lbf.
RA: 1.
Weight–Loco: 37.1 tons.
   –Tender: 30.65 tons.
Valve Gear: Stephenson. Slide valves.
BR Power Classification: 2F.

Dual (air/vacuum) brakes.

BR	LNER	GER		
65462	7564–5462	564	North Norfolk Railway	Stratford 1912

▲ One of four locomotives from the national collection that are currently based at Barrow Hill, Class J17 0-6-0 8217 stands on the roundhouse turntable on 12 May 2022. **Ian Beardsley**

▼ Class J27 0-6-0 65894 leads a mixed freight train away from Loughborough on 1 October 2022, the final day of the Great Central Railway's Autumn Steam Gala that year. **Peter Foster**

CLASS J17 — 0-6-0

Built: 1900–11. Holden GER Class G58. 90 built (65500–589).
Boiler Pressure: 180 lbf/sq in superheated. **Weight –Loco:** 45.4 tons.
Wheel Diameter: 4' 11". **–Tender:** 38.25 tons.
Cylinders: 19" x 26" (I). **Valve Gear:** Stephenson. Slide valves.
Tractive Effort: 24340 lbf. **BR Power Classification:** 4F.
RA: 4.

No train brakes.

BR	LNER	GER		
65567	8217–5567	1217	Barrow Hill Roundhouse (N)	Stratford 1905

CLASS J27 — 0-6-0

Built: 1906–23. Worsdell NER Class P3. 115 built.
Boiler Pressure: 180 lbf/sq in superheated. **Weight–Loco:** 47 tons.
Wheel Diameter: 4' 7¼". **–Tender:** 37.6 tons.
Cylinders: 18½" x 26" (I). **Valve Gear:** Stephenson. Piston valves.
Tractive Effort: 24640 lbf. **BR Power Classification:** 4F.
RA: 5.

BR	LNER		
65894	2392–5894	North Yorkshire Moors Railway	Darlington 1923

CLASS Y5 — 0-4-0ST

Built: 1874–1903. Neilson & Company design for GER (Class 209). 8 built. Survivor sold in 1917.
Boiler Pressure: 140 lbf/sq in. **Weight:** 21.2 tons.
Wheel Diameter: 3' 7". **Cylinders:** 12" x 20" (O).
Valve Gear: Stephenson. Slide valves. **Tractive Effort:** 7970 lbf.
RA: 1.

GER		
229	Flour Mill Workshop, Bream	N 2119/1876

CLASS J94. 68077/078 (LNER 8077/078) – see War Department Steam Locomotives.

CLASS Y7 — 0-4-0T

Built: 1888–1923. Worsdell NER Class H. 24 built.
Boiler Pressure: 160 lbf/sq in. **Weight:** 22.7 tons.
Wheel Diameter: 4' 0". **Cylinders:** 14" x 20" (I).
Valve Gear: Joy. Slide valves. **Tractive Effort:** 11140 lbf.
BR Power Classification: 0F. **RA:** 1.

BR	LNER	NER		
68088	985–8088		Mid Suffolk Light Railway	Darlington 1205/1923
–	1310	1310	Middleton Railway	Gateshead 38/1891

CLASS Y9 — 0-4-0ST

Built: 1882–99. Drummond NBR Class G. 35 built.
Boiler Pressure: 130 lbf/sq in. **Weight:** 27.8 tons.
Wheel Diameter: 3' 8". **Cylinders:** 14" x 20" (I).
Valve Gear: Stephenson. Slide valves. **Tractive Effort:** 9840 lbf.
BR Power Classification: 0F. **RA:** 2.

BR	LNER	NBR		
68095	10094–8095	42–894–1094	Bo'ness & Kinneil Railway	Cowlairs 1887

CLASS Y1 — 4wVBGT

Built: 1925–33. Sentinel geared loco. 24 built.
Boiler Pressure: 275 lbf/sq in superheated.
Wheel Diameter: 2' 6".
Valve Gear: Rotary cam. Poppet valves.
BR Power Classification: 0F.
Weight: 19.8 tons.
Cylinders: 6¾" x 9" (I).
Tractive Effort: 7260 lbf.
RA: 1.

BR	LNER		
68153	59–8153	Middleton Railway	S 8837/1933

Also carried DEPARTMENTAL LOCOMOTIVE No. 54.

CLASS J69 — 0-6-0T

Built: 1890–1904. Holden GER Class S56. 126 locomotives (including many rebuilt from J67).
Boiler Pressure: 180 lbf/sq in.
Wheel Diameter: 4' 0".
Valve Gear: Stephenson. Slide valves.
BR Power Classification: 2F.
Weight: 42.45 tons.
Cylinders: 16½" x 22" (I).
Tractive Effort: 19090 lbf.
RA: 3.

Air brakes.

BR	LNER	GER		
68633	7087–8633	87	Bressingham Steam Museum (N)	Stratford 1249/1904

CLASS J52 — 0-6-0ST

Built: 1897–1909. Ivatt GNR Class J13. Many rebuilt from Stirling locomotives (built 1892–97).
Boiler Pressure: 170 lbf/sq in.
Wheel Diameter: 4' 8".
Valve Gear: Stephenson. Slide valves.
BR Power Classification: 3F.
Weight: 51.7 tons.
Cylinders: 18" x 26" (I).
Tractive Effort: 21740 lbf.
RA: 5.

BR	LNER	GNR		
68846	4247–8846	1247	National Railway Museum, York (N)	SS 4492/1899

CLASS J72 — 0-6-0T

Built: 1898–1925. Worsdell NER Class E1. Further batch built 1949–51 by BR. 113 built.
Boiler Pressure: 140 lbf/sq in.
Wheel Diameter: 4' 1¼".
Valve Gear: Stephenson. Slide valves.
BR Power Classification: 2F.
Weight: 38.6 tons.
Cylinders: 17" x 24" (I).
Tractive Effort: 16760 lbf.
RA: 5.

69023–Departmental No. 59   1861 Shed, Darlington   Darlington 2151/1951

CLASS N2 — 0-6-2T

Built: 1920–29. Gresley GNR Class N2. 107 built (69490–596).
Boiler Pressure: 170 lbf/sq in superheated.
Wheel Diameter: 5' 8", 3' 8".
Valve Gear: Stephenson. Piston valves.
BR Power Classification: 3MT.
Weight: 70.25 tons.
Cylinders: 19" x 26" (I).
Tractive Effort: 19950 lbf.
RA: 6.

BR	LNER	GNR		
69523	4744–9523	1744	North Norfolk Railway	NBL 22600/1921

▲ North Eastern Railway 1001 Class 0-6-0 1275 is pictured at the National Railway Museum, York on 29 January 2024. **Robert Pritchard**

▼ Great Northern Railway Class A2 4-2-2 1 stands on display around the turntable in the Great Hall at the National Railway Museum, York on 29 January 2024. **Robert Pritchard**

CLASS N7   0-6-2T

Built: 1915–28. Hill GER Class L77. 134 built (69600–733). 69621 rebuilt to N7/4 1946.
Boiler Pressure: 180 lbf/sq in superheated.   **Weight:** 61.8 tons.
Wheel Diameters: 4′ 10″, 3′ 9″.   **Cylinders:** 18″ x 24″ (I).
Valve Gear: Walschaerts (inside). Piston valves.   **Tractive Effort:** 20510 lbf.
RA: 5.   **BR Power Classification:** 3MT.

Dual (air/vacuum) brakes.

BR	LNER	GER		
69621	999E–7999–9621	999	East Anglian Railway Museum	Stratford 1924

CLASS X1   2-2-4T

Built: 1869 by NER as 2-2-2WT. Rebuilt 1892 to 2-cylinder compound 4-2-2T and rebuilt as 2-2-4T in 1902 and used for pulling inspection saloons. NER Class 66.
Boiler Pressure: 175 lbf/sq in.   **Weight:** 44.95 tons.
Wheel Diameters: 3′ 7″, 5′ 7¾″, 3′ 1¼″.   **Cylinders:** 13″ x 24″ (hp) + 18½″ x 20″ (lp) (I).
Valve Gear: Stephenson. Slide valves.   **Tractive Effort:** 6390 lbf.

LNER	NER			
66	1478–66	AEROLITE	National Railway Museum, Shildon (N)	Gateshead 1869

NER 901 CLASS   2-4-0

Built: 1872–82. Fletcher design. 55 built.
Boiler Pressure: 160 lbf/sq in.   **Weight–Loco:** 39.7 tons.
Wheel Diameters: 4′ 6″, 7′ 0″.   **–Tender:** 29.9 tons.
Cylinders: 18″ x 24″ (I).   **Valve Gear:** Stephenson. Slide valves.
Tractive Effort: 12590 lbf.

LNER	NER		
910	910	Stainmore Railway (N)	Gateshead 1875

NER 1001 CLASS   0-6-0

Built: 1864–75. Bouch design for Stockton & Darlington Railway.
Boiler Pressure: 130 lbf/sq in.   **Weight–Loco:** 35 tons.
Wheel Diameter: 5′ 0½″.   **Cylinders:** 17″ x 26″ (I).
Valve Gear: Stephenson. Slide valves.   **Tractive Effort:** 13720 lbf.

LNER	NER		
1275	1275	National Railway Museum, York (N)	Glasgow 707/1874

CLASS E5   2-4-0

Built: 1885. Tennant NER 1463 Class. 20 built.
Boiler Pressure: 160 lbf/sq in.   **Weight–Loco:** 42.1 tons.
Wheel Diameters: 4′ 6″, 7′ 0″.   **–Tender:** 32.1 tons.
Cylinders: 18″ x 24″ (I).   **Valve Gear:** Stephenson. Slide valves.
Tractive Effort: 12590 lbf.

LNER	NER		
1463	1463	Head of Steam, Darlington Railway Museum (N)	Darlington 1885

CLASS D17/1 — 4-4-0

Built: 1893–97. Worsdell NER Class M1 (later Class M). 20 built.
Boiler Pressure: 160 lbf/sq in. **Weight–Loco:** 52 tons.
Wheel Diameters: 3' 7¼", 7' 1¼".   **–Tender:** 41 tons.
Cylinders: 19" x 26" (I). **Valve Gear:** Stephenson. Slide valves.
Tractive Effort: 14970 lbf. **RA:** 6.

LNER	NER		
1621	1621	National Railway Museum, Shildon (N)	Gateshead 1893

CLASS C2 — "KLONDYKE" — 4-4-2

Built: 1898–1903. HA Ivatt GNR Class C1. 22 built.
Boiler Pressure: 170 lbf/sq in superheated. **Weight–Loco:** 62 tons.
Wheel Diameters: 3' 8", 6' 8", 3' 8". **–Tender:** 42.1 tons.
Cylinders: 19" x 24" (O). **Valve Gear:** Stephenson. Piston valves.
Tractive Effort: 15650 lbf. **RA:** 4.

LNER	GNR			
3990	990	HENRY OAKLEY	National Railway Museum, York (N)	Doncaster 769/1898

GNR CLASS A2 — 4-2-2

Built: 1870–93. Stirling design. 47 built. 1 is currently matched with a GNR "Stirling" tender (built 1893). The GNR "Stirling Goods" tender that had been paired with it is currently stored at the National Railway Museum, Shildon.
Boiler Pressure: 140 lbf/sq in. **Weight–Loco:** 38.5 tons.
Wheel Diameters: 3' 10", 8' 1", 4' 1". **–Tender:** 30 tons.
Cylinders: 18" x 28" (O). **Valve Gear:** Stephenson. Slide valves.
Tractive Effort: 11130 lbf.

1	National Railway Museum, York (N)	Doncaster 50/1870

STOCKTON & DARLINGTON RAILWAY — 0-4-0

Built: 1825–26. George Stephenson design. 6 built.
Boiler Pressure: 50 lbf/sq in. **Weight–Loco:** 6.5 tons.
Wheel Diameter: 3' 11". **–Tender:**
Cylinders: 9½" x 24" (O). **Tractive Effort:** 2050 lbf.

1	LOCOMOTION	National Railway Museum, Shildon (N)	RS 1/1825

1 was originally named ACTIVE.

STOCKTON & DARLINGTON RAILWAY — 0-6-0

Built: 1845. Timothy Hackworth design.
Boiler Pressure: 75 lbf/sq in. **Weight–Loco:** 6.5 tons.
Wheel Diameter: 4' 0". **Cylinders:** 14½" x 24" (O).
Tractive Effort: 6700 lbf.

25	DERWENT	Head of Steam, Darlington Railway Museum (N)	Kitching 1845

1.5. BRITISH RAILWAYS STANDARD STEAM LOCOMOTIVES

GENERAL

From 1951 onwards, British Railways produced a series of standard steam locomotives under the jurisdiction of RA Riddles. Examples of most classes have been preserved, the exceptions being the Class 6MT "Clan" Pacifics, the Class 3MT 2-6-0s (77000 series), the Class 3MT 2-6-2Ts (82000 series) and the Class 2MT 2-6-2Ts (84000 series).

NUMBERING SYSTEM

Tender engines were numbered in the 70000 series and tank engines in the 80000 series, the exceptions being the Class 9F 2-10-0s, which were numbered in the 92000 series.

CLASSIFICATION SYSTEM

British Railways standard steam locomotives were referred to by power classification like LMS locomotives. All locomotives were classed as "MT", denoting "mixed traffic", except for 71000 and the Class 9F 2-10-0s. The latter, although freight locos, were often used on passenger trains on summer Saturdays.

▲ Bluebell-based Class 5MT 4-6-0 73082 CAMELOT heads a mixed freight train south along the Great Central Railway near Swithland Sidings on 29 January 2023. **Martyn Tattam**

CLASS 7MT BRITANNIA 4-6-2

Built: 1951–54. 55 built (70000–054).
Boiler Pressure: 250 lbf/sq in superheated. **Weight–Loco:** 94 tons.
Wheel Diameters: 3' 0", 6' 2", 3' 3½".   **–Tender:** 49.15 tons.
Cylinders: 20" x 28" (O).   **Valve Gear:** Walschaerts. Piston valves.
Tractive Effort: 32160 lbf.   **RA:** 7

x   Dual (air/vacuum) brakes.

70000 x	BRITANNIA	LNWR Heritage, Crewe	Crewe 1951
70013	OLIVER CROMWELL	Great Central Railway (N)	Crewe 1951

CLASS 8P 4-6-2

Built: 1954. 1 built.
Boiler Pressure: 250 lbf/sq in superheated. **Weight–Loco:** 101.25 tons.
Wheel Diameters: 3' 0", 6' 2", 3' 3½".   **–Tender:** 53.7 tons.
Cylinders: 18" x 28" (3).   **Valve Gear:** British Caprotti (outside). Poppet valves.
Tractive Effort: 39080 lbf.   **RA:** 8.

Dual (air/vacuum) brakes.

71000	DUKE OF GLOUCESTER	Tyseley Locomotive Works	Crewe 1954

CLASS 5MT 4-6-0

Built: 1951–57. 172 built (73000–171).
Boiler Pressure: 225 lbf/sq in superheated. **Weight–Loco:** 76 tons.
Wheel Diameters: 3' 0", 6' 2".   **–Tender:** 50.25 or 52.5 tons.
Cylinders: 19" x 28" (O).
Valve Gear: Walschaerts. Piston valves (* outside British Caprotti. Poppet valves).
Tractive Effort: 26120 lbf.   **RA:** 5.

x   Dual (air/vacuum) brakes.

73050 x	"CITY OF PETERBOROUGH"	Nene Valley Railway	Derby 1954
73082	CAMELOT	Bluebell Railway	Derby 1955
73096		Mid Hants Railway	Derby 1955
73129 *		Midland Railway-Butterley	Derby 1956
73156		Great Central Railway	Doncaster 1956

CLASS 4MT 4-6-0

Built: 1951–57. 80 built (75000–079).
Boiler Pressure: 225 lbf/sq in superheated. **Weight–Loco:** 67.9 tons.
Wheel Diameters: 3' 0", 5' 8".   **–Tender:** 42.15 or 50.25 tons.
Cylinders: 18" x 28" (O).   **Valve Gear:** Walschaerts. Piston valves.
Tractive Effort: 25520 lbf.   **RA:** 4.

*   Fitted with double chimney.

75014	"BRAVEHEART"	Dartmouth Steam Railway	Swindon 1951
75027		Bluebell Railway	Swindon 1954
75029 *	"THE GREEN KNIGHT"	North Yorkshire Moors Railway	Swindon 1954
75069 *		Severn Valley Railway	Swindon 1955
75078 *		Keighley & Worth Valley Railway	Swindon 1956
75079 *		Mid Hants Railway	Swindon 1956

CLASS 4MT 2-6-0

Built: 1952–57. 115 built (76000–114).
Boiler Pressure: 225 lbf/sq in superheated.
Wheel Diameters: 3' 0", 5' 3".
Cylinders: 17½" x 26" (O).
Tractive Effort: 24 170 lbf.
Weight–Loco: 59.75 tons.
        –Tender: 42.15 tons.
Valve Gear: Walschaerts. Piston valves.
RA: 4.

76017	Southall Depot	Horwich 1953
76077	Gloucestershire Warwickshire Railway	Horwich 1956
76079	North Yorkshire Moors Railway	Horwich 1957
76084	North Norfolk Railway	Horwich 1957

76077 is currently under overhaul at Locomotive Maintenance Services, Loughborough.

CLASS 2MT 2-6-0

Built: 1952–56. 65 built (78000–064). These locomotives were almost identical to the Ivatt LMS Class 2MT 2-6-0s (46400–46527).
Boiler Pressure: 200 lbf/sq in superheated.
Wheel Diameters: 3' 0", 5' 0".
Cylinders: 16½" x 24" (O).
Tractive Effort: 18 510 lbf.
Weight–Loco: 49.25 tons.
        –Tender: 36.85 tons.
Valve Gear: Walschaerts. Piston valves.
RA: 3.

78018	Great Central Railway	Darlington 1954
78019	Great Central Railway	Darlington 1954
78022	Keighley & Worth Valley Railway	Darlington 1954

CLASS 4MT 2-6-4T

Built: 1951–57. 155 built (80000–154).
Boiler Pressure: 225 lbf/sq in superheated.
Wheel Diameters: 3' 0", 5' 8", 3' 0".
Valve Gear: Walschaerts. Piston valves.
RA: 4.
Weight: 86.65 tons.
Cylinders: 18" x 28" (O).
Tractive Effort: 25 520 lbf.

80002	Keighley & Worth Valley Railway	Derby 1952
80064	West Somerset Railway	Brighton 1953
80072	Llangollen & Corwen Railway	Brighton 1953
80078	Mid Norfolk Railway	Brighton 1954
80079	Severn Valley Railway	Brighton 1954
80080	Ecclesbourne Valley Railway	Brighton 1954
80097	East Lancashire Railway	Brighton 1954
80098	Midland Railway-Butterley	Brighton 1954
80100	Bluebell Railway	Brighton 1955
80104	Swanage Railway	Brighton 1955
80105	Bo'ness & Kinneil Railway	Brighton 1955
80135	North Yorkshire Moors Railway	Brighton 1956
80136	North Yorkshire Moors Railway	Brighton 1956
80150	Mid Hants Railway	Brighton 1956
80151	Bluebell Railway	Brighton 1957

80078 is on loan from Sonic Rail Services, Burnham-on-Crouch.
80080 is on loan from the Midland Railway-Butterley.
80104 is currently under overhaul at Tyseley Locomotive Works.

▲ Class 4MT 2-6-0 76079 arrives at Grosmont with one of the North Yorkshire Moors Railway's services from Whitby to Pickering on 2 August 2022. **Alisdair Anderson**

▼ Shortly after departing East Grinstead, Class 4MT 2-6-4T 80151 crosses Imberhorne Viaduct with one of the Bluebell Railway's services to Sheffield Park on 20 March 2022. **Jon Bowers**

CLASS 9F   2-10-0

Built: 1954–60. 251 built (92000–250). 92220 EVENING STAR was the last steam locomotive to be built for British Railways.
Boiler Pressure: 250 lbf/sq in superheated.
Wheel Diameters: 3' 0", 5' 0".
Cylinders: 20" x 28" (O).
Tractive Effort: 39670 lbf.
Weight–Loco: 86.7 tons.
             –Tender: 52.5 or 55.25 tons.
Valve Gear: Walschaerts. Piston valves.
RA: 9.

* Fitted with a single chimney. All other surviving members of the class have double chimneys.

92134 *		North Yorkshire Moors Railway	Crewe 1957
92203	"BLACK PRINCE"	North Norfolk Railway	Swindon 1959
92207	"MORNING STAR"	North Dorset Railway Trust, Shillingstone	Swindon 1959
92212		Mid Hants Railway	Swindon 1959
92214		Great Central Railway	Swindon 1959
92219		Strathspey Railway	Swindon 1960
92220	EVENING STAR	National Railway Museum, York (N)	Swindon 1960
92240		Bluebell Railway	Crewe 1958
92245		NL Engineering (North West), Blackrod	Crewe 1958

92207 is currently undergoing overhaul at Somerset & Dorset Steam, Poole.
92212 is currently undergoing overhaul at the Midland Railway-Butterley.

▲ During a photographic charter at the Great Central Railway on 24 November 2023, Class 9F 2-10-0 92214 approaches Quorn & Woodhouse with a train of mineral wagons. **Robert Falconer**

1.6. WAR DEPARTMENT STEAM LOCOMOTIVES

GENERAL

During the Second World War, the War Department (WD) of the British Government acquired and used a considerable number of steam locomotives. On the cessation of hostilities, many of these locomotives were sold for further service, both to industrial users and other railway administrations. The bulk of WD steam locomotives preserved date from this period. By 1952, many of the large wartime fleet of steam locomotives had been disposed of and those remaining were renumbered into a new series. From 1 April 1964, the WD became the Army Department of the Ministry of Defence, with consequent renumbering taking place in 1968. The locomotives considered to be main line locomotives built to "Austerity" designs are included here. Also included in this section are the steam locomotives built to WD "Austerity" designs for industrial users. Only those locomotives currently resident in Great Britain are shown.

CLASS WD　　　　　　　AUSTERITY　　　　　　　2-10-0

Built: 1943–45 by North British. 150 built. Many sold to overseas railways. 25 sold to BR in 1948 and numbered 90750–774.
Boiler Pressure: 225 lbf/sq in superheated.　**Weight–Loco:** 78.3 tons.
Wheel Diameters: 3′ 2″, 4′ 8½″.　　　　　　　　–Tender: 55.5 tons
Cylinders: 19″ x 28″ (O).　　　　　　**Valve Gear:** Walschaerts. Piston valves.
Tractive Effort: 34 210 lbf.　　　　　**BR Power Classification:** 8F.

g　Hellenic Railways (Greece) number.

AD/Overseas	WD				
600	3651–73651	GORDON		Severn Valley Railway	NBL 25437/1943
Lb951 g	3652–73652			North Norfolk Railway	NBL 25438/1943
Lb960 g	3672–73672	"DAME VERA LYNN"	North Yorkshire Moors Railway	NBL 25458/1944

3652–73652–Lb951 carries the number 90775 and the name "THE ROYAL NORFOLK REGIMENT".

CLASS WD　　　　　　　AUSTERITY　　　　　　　2-8-0

Built: 1943–45 by North British & Vulcan Foundry. 935 built. Many sold to overseas railways. 200 sold to LNER in 1946. These became LNER 3000–3199 and BR 90000–100, 90422–520. A further 533 were sold to BR in 1948 and numbered 90101–421, 90521–732.
Boiler Pressure: 225 lbf/sq in superheated.　**Weight–Loco:** 70.25 tons.
Wheel Diameters: 3′ 2″, 4′ 8½″.　　　　　　　　–Tender: 55.5 tons.
Cylinders: 19″ x 28″ (O).　　　　　　**Valve Gear:** Walschaerts. Piston valves.
Tractive Effort: 34 210 lbf.　　　　　**BR Power Classification:** 8F.

This locomotive was purchased from Swedish State Railways (SJ), having previously seen service with Netherlands Railways (NS). It has been restored to BR condition.

Present	SJ	NS	WD		
90733	1931	4464	79257	Keighley & Worth Valley Railway	VF 5200/1945

CLASS 50550　　　　　　　　　　　　　　　　　0-6-0ST

Built: 1941–42. 8 built. Originally intended for Stewarts and Lloyd Minerals, but only 1 delivered. 3 taken on by WD, becoming 65–67. 4 went to other industrial users and 2 of these survive.
Boiler Pressure: 170 lbf/sq in.　　　　**Weight:** 48.35 tons.
Wheel Diameter: 4′ 5″.　　　　　　　　**Cylinders:** 18″ x 26″ (I).
Valve Gear: Stephenson. Slide valves.　**Tractive Effort:** 22 150 lbf.

WD	Present		
–	Unnumbered	Dean Forest Railway	HE 2411/1941
–	GUNBY	Dean Forest Railway	HE 2413/1942
66–70066	S112 "SPITFIRE"	Embsay & Bolton Abbey Railway	HE 2414/1942

66–70066–S112 is currently under overhaul at NL Engineering (North West), Blackrod.

▲ Class WD Austerity 2-10-0 600 GORDON stands on display in the Engine House at Highley, on the Severn Valley Railway, on 19 May 2022. **Ian Beardsley**

▼ Class WD Austerity 0-6-0ST 66 (HE 3890/1964) is seen working one of the shuttle services at the Buckinghamshire Railway Centre on 17 July 2022. **Ian Beardsley**

CLASS WD AUSTERITY 0-6-0ST

Built: 1943–53 for Ministry of Supply and War Department. 391 built. 75 bought by LNER and classified J94. Many others passed to industrial users. The design of this class was derived from the 50550 Class of Hunslet locomotives (see page 67).
Boiler Pressure: 170 lbf/sq in.   **Weight:** 48.25 tons.
Wheel Diameter: 4′ 3″.   **Cylinders:** 18″ x 26″ (I).
Valve Gear: Stephenson. Slide valves.   **Tractive Effort:** 23870 lbf.
BR Power Classification: 4F.   **RA:** 5.

§   Oil fired.   x   Dual (air/vacuum) brakes.
†   Rebuilt as 0-6-0 tender locomotive.   *   Rebuilt in preservation as a side tank.

BR	LNER	WD		
68078	8078	71463	Hope Farm, Sellindge	AB 2212/1946
68077	8077	71466	Spa Valley Railway	AB 2215/1946

WD/AD	Present		
71480	Unnumbered	Tyseley Locomotive Works	RSH 7289/1945
71499	Unnumbered	NL Engineering (North West), Blackrod	HC 1776/1944
71505–118 x§	BRUSSELS LONGMOOR MILITARY RAILWAY	Keighley & Worth Valley Railway	HC 1782/1945
71515		Pontypool & Blaenavon Railway	RSH 7169/1944
71516	"WELSH GUARDSMAN"	Severn Valley Railway	RSH 7170/1944
71529–165	W.P.R No. 15 "EARL DAVID"	Vale of Berkeley Railway	AB 2183/1945
75006		Nene Valley Railway	HE 2855/1943
75008 x	"SWIFTSURE"	Kent & East Sussex Railway	HE 2857/1943
75015	48	Aln Valley Railway	HE 2864/1943
75019–168	"LORD PHIL"	Midland Railway-Butterley	HE 2868/1943
			rebuilt HE 3883/1963
75030	Unnumbered	Caledonian Railway	HE 2879/1943
75031–101	No. 17	Locomotive Maintenance Services, Loughborough	HE 2880/1943
75041–107†	2890	East Lancashire Railway	HE 2890/1943
			rebuilt HE 3882/1962
75050	No. 35 "NORMAN"	East Lancashire Railway	RSH 7086/1943
75061	No. 9 CAIRNGORM	Strathspey Railway	RSH 7097/1943
75062	49	Tanfield Railway	RSH 7098/1943
75091	68067	Llangollen & Corwen Railway	HC 1752/1943
75105	"WALKDEN"	Ribble Steam Railway	HE 3155/1944
75113–132	SAPPER	Kent & East Sussex Railway	HE 3163/1944
			rebuilt HE 3885/1964
75118–134	S134 "WHELDALE"	Embsay & Bolton Abbey Railway	HE 3168/1944
75130	ANTWERP	Hope Farm, Sellindge	HE 3180/1944
75133–138	Unnumbered	Flour Mill Workshop, Bream	HE 3183/1944
75141–139	68006	Barrow Hill Roundhouse	HE 3192/1944
			rebuilt HE 3888/1964
75142–140	3193 "NORFOLK REGIMENT"	Northampton & Lamport Railway	HE 3193/1944
			rebuilt HE 3887/1964
75158–144	"THE DUKE"	Ecclesbourne Valley Railway	WB 2746/1944
75161	Unnumbered	Caledonian Railway	WB 2749/1944
75170	2758	Cefn Coed Colliery Museum	WB 2758/1944
75171–147	Unnumbered	Caledonian Railway	WB 2759/1944
75178		Bodmin Railway	WB 2766/1945
75186–150	ROYAL PIONEER	Peak Rail	RSH 7136/1944
			rebuilt HE 3892/1969
75189–152	RENNES	Dean Forest Railway	RSH 7139/1944
			rebuilt HE 3880/1962
75254–175		Bo'ness & Kinneil Railway	WB 2777/1945
75256	No. 20	Tanfield Railway	WB 2779/1945
75282–181	"HAULWEN"	Gwili Railway	VF 5272/1945
			rebuilt HE 3879/1961
75319	72	Mountsorrel & Rothley Community Heritage Centre	VF 5309/1945
190–90		Colne Valley Railway	HE 3790/1952

191–91	No. 23 "HOLMAN F. STEPHENS"	Kent & East Sussex Railway	HE 3791/1952
192–92 x	WAGGONER	Isle of Wight Steam Railway	HE 3792/1953
193–93	Unnumbered	Ribble Steam Railway	HE 3793/1953
194–94	"CUMBRIA"	Ribble Steam Railway	HE 3794/1953
197 x	No. 25 "NORTHIAM"	Kent & East Sussex Railway	HE 3797/1953
198–98 x	ROYAL ENGINEER	Isle of Wight Steam Railway	HE 3798/1953
200	Unnumbered	Colne Valley Railway	HE 3800/1953

In addition to the 391 locomotives built for the Ministry of Supply and the War Department, a further 93 were built for industrial users, those that survive being:

No. 60		Aln Valley Railway	HE 3686/1949
WHISTON		Foxfield Railway	HE 3694/1950
RESPITE		Ribble Steam Railway	HE 3696/1950
REPULSE		Lakeside & Haverthwaite Railway	HE 3698/1950
NORMA		Cambrian Heritage Railways, Oswestry	HE 3770/1952
8 "SIR ROBERT PEEL"		Embsay & Bolton Abbey Railway	HE 3776/1952
68030		North Yorkshire Moors Railway	HE 3777/1952
1 *		Mid Hants Railway	HE 3781/1952
No. 69		Stephenson Steam Railway	HE 3785/1953
N.C.B. MONCKTON No.1		Embsay & Bolton Abbey Railway	HE 3788/1953
"WILBERT REV.W.AWDRY"		Dean Forest Railway	HE 3806/1953
3809		Great Central Railway	HE 3809/1954
GLENDOWER		South Devon Railway	HE 3810/1954
No. 19		Bo'ness & Kinneil Railway	HE 3818/1954
WARRIOR		Dean Forest Railway	HE 3823/1954
68009		Stainmore Railway	HE 3825/1954
Unnumbered		Gwili Railway	HE 3829/1955
No. 5		Bo'ness & Kinneil Railway	HE 3837/1955
WIMBLEBURY		Foxfield Railway	HE 3839/1956
PAMELA		Garw Valley Railway	HE 3840/1956
No. 22 x		North Norfolk Railway	HE 3846/1956
JUNO		National Railway Museum, Shildon	HE 3850/1958
CADLEY HILL No. 1		Leicestershire County Museum store, Snibston	HE 3851/1962
65		Dean Forest Railway	HE 3889/1964
66		Buckinghamshire Railway Centre	HE 3890/1964

HC 1752/1943 is on loan from the Great Central Railway.
HE 3168/1944 is currently under overhaul at Statfold Engineering.
HE 3776/1952 is under overhaul at NL Engineering (North West), Blackrod.
HE 3846/1956 is on loan from the Appleby–Frodingham RPS, Scunthorpe.
HE 3850/1958 is on loan from the Isle of Wight Steam Railway.

SHROPSHIRE & MONTGOMERY RAILWAY 0-4-2WT

Built: 1893 by Alfred Dodman & Company for William Birkitt. Sold to Shropshire & Montgomery Railway in 1911 when it was rebuilt from 2-2-2WT.
Boiler Pressure: 60 lbf/sq in. **Weight**: 5.5 tons.
Wheel Diameters: 2' 3", 2'3". **Cylinders**: 4" x 9" (I).

In 1950, after being requisitioned by the War Department in the Second World War, this locomotive and three others (LNWR coal engines) became BR (WR) stock when this line was nationalised. The locomotives were then withdrawn.

1	GAZELLE	Kent & East Sussex Railway (N)	Dodman/1893

1.7. UNITED STATES ARMY TRANSPORTATION CORPS STEAM LOCOMOTIVES

GENERAL

During World War II many locomotives were constructed by various American builders for the USATC. Many saw use on Britain's railways, particularly in the period 1943–45. After the war many of these locos were sold to overseas railway administrations, but several have now been repatriated to the British Isles. Only those locos currently resident in Great Britain are shown here.

CLASS S160   2-8-0

Built: 1942–45 by various American builders. It is estimated that 2120 were built.
Boiler Pressure: 225 lbf/sq in superheated. **Weight–Loco:** 73 tons.
Wheel Diameters: 3' 2", 4' 9".   **–Tender:** 52.1 tons.
Cylinders: 19" x 26" (O).   **Tractive Effort:** 31 490 lbf.
Valve Gear: Walschaerts. Piston valves.

USATC	Overseas Railway		
1631	MAV (Hungarian Railways) 411.388	Reid Freight Services, Cockshute Sidings, Stoke-on-Trent	AL 70284/1942
2138	MAV (Hungarian Railways) 411.009	*Location unknown*	AL 70620/1943
2253	PKP (Polish Railways) Tr203.288	Dartmouth Steam Railway	BLW 69496/1943
2364	MAV (Hungarian Railways) 411.337	*Location unknown*	BLW 69621/1943
3278	FS (Italian State Railways) 736.073	Churnet Valley Railway	AL 71533/1944
5197	Chinese State Railways KD6.463	Churnet Valley Railway	Lima 8856/1945
5820	PKP (Polish Railways) Tr203.474	Keighley & Worth Valley Railway	Lima 8758/1945
6046	MAV (Hungarian Railways) 411.144	Churnet Valley Railway	BLW 72080/1945

2253 carries the name "OMAHA".
3278 carries the name "FRANKLYN D. ROOSEVELT".

Only the frames of 2364 survive.

3278 is on long-term loan from Tyseley Locomotive Works. This locomotive passed to Hellenic Railways (Greece) and was numbered 575. Formerly Baldwin 70340.

See the Southern Railway section for Class USATC S100 0-6-0Ts.

1.8. NEW BUILD STEAM LOCOMOTIVES

GENERAL

The following is a list of new build steam locomotive projects that have either been completed, are expected to be completed within two years or at least a have frames in place. Technical details refer to the original locomotives and the new build locomotives may differ from these.

1.8.1. COMPLETED NEW BUILD STEAM LOCOMOTIVES

GWR 2900 CLASS   SAINT   4-6-0

Original Class Built: 1902–13. Churchward design. 77 built (2910–55, 2971–90, 2998). The new build locomotive was rebuilt from GWR 4900 Class 4-6-0 4942 MAINDY HALL.
Boiler Pressure: 225 lbf/sq in superheated.   **Weight–Loco:** 72 tons.
Wheel Diameters: 3' 2", 6' 8½".   **–Tender:** 43.15 tons.
Cylinders: 18½" x 30" (O).   **Valve Gear:** Stephenson.
Tractive Effort: 24390 lbf.   **Restriction:** Red.
Power Classification: D (4P).

2999   LADY OF LEGEND   Didcot Railway Centre   Swindon 1929, rebuilt Didcot 3540/2018

GWR 6800 CLASS   GRANGE   4-6-0

Original Class Built: 1936–39. Collett design. 80 built (6800–79). The new build locomotive uses the boiler from GWR 6959 Class 4-6-0 7927 WILLINGTON HALL.
Boiler Pressure: 225 lbf/sq in superheated.   **Weight–Loco:** 74 tons.
Wheel Diameters: 3' 0", 5' 8".   **–Tender:** 40 tons.
Cylinders: 18½" x 30" (O).   **Valve Gear:** Stephenson. Piston valves.
Tractive Effort: 28875 lbf.   **Restriction:** Red.
Power Class: D (5MT).

6880   BETTON GRANGE   Tyseley Locomotive Works   Tyseley Locomotive Works 2024

GWR 9351 CLASS   2-6-0

Rebuilt from 5101 Class 2-6-2T 5193 by the West Somerset Railway.
Boiler Pressure: 225 lbf/sq in superheated.   **Weight–Loco:** 63.85 tons.
Wheel Diameters: 3' 2", 5' 8".   **–Tender:** 40 tons.
Cylinders: 18" x 30" (O).   **Valve Gear:** Stephenson. Piston valves.
Tractive Effort: 28880 lbf.   **Restriction:** Blue.
Power Classification: C.

9351   West Somerset Railway   Swindon 1934, rebuilt WSR/2006

LNER CLASS A1   4-6-2

Original Class Built: 1948–49. Peppercorn development of Thompson A1/1.
Boiler Pressure: 250 lbf/sq in superheated.   **Weight–Loco:** 104.7 tons.
Wheel Diameters: 3' 2", 6' 8", 3' 8".   **–Tender:** 66.1 tons.
Cylinders: 19" x 26" (3).   **Valve Gear:** Walschaerts. Piston valves.
Tractive Effort: 37400 lbf.   **BR Power Classification:** 8P.
RA: 9.

New build locomotive has dual (air/vacuum) brakes.

60163   TORNADO   Darlington Locomotive Works   Darlington Hope Street 2195/2008

▲ The Great Western Society's new build GWR 2900 Class 4-6-0 2999 LADY OF LEGEND stands on the shed apron at Didcot Railway Centre on 26 August 2023. **Martyn Tattam**

▼ New build GWR 9351 Class 2-6-0 9351 climbs Washford bank with the West Somerset Railway's 10.15 Bishops Lydeard–Minehead service on 20 March 2022 . **Nick Gilliam**

1.8.2. NEW BUILD STEAM LOCOMOTIVES UNDER CONSTRUCTION

GWR DESIGN

3800 CLASS   COUNTY   4-4-0

Original Class Built: 1904–12. Churchward design. 40 built (3800–39). The new build locomotive is using the boiler from GWR 5205 Class 2-8-0 5227 and major parts from two other GWR donor locomotives – 2800 Class 2-8-0 2861 and 5101 Class 2-6-2T 4115.
Boiler Pressure: 200 lbf/sq in superheated.   **Weight–Loco**: 55.3 tons.
Wheel Diameters: 3' 2", 6' 8½".   **–Tender**: 36.75 tons.
Cylinders: 18" x 30" (O).   **Valve Gear**: Stephenson. Piston valves.
Tractive Effort: 20 530 lbf.   **Restriction**: Red.
Power Class: C.

3840   COUNTY OF MONTGOMERY   Tyseley Locomotive Works   Under construction

4700 CLASS   2-8-0

Original Class Built: 1919–23. Churchward design. 9 built (4700–08). This new build locomotive will use parts from three GWR donor locomotives – 4073 Class 7027 THORNBURY CASTLE, 5101 Class 2-6-2T 4115 and 5205 Class 2-8-0T 5227 – but has completely new frames.
Boiler Pressure: 225 lbf/sq in superheated.   **Weight–Loco**: 82 tons.
Wheel Diameters: 3' 2", 5' 8".   **–Tender**: 46 tons.
Cylinders: 19" x 30" (O).   **Valve Gear**: Stephenson. Piston valves.
Tractive Effort: 30 460 lbf.   **Restriction**: Red.
Power Classification: D (7F).

4709   Tyseley Locomotive Works   Under construction

LMS DESIGN

LNWR   BLOOMER   2-2-2

Original Class Built: 1851–62. 74 built; 31 "Small Bloomers" and 40 "Large Bloomers" and three "Special Bloomers". James McConnel design for express passenger work between London and Birmingham, and later Rugby and Stafford.
Boiler Pressure: 100 lbf/sq.   **Weight–Loco**: 29.5 tons.
Wheel Diameters: 4' 6", 7', 4'.   **–Tender**:
Cylinders: 16" x 22" (I).   **Valve Gear**: Stephenson.
Tractive Effort:

670   Tyseley Locomotive Works   Under construction

LNWR   GEORGE THE FIFTH   4-4-0

Original Class Built: 1910–15. Bowen-Cooke design. 80 built. In addition, 10 Queen Mary class 4-4-0s were rebuilt as George the Fifths.
Boiler Pressure: 180 lbf/sq.   **Weight–Loco**: 60 tons.
Wheel Diameters: 3' 3", 6', 9".   **–Tender**:
Cylinders: 20.5" x 26" (I).   **Valve Gear**: Joy.
Tractive Effort: 20 640 lbf.

2013–22013   PRINCE GEORGE   Crewe Heritage Centre   Under construction

LNER DESIGN

CLASS P2 — 2-8-2

Original Class Built: 1934–36. Gresley design. 6 built (2001–06).
Boiler Pressure: 220 lbf/sq in superheated. **Weight–Loco:** 107.15 tons.
Wheel Diameters: 3′ 2″, 6′ 2″, 3′ 8″. **–Tender:** 60.35 tons.
Cylinders: 21″ x 26″ (3).
Valve Gear: Lentz. Rotary (2001); Walschaerts. Piston valves (2002–06).
Tractive Effort: 43 462 lbf.

2007	PRINCE OF WALES	Darlington Locomotive Works	Under construction

CLASS B17 — 4-6-0

Original Class Built: 1928–37. Gresley design. 73 built (2800–2872).
Boiler Pressure: 200 lbf/sq in superheated. **Weight–Loco:** 77.25 tons.
Wheel Diameters: 3′ 2″, 6′ 8″. **–Tender:** 39 tons.
Cylinders: 17½″ x 26″ (3). **Valve Gear:** Gresley conjugated.
Tractive Effort: 25 380 lbf. **RA:** 5

Class B17/6: Rebuilt with Diagram 100A boilers. Details as above except:
Boiler Pressure: 225 lbf/sq in superheated. **Weight – Tender:** 52 tons.
Tractive Effort: 28 553 lbf.

61673	SPIRIT OF SANDRINGHAM	CTL Seal, Sheffield	Under Construction

BRITISH RAILWAYS DESIGN

CLASS 6MT — CLAN — 4-6-2

Original Class Built: 1951–52. 10 built (72000–09).
Boiler Pressure: 225 lbf/sq in superheated. **Weight–Loco:** 88.5 tons.
Wheel Diameters: 3′ 2″, 6′ 2″, 3′ 3½″. **–Tender:** 49.15 tons.
Cylinders: 19½″ x 28″ (O). **Valve Gear:** Walschaerts. Piston valves.
Tractive Effort: 27 520 lbf. **RA:** 6

72010	HENGIST	CTL Seal, Sheffield	Under construction

CLASS 3MT — 2-6-2T

Original Class Built: 1952–55. 45 built (82000–44).
Boiler Pressure: 200 lbf/sq in superheated. **Weight:** 74.05 tons.
Wheel Diameters: 3′ 0″, 5′ 3″, 3′ 0″. **Cylinders:** 17½″ x 26″ (O).
Valve Gear: Walschaerts. Piston valves. **Tractive Effort:** 21 490 lbf.
RA: 4.

82045	Severn Valley Railway	Under construction

CLASS 2MT — 2-6-2T

Original Class Built: 1953–57. 30 built (84000–29). This new build locomotive is being rebuilt from BR 2MT 2-6-0 78059.
Boiler Pressure: 200 lbf/sq in superheated. **Weight:** 66.25 tons.
Wheel Diameters: 3′ 0″, 5′ 0″, 3′ 0″. **Cylinders:** 16½″ x 24″ (O).
Valve Gear: Walschaerts. Piston valves. **Tractive Effort:** 18 510 lbf.
RA: 1.

84030	Bluebell Railway	Under construction

▲ New build BR Class 6MT 4-6-2 72010 HENGIST is seen under construction at CTL Seal, Sheffield on 23 April 2022. **Robert Pritchard**

▼ The 1934 replica of Liverpool & Manchester Railway 0-2-2 1 ROCKET stands on display in the Great Hall at the National Railway Museum, York on 29 January 2024. **Robert Pritchard**

1.9. REPLICA STEAM LOCOMOTIVES

GENERAL

Details are included of steam locomotives which would have been included in the preceding chapters had the original locomotive survived or does survive. Locomotives are listed under the heading of the original Railway/Manufacturer. Only locomotives which work, previously worked or can be relatively easily made to work are included.

1.9.1 COMPLETED REPLICA STEAM LOCOMOTIVES

STOCKTON & DARLINGTON RAILWAY   0-4-0
Built: 1975.
Boiler Pressure: 50 lbf/sq in.
Wheel Diameter: 3' 11".
Cylinders: 9½" x 24" (O).
Weight—Loco: 6.5 tons.
—Tender:
Tractive Effort: 2050 lbf.

| 1 | LOCOMOTION | Head of Steam, Darlington Railway Museum | Loco Ent 1/1975 |

1 was originally named ACTIVE.
Currently under overhaul at Locomotive Maintenance Services, Loughborough.

LIVERPOOL & MANCHESTER RAILWAY   0-2-2
Built: 1934/79.
Boiler Pressure: 50 lbf/sq in.
Wheel Diameters: 4' 8½", 2' 6".
Cylinders: 8" x 17" (O).
Weight—Loco: 4.25 tons.
—Tender: 5.2 tons.
Tractive Effort: 820 lbf.

§   Sectioned.

| 1 | ROCKET § | National Railway Museum, York (N) | RS 4089/1934 |
| 1 | ROCKET | National Railway Museum, York (N) | Loco Ent 2/1979 |

LIVERPOOL & MANCHESTER RAILWAY   0-4-0
Built: 1979.
Boiler Pressure: 50 lbf/sq in.
Wheel Diameter: 4' 6".
Cylinders: 7" x 18" (O).
Weight—Loco: 4.25 tons.
—Tender: 5.2 tons.
Tractive Effort: 690 lbf.

| SANS PAREIL | National Railway Museum, Shildon | Shildon 1980 |

LIVERPOOL & MANCHESTER RAILWAY   2-2-0
Built: 1992 (original dated from 1832).
Boiler Pressure: 100 lbf/sq in (original 50 lbf/sq in).
Wheel Diameters: 5'.
Cylinders: 9" x 22" (O).
Weight—Loco: 8 tons.
—Tender: 4 tons.
Tractive Effort:

| PLANET | 9 | Science & Industry Museum, Manchester | Manchester 1992 |

BRAITHWAITE & ERICSSON & COMPANY   0-2-2WT
Built: 1929 (using parts from 1829 original)/1980.
Boiler Pressure:
Wheel Diameter:
Cylinders:
Weight—Loco:
—Tender:
Tractive Effort:

| NOVELTY | Science & Industry Museum, Manchester (N) | Science Museum 1929 |
| NOVELTY | Swedish Railway Museum, Gävle, Sweden | Loco Ent 3/1980 |

GREAT WESTERN RAILWAY   2-2-2

Built: 1925 (using parts from 1837 original).   **Gauge:** 7' 0¼".
Boiler Pressure: 90 lbf/sq in.   **Weight–Loco:** 23.35 tons.
Wheel Diameters: 4' 0", 7' 0", 4' 0".   **–Tender:** 6.5 tons.
Cylinders: 16" x 16" (I).   **Tractive Effort:** 3730 lbf.

NORTH STAR	STEAM – Museum of the Great Western Railway (N)	Swindon 1925

GREAT WESTERN RAILWAY   2-2-2

Built: 2005.   **Gauge:** 7' 0¼".
Boiler Pressure: 50 lbf/sq in.   **Weight–Loco:** 23.35 tons.
Wheel Diameters: 4' 0", 7' 0", 4' 0".   **–Tender:** 6.5 tons.
Cylinders: 15" x 18" (I).   **Tractive Effort:** 2050 lbf.

FIRE FLY	Didcot Railway Centre	Didcot/Bristol 2005

GREAT WESTERN RAILWAY   4-2-2

Built: 1985.   **Gauge:** 7' 0¼".
Boiler Pressure: **Weight–Loco:** 35.5 tons.
Wheel Diameters: 4' 6", 8' 0", 4' 6".   **–Tender:**
Cylinders: 18" x 24" (I).   **Tractive Effort:** 7920 lbf.

IRON DUKE	Didcot Railway Centre (N)	Resco 1985

SOUTHERN RAILWAY CLASS H2   4-4-2

Original Class Built: 1911–12. Billinton development of Marsh H1 Class. 6 built (32421–426). The replica locomotive uses the boiler from a GNR C1 Atlantic, which is similar to the LBSCR class.
Boiler Pressure: 170 lbf/sq in.   **Weight–Loco:** 68.25 tons.
Wheel Diameters: 3' 6", 6' 7½".   **–Tender:** 39.25 tons.
Cylinders: 21" x 26" (O).   **Valve Gear:** Stephenson. Piston valves.
Tractive Effort: 20840 lbf.   **BR Power Classification:** 3P.

Dual (air/vacuum) brakes.

BR	SR	LBSCR			
32424	B424–2424	424	BEACHY HEAD	Bluebell Railway	Bluebell Railway 2024

1.9.2. REPLICA STEAM LOCOMOTIVES UNDER CONSTRUCTION

GWR DESIGN

1000 CLASS   COUNTY   4-6-0

Original Class Built: 1945–47. Hawksworth design. 30 built (1000–29). The replica locomotive uses the frames from GWR 6959 Class 4-6-0 7927 WILLINGTON HALL and the firebox from LMS Class 8F 2-8-0 48518.
Boiler Pressure: 250 lbf/sq in superheated.   **Weight–Loco:** 76.85 tons.
Wheel Diameters: 3' 0", 6'3".   **–Tender:** 49 tons.
Cylinders: 18½" x 30" (O).   **Valve Gear:** Stephenson. Piston valves.
Tractive Effort: 29090 lbf.   **Restriction:** Red.
BR Power Classification: D (6MT).

1014	COUNTY OF GLAMORGAN	Didcot Railway Centre	Under construction

LMS DESIGN

CLASS 6P (formerly 5XP)   PATRIOT   4-6-0

Original Class Built: 1930–34. Fowler design. The first two members of the class were rebuilt from LNWR "Claughtons". 52 built (45500–51). This will be the 53rd locomotive built but will assume the identity of a former member of the class.
Boiler Pressure: 200 lbf/sq in superheated.   **Weight–Loco:** 80.75 tons.
Wheel Diameters: 3′ 3″, 6′9″.   **–Tender:** 42.70 tons.
Cylinders: 18″ x 26″ (3).   **Valve Gear:** Walschaerts. Piston valves.
Tractive Effort: 26 520 lbf.   **Restriction:** Red.
BR Power Classification: 6P.

BR	LMS		
45551	5551	THE UNKNOWN WARRIOR Tyseley Locomotive Works	Under construction

LNER DESIGN

CLASS D7   4-4-0

Original Class Built: 1887–94. Parker GCR Class 2/2A. 31 built (5561–67, 5682–93, 5700–11).
Boiler Pressure: 160 lbf/sq in.   **Weight–Loco:** 46 tons.
Wheel Diameters: 3′ 6″, 6′ 9″.   **–Tender:** 37.3 tons.
Cylinders: 18″ x 26″ (O).   **Valve Gear:** Stephenson: Slide valves.
Tractive Effort: 14 144 lbf.

LNER	GCR	MS&LR		
567–5567	567	567	Private site, Rugby	Under construction

CLASS F5   2-4-2T

Original Class Built: 1911–20. Holden design. 32 rebuilt (67188–67219) from GER Class M15s.
Boiler Pressure: 180 lbf/sq in.   **Weight–Loco:** 54 tons.
Wheel Diameters: 3′ 9″, 5′ 4″, 3′ 9″.
Cylinders: 17½″ x 24″ (I).   **Valve Gear:** Stephenson: Slide valves.
Tractive Effort: 17 571 lbf.

BR	LNER	GER		
67218	7789–7218	789	Tyseley Locomotive Works	Under construction

CLASS G5   0-4-4T

Original Class Built: 1894–1901. Wilson Worsdell NER design for branch line and suburban use. 110 built (67240–349). LNER 7306 was one of two members of the class withdrawn in 1948 and never received its allocated BR number 67306. The original was built at Darlington in 1897.
Boiler Pressure: 160 lbf/sq in.   **Weight:** 54.20 tons.
Wheel Diameters: 3′ 1¼″, 5′ 1¼″.   **Cylinders:** 18″ x 24″ (I).
Valve Gear: Stephenson. Slide valves.   **Tractive Effort:** 17 200 lbf.
BR Power Classification: 1P.   **RA:** 4.

LNER	NER		
1759–7306	1759	Class G5 Locomotive Company, Shildon	Under construction

PLATFORM 5 MAIL ORDER
www.platform5.com

Diesel & Electric
LOCO REGISTER
6th Edition

A complete list of all diesel and electric locomotives operated by British Railways, its constituents and successors, that have been capable of working on the main line railway network, including shunters and departmental locomotives.

Detailed entries list every number carried, entry to service and withdrawal dates and every official name carried.

Scrapping information has also been included. The book now contains scrapping details for approaching 5000 locomotives, showing where and when they were disposed of. Well illustrated. 256 pages. Published 2024.

Cover Price £25.95. Mail Order Price £22.95 plus P&P.

If ordering at www.platform5.com use the promotion code **REG6** at the basket.

ORDER BY POST, TELEPHONE OR AT www.platform5.com

POSTAGE & PACKING: 10% UK; 30% Europe; 50% Rest of World. Cheques payable to Platform 5 Publishing Ltd.

**Mail Order Department (PL), Platform 5 Publishing Ltd,
52 Broadfield Road, SHEFFIELD, S8 0XJ, ENGLAND. Tel: 0114 255 8000**

2. DIESEL LOCOMOTIVES

GENERAL

It was not until the mid-1950s that diesel locomotives appeared in great numbers. During the 1930s, however, several small building programmes were authorised, particularly on the LMS with diesel shunting locomotives. A few locomotives survive from this period, along with several others built in the immediate post-war period. During World War II, a large proportion of LMS locomotives were transferred to the War Department, which also authorised the construction of further orders. Many of these were shipped across the English Channel and subsequently lost in action. It is possible that some survive undiscovered. Notification of these would be gratefully appreciated. Those known to survive are listed in Section 2.1.

From the mid-1950s, the re-equipment of the railway network began in earnest and vast numbers of new, mainly diesel, locomotives were constructed by British Railways and private contractors. Those from this period now considered to be preserved can be found in Section 2.3. Some examples from this period are still in service with main line and industrial users; details of these can be found in the Platform 5 "British Railways Pocket Book 1: Locomotives" or the bound volume "British Railways Locomotives & Coaching Stock".

WHEEL ARRANGEMENT

The Whyte notation is used for diesel shunting locomotives with coupled driving wheels (see steam section). For other shunting and main line diesel and electric locomotives, the system whereby the number of powered axles on a bogie or frame is denoted by a letter (A = 1, B = 2, C = 3 etc) and the number of unpowered axles is denoted by a number is used. The letter "o" after a letter indicates that each axle is individually powered and a + sign indicates that the bogies are intercoupled.

DIMENSIONS

SI units are generally used. Imperial units are sometimes given in parentheses.

TRACTIVE EFFORT

Continuous and maximum tractive efforts are generally quoted for vehicles with electric transmission.

BRAKES

Locomotives are assumed to have train vacuum brakes unless otherwise stated.

NUMBERING SYSTEMS

Prior to nationalisation, each railway company allocated locomotive numbers in accordance with its own policy. After nationalisation in 1948, a common system was devised and internal combustion locomotives were allocated five figure numbers in the series 10000–19999.

Diesel locomotives built prior to nationalisation or to pre-nationalisation designs are arranged generally in order of the 1948 numbers, with those withdrawn before 1948 listed at the beginning of each section. In 1957, a new numbering scheme was introduced for locomotives built to British Railways specifications and details of this are given in the introduction to the British Railways section.

2.1. LONDON MIDLAND & SCOTTISH RAILWAY DIESEL LOCOMOTIVES

DIESEL MECHANICAL 0-4-0

Built: 1934 by English Electric at Preston Works for Drewry Car Company.
Engine: Allan 8RS18 of 119 kW (160 hp) at 1200 rpm (now fitted with a Gardner 6L3 of 114 kW (153 hp)).
Transmission: Mechanical. Wilson four-speed gearbox driving a rear jackshaft.
Maximum Tractive Effort: 50 kN (11 200 lbf).   **Weight:** 25.8 tonnes.
Maximum Speed: 12 mph.   **Wheel Diameter:** 914 mm.

No train brakes.

LMS	WD	AD		
7050	224–70224–846	240	National Railway Museum, York (N)	DC 2047/EE/DK 847 1934

DIESEL MECHANICAL 0-6-0

Built: 1932 by Hunslet Engine Company (taken into stock 1933).
Engine: MAN 112 kW (150 hp) at 900 rpm (now fitted with a Maclaren/Ricardo 98 kW engine).
Transmission: Mechanical. Hunslet constant mesh four-speed gearbox.
Maximum Tractive Effort: **Weight:** 21.7 tonnes.
Maximum Speed: 30 mph.   **Wheel Diameter:** 914 mm.

Built without train brakes, but vacuum brakes now fitted.

LMS	WD		
7401–7051	27–70227	Middleton Railway	HE 1697/1932

▲ Class 11 12082 stands in the shed yard at Ropley on the Mid Hants Railway on 28 August 2023.
Phil Barnes

DIESEL ELECTRIC 0-6-0

Built: 1935 by English Electric. 11 built, 3 taken over by BR as 12000–002 (LMS 7074/76/79) and scrapped 1956–62. Others sold to WD for use in France.
Engine: English Electric 6K of 261 kW (350 hp) at 675 rpm.
Transmission: Electric. Two axle-hung traction motors with a single reduction drive.
Maximum Tractive Effort: 147 kN (33 000 lbf).   **Weight:** 52 tonnes.
Maximum Speed: 30 mph.   **Wheel Diameter:** 1232 mm.

No train brakes.

LMS	WD			
7069	18		Private site, Malvern	EE/HL 3841 1935

DIESEL ELECTRIC 0-6-0

Built: 1939–42 at Derby. 40 built, 30 taken over by BR as 12003–032 (LMS 7080–99, 7110–19) and scrapped 1964–67. Others sold to WD for use in Italy and Egypt. Four were operated by FS (Ne 700.001–004) in Italy.
Engine: English Electric 6KT of 261 kW (350 hp) at 680 rpm.
Transmission: Electric. One traction motor with jackshaft drive.
Maximum Tractive Effort: 147 kN (33 000 lbf).   **Weight:** 56 tonnes.
Maximum Speed: 20 mph.   **Wheel Diameter:** 1295 mm.

Built without train brakes, but air brakes now fitted.

LMS	WD	FS	Present		
7103	52–70052	Ne 700.001	Unnumbered	Museo Ferroviario Piemontese store, Torino (Turin) Ponte Mosca station, Italy	Derby 1941
7106	55–70055	Ne 700.003	Unnumbered	Trasporto Ferroviario Toscano, Arezzo Pescaiola, Italy	Derby 1941

BR CLASS 11   DIESEL ELECTRIC 0-6-0

Built: 1945–52. LMS design. 120 built. The first order for 20 was for the WD, 14 being delivered as 260–268/70269–273, the balance passing to the LMS as 7120–7125 (BR 12033–038). 260–268 were renumbered 70260–268 and 70260–269 were sold to the NS (Netherlands Railways) in 1946.
Engine: English Electric 6KT of 261 kW (350 hp) at 680 rpm.
Transmission: Electric. Two EE 506 axle-hung traction motors.
Maximum Tractive Effort: 156 kN (35 000 lbf).
Continuous Tractive Effort: 49.4 kN (11 100 lbf) at 8.8 mph.
Wheel Diameter: 1232 mm.   **Weight:** 56 tonnes.
Power at Rail: 183 kW (245 hp).   **Maximum Speed:** 20 mph.

No train brakes except 70272, 12099 and 12131, which have since been fitted with vacuum brakes, and 12083, which has since been fitted with air brakes.

BR	WD	AD		
–	70269		Netherlands National Railway Museum, Utrecht	Derby 1944
–	70272–878	601	Lakeside & Haverthwaite Railway	Derby 1944
12052			Caledonian Railway	Derby 1949
12077			Midland Railway-Butterley	Derby 1950
12082			Mid Hants Railway	Derby 1950
12083			Battlefield Line	Derby 1950
12088			Aln Valley Railway, Alnwick	Derby 1950
12093			Caledonian Railway	Derby 1951
12099			Severn Valley Railway	Derby 1952
12131			North Norfolk Railway	Darlington 1952

2.2. SOUTHERN RAILWAY DIESEL LOCOMOTIVES

BR CLASS 12   DIESEL ELECTRIC   0-6-0

Built: 1949–52. Based on pre-war LMS design. Bulleid Firth Brown wheels. 26 built.
Engine: English Electric 6KT of 350 hp at 680 rpm.
Transmission: Electric. Two EE 506A axle-hung traction motors.
Maximum Tractive Effort: 107 kN (24000 lbf).
Continuous Tractive Effort: 36 kN (8000 lbf) at 10.2 mph.
Wheel Diameter: 1370 mm.   **Weight:** 45 tonnes.
Power at Rail: 163 kW (218 hp).   **Maximum Speed:** 27 mph.

No train brakes.

15224   Spa Valley Railway   Ashford 1949

2.3. BRITISH RAILWAYS DIESEL LOCOMOTIVES

NUMBERING & CLASSIFICATION SYSTEM

In 1957, British Railways introduced a new numbering system, which applied to all diesel locomotives except those built to pre-nationalisation designs. Each locomotive was allocated a number of up to four digits prefixed with a "D". Diesel electric shunters numbered in the 13xxx series had the "1" replaced by a "D", while diesel mechanical shunters numbered in the 11xxx series were allocated numbers in the D2xxx series.

When all steam locomotives had been withdrawn, the prefix letter was officially eliminated from the number of diesel locomotives, although it continued to be carried on many of them. For this reason, no attempt is made to distinguish between those locomotives that did or did not have the "D" prefix removed. Similarly, in preservation, no distinction is made between locomotives which do or do not carry a "D" prefix at present.

British Railways also introduced a new classification system for diesel locomotives. Each main line diesel locomotive class was designated a "Type" based on engine horsepower. This broadly took the following form:

Type	Engine Horsepower (hp)	Number Range
1	800–1000	D8000–D8999
2	1001–1499	D5000–D6499
3	1500–1999	D6500–D7499/D7900–D7999
4	2000–2999	D1 –D1999
5	3000+	D9000–D9499
Shunting	150/300	D2000–D2999
Shunting	350/400	D3000–D4999
Shunting/trip	650	D9500–D9999

In 1968, British Railways introduced a two digit numerical class code for diesel locomotives. With the introduction of modern communications, each locomotive was allocated a new five digit number comprising the two digit class number followed by a three digit serial number. These started to be applied in 1972 and several locomotives have carried more than one number in this scheme.

In this section, classes are listed in 1968 two digit class number order. Locomotives are listed in 1957 number order within each class apart from Classes 09, 24, 25, 26, 31, 33, 37, 45 and 47, which are listed within sub-class groups (but still in 1957 number order within that sub-class). A number of diesel shunting locomotives were withdrawn prior to the classification system being introduced and these are listed at the beginning of this section. Experimental and civil engineers' main line locomotives are listed in Sections 2.4 and 2.5.

UNCLASSIFIED   HUDSWELL-CLARKE   0-6-0

Built: 1955–61 by Hudswell-Clarke & Company, Leeds. 20 built.
Engine: Gardner 8L3 of 152 kW (204 hp) at 1200 rpm.
Transmission: Mechanical. SSS powerflow double synchro.
Maximum Tractive Effort: 85.7 kN (19245 lbf).
Continuous Tractive Effort: 76 kN (17069 lbf) at 3.72 mph.
Weight: 34 tonnes.   **Wheel Diameter:** 1067 mm.
Maximum Speed: 25 mph.

D 2511	Keighley & Worth Valley Railway	HC D 1202/1961

UNCLASSIFIED   NORTH BRITISH   0-4-0

Built: 1957–61 by North British Locomotive Company, Glasgow. 73 built.
Engine: MAN W6V 17.5/22A of 168 kW (225 hp) at 1100 rpm.
Transmission: Mechanical. Voith L33YU.
Maximum Tractive Effort: 89.4 kN (20080 lbf).
Continuous Tractive Effort: 53.4 kN (12000 lbf) at 4 mph.
Weight: 28 tonnes.   **Wheel Diameter:** 1067 mm.
Maximum Speed: 15 mph.

D 2767	Bo'ness & Kinneil Railway	NBL 28020/1960
D 2774	Strathspey Railway	NBL 28027/1960

CLASS 01   0-4-0

Built: 1956 by Andrew Barclay, Kilmarnock. 4 built.
Engine: Gardner 6L3 of 114 kW (153 hp) at 1200 rpm.
Transmission: Mechanical. Wilson SE4 epicyclic gearbox.
Maximum Tractive Effort: 56.8 kN (12750 lbf).   **Weight:** 25.5 tonnes.
Wheel Diameter: 965 mm.   **Maximum Speed:** 14 mph.

No train brakes.

11503–D 2953	Peak Rail	AB 395/1956
11506–D 2956	East Lancashire Railway	AB 398/1956

CLASS 02   0-4-0

Built: 1960–61 by Yorkshire Engine Company, Sheffield. 20 built.
Engine: Rolls Royce C6NFL of 127 kW (170 hp) at 1800 rpm.
Transmission: Hydraulic. Rolls Royce CF 10000.
Maximum Tractive Effort: 66.8 kN (15000 lbf).
Continuous Tractive Effort: 61 kN (13700 lbf) at 1.4 mph.
Weight: 28.6 tonnes.
Wheel Diameter: 1067 mm.   **Maximum Speed:** 19.5 mph.

D 2853–02003	Barrow Hill Roundhouse	YE 2812/1960
D 2854	Peak Rail	YE 2813/1960
D 2858	Midland Railway-Butterley	YE 2817/1960
D 2860	National Railway Museum, York (N)	YE 2843/1961
D 2866	Peak Rail	YE 2849/1961
D 2867	Northampton Ironstone Railway	YE 2850/1961
D 2868	Barrow Hill Roundhouse	YE 2851/1961

CLASS 03 0-6-0

Built: 1957–62 at Doncaster and Swindon. 230 built.
Engine: Gardner 8L3 of 152 kW (204 hp) at 1200 rpm. Replaced with Deutz VM V12 (300–350 hp) on D 2128 and D 2134 whilst in industrial use in Belgium. D 2128 has since been re-engined with a Cummins NT855 of 260 kW (350 hp) at 1800 rpm and hydraulic transmission.
Transmission: Mechanical. Wilson CA5 epicyclic gearbox.
Maximum Tractive Effort: 68 kN (15 300 lbf).   **Weight**: 31 tonnes.
Wheel Diameter: 1092 mm.   **Maximum Speed**: 28 mph.

- a   Air braked only.
- x   Dual (air/vacuum) braked.
- §   Modified with cut down cab for working on Burry Port & Gwendraeth Valley Line.

11205–D 2018–03018		Mangapps Railway Museum	Swindon 1958
11207–D 2020–03020		Sonic Rail Services, Burnham-on-Crouch	Swindon 1958
11209–D 2022–03022		Swindon & Cricklade Railway	Swindon 1958
11210–D 2023		Kent & East Sussex Railway	Swindon 1958
11211–D 2024		Kent & East Sussex Railway	Swindon 1958
D 2027–03027		Peak Rail	Swindon 1958
D 2037–03037		Royal Deeside Railway	Swindon 1959
D 2041		Colne Valley Railway	Swindon 1959
D 2046		Colne Valley Railway	Doncaster 1958
D 2051		Telford Steam Railway	Doncaster 1959
D 2059–03059 x		Isle of Wight Steam Railway	Doncaster 1959
D 2062–03062		East Lancashire Railway	Doncaster 1959
D 2063–03063 x		Mid Norfolk Railway	Doncaster 1959
D 2066–03066 x		Barrow Hill Roundhouse	Doncaster 1959
D 2069–03069		Chinnor & Princes Risborough Railway	Doncaster 1959
D 2072–03072		Lakeside & Haverthwaite Railway	Doncaster 1959
D 2073–03073 x		Crewe Heritage Centre	Doncaster 1959
D 2078–03078 x		Stephenson Steam Railway	Doncaster 1959
D 2079–03079		Derwent Valley Light Railway	Doncaster 1960
D 2081–03081		Mangapps Railway Museum	Doncaster 1960
D 2089–03089 x		Mangapps Railway Museum	Doncaster 1960
D 2090–03090		National Railway Museum, Shildon (N)	Doncaster 1960
D 2094–03094 x		Royal Deeside Railway	Doncaster 1960
D 2099–03099		Peak Rail	Doncaster 1960
D 2112–03112 x		Rother Valley Railway	Doncaster 1960
D 2113–03113		Peak Rail	Doncaster 1960
D 2117		Lakeside & Haverthwaite Railway	Swindon 1959
D 2118		Great Central Railway (Nottingham)	Swindon 1959
D 2119–03119 §		Epping Ongar Railway	Swindon 1959
D 2120–03120 §		Fawley Hill Railway	Swindon 1959
D 2128–03128		Somerset & Dorset Railway Heritage Trust, Midsomer Norton Station	Swindon 1960
D 2133		West Somerset Railway	Swindon 1960
D 2134–03134 a		Royal Deeside Railway	Swindon 1960
D 2138		Midland Railway-Butterley	Swindon 1960
D 2139		Peak Rail	Swindon 1960
D 2141–03141 §		Gwendraeth Valley Railway	Swindon 1960
D 2144–03144 §x		Wensleydale Railway	Swindon 1960
D 2145–03145 §		Moreton Park Railway	Swindon 1960
D 2148		Ribble Steam Railway	Swindon 1960
D 2152–03152 §		Swindon & Cricklade Railway	Swindon 1960
D 2158–03158 x		Mangapps Railway Museum	Swindon 1960
D 2162–03162 x		Llangollen & Corwen Railway	Swindon 1960
D 2170–03170 x		Epping Ongar Railway	Swindon 1960
D 2178		Gwili Railway	Swindon 1962
D 2179–03179 x	CLIVE	Rushden Transport Museum	Swindon 1962
D 2180–03180 x		Peak Rail	Swindon 1962
D 2182		Gloucestershire Warwickshire Railway	Swindon 1962
D 2184		Colne Valley Railway	Swindon 1962
D 2189–03189		Ribble Steam Railway	Swindon 1961

▲ Making a rare appearance away from its base at the Moreton Park Railway, 03145 stands at Lydney Junction during the Dean Forest Railway's diesel gala on 9 September 2023. **Darren Ford**

▼ 08164 "PRUDENCE" is seen stabled at the East Lancashire Railway's Buckley Wells depot on 9 February 2024 . **Tom McAtee**

D 2192	Dartmouth Steam Railway	Swindon 1961
D 2196–03196 x	Aysgarth Station	Swindon 1961
D 2197–03197 x	Mid Norfolk Railway	Swindon 1961
D 2199 a	Peak Rail	Swindon 1961
Dept 92–D 2371–03371 x	Dartmouth Steam Railway	Swindon 1958
D 2399–03399 x	Mangapps Railway Museum	Doncaster 1961

D 2118 currently carries the number 03118, which it would have received had it remained in BR service for longer.

D 2069–03069 is on loan from the Vale of Berkeley Railway, Sharpness.
D 2128–03128 is on loan from Andrew Briddon Locomotives, Darley Dale.
D 2197–03197 is on loan from Sonic Rail Services, Burnham-on-Crouch.

CLASS 04   0-6-0

Built: 1952–62. Drewry design built by Vulcan Foundry & Robert Stephenson & Hawthorns. 140 built.
Engine: Gardner 8L3 of 152 kW (204 hp) at 1200 rpm.
Transmission: Mechanical. Wilson CA5 epicyclic gearbox.
Maximum Tractive Effort: 69.7 kN (15 650 lbf) (* 75.0 kN (16 850 lbf)).
Weight: 32 tonnes.
Wheel Diameter: 1067 mm (* 991 mm) or 1092 mm (D 2274–D 2339 as built).
Maximum Speed: 25.8 mph (* 25 mph, † 27.5 mph).

11103–D 2203 *		Mangapps Railway Museum	DC/VF 2400/D145/1952
11106–D 2205 *		Peak Rail	DC/VF 2486/D212/1953
11108–D 2207 *		North Yorkshire Moors Railway	DC/VF 2482/D208/1953
11135–D 2229	Unnumbered	Peak Rail	DC/VF 2552/D278/1955
11215–D 2245		Derwent Valley Light Railway	DC/RSH 2577/7864/1956
11216–D 2246		South Devon Railway	DC/RSH 2578/7865/1956
D 2271		South Devon Railway	DC/RSH 2615/7913/1958
D 2272		Peak Rail	DC/RSH 2616/7914/1958
D 2279 †		East Anglian Railway Museum	DC/RSH 2656/8097/1960
D 2280 †	Unnumbered	Gloucestershire Warwickshire Railway	DC/RSH 2657/8098/1960
D 2284 †		Peak Rail	DC/RSH 2661/8102/1960
D 2289	Unnumbered	Peak Rail	DC/RSH 2669/8122/1960
D 2298		Buckinghamshire Railway Centre	DC/RSH 2679/8157/1960
D 2302		Moreton Park Railway	DC/RSH 2683/8161/1960
D 2310		Battlefield Line	DC/RSH 2691/8169/1960
D 2324		Nemesis Rail, Burton-on-Trent	DC/RSH 2705/8183/1961
D 2325		Mangapps Railway Museum	DC/RSH 2706/8184/1961
D 2334		Mid Norfolk Railway	DC/RSH 2715/8193/1961
D 2337		Peak Rail	DC/RSH 2718/8196/1961

11215–D 2245 is on loan from the Battlefield Line.

CLASS 05   0-6-0

Built: 1955–61 by Hunslet Engine Company, Leeds. 69 built.
Engine: Gardner 8L3 of 152 kW (204 hp) at 1200 rpm.
Transmission: Mechanical. Hunslet gearbox.
Maximum Tractive Effort: 64.6 kN (14 500 lbf). **Weight:** 31 tonnes.
Wheel Diameter: 1121 (* 1016) mm. **Maximum Speed:** 18 mph.

11140–D 2554–05001–97803 *	Isle of Wight Steam Railway	HE 4870/1956
D 2578	Moreton Park Railway	HE 5460/1958 rebuilt HE 6999/1968
D 2587	Peak Rail	HE 5636/1959 rebuilt HE 7180/1969
D 2595	Ribble Steam Railway	HE 5644/1960 rebuilt HE 7179/1969

CLASS 06   0-4-0

Built: 1958–60 by Andrew Barclay, Kilmarnock. 35 built.
Engine: Gardner 8L3 of 152 kW (204 hp) at 1200 rpm.
Transmission: Mechanical. Wilson CA5 epicyclic gearbox.
Maximum Tractive Effort: 88 kN (19800 lbf).   **Weight:** 37 tonnes.
Wheel Diameter: 1092 mm.   **Maximum Speed:** 23 mph.

D 2420–06003–97804	Peak Rail	AB 435/1959

CLASS 07   0-6-0

Built: 1962 by Ruston & Hornsby, Lincoln. 14 built.
Engine: Paxman 6RPHL Mk III of 205 kW (275 hp) at 1360 rpm.
Transmission: Electric. One AEI RTB 6652 traction motor.
Maximum Tractive Effort: 126 kN (28240 lbf).
Continuous Tractive Effort: 71 kN (15950 lbf) at 4.38 mph.
Power at Rail: 142 kW (190 hp).   **Weight:** 43.6 tonnes.
Wheel Diameter: 1067 mm.   **Maximum Speed:** 20 mph.

x   Dual (air/vacuum) braked.

D 2985–07001 x	Peak Rail	RH 480698/1962
D 2989–07005 x	Great Central Railway	RH 480690/1962
D 2994–07010	Avon Valley Railway	RH 480695/1962
D 2995–07011 x	St Leonards Railway Engineering	RH 480696/1962
D 2996–07012	Barrow Hill Roundhouse	RH 480697/1962
D 2997–07013 x	East Lancashire Railway	RH 480698/1962

CLASS 08   0-6-0

Built: 1952–62. Built at Derby, Darlington, Crewe, Horwich & Doncaster. 996 built.
Engine: English Electric 6KT of 298 kW (400 hp) at 680 rpm.
Transmission: Electric. Two EE 506 axle-hung traction motors.
Maximum Tractive Effort: 156 kN (35000 lbf).
Continuous Tractive Effort: 49.4 kN (11100 lbf) at 8.8 mph.
Power at Rail: 194 kW (260 hp).   **Weight:** 50 tonnes.
Wheel Diameter: 1372 mm.   **Maximum Speed:** 15 mph.

x   Dual (air/vacuum) braked.   a   Air-braked only.
§   modified with cut down cab for working on Burry Port & Gwendraeth Valley Line.

D 3101 built without train brakes.

13000–D 3000		HNRC, Worksop	Derby 1952
13002–D 3002		Plym Valley Railway	Derby 1952
13014–D 3014		Dartmouth Steam Railway	Derby 1952
13018–D 3018–08011	"HAVERSHAM"	Chinnor & Princes Risborough Railway	Derby 1953
13019–D 3019		Cambrian Railway Trust, Llynclys	Derby 1953
13022–D 3022–08015		Severn Valley Railway	Derby 1953
13023–D 3023–08016		Peak Rail	Derby 1953
13029–D 3029–08021		Tyseley Locomotive Works	Derby 1953
13030–D 3030–08022	"LION"	Cholsey & Wallingford Railway	Derby 1953
13044–D 3044–08032		Mid Hants Railway	Derby 1954
13059–D 3059–08046 x	"BRECHIN CITY"	Caledonian Railway	Derby 1954
13067–D 3067–08054		Embsay & Bolton Abbey Railway	Darlington 1953
13074–D 3074–08060	"UNICORN"	Cholsey & Wallingford Railway	Darlington 1953
13079–D 3079–08064		National Railway Museum, Shildon (N)	Darlington 1954
13101–D 3101		Great Central Railway	Derby 1955
13167–D 3167–08102		Lincolnshire Wolds Railway	Derby 1955
13174–D 3174–08108	"Dover Castle"	Kent & East Sussex Railway	Derby 1955
13180–D 3180–08114		Epping Ongar Railway	Derby 1955
13190–D 3190–08123		Cholsey & Wallingford Railway	Derby 1955
13201–D 3201–08133		Severn Valley Railway	Derby 1955
13232–D 3232–08164	"PRUDENCE"	East Lancashire Railway	Darlington 1956
13236–D 3236–08168		Nemesis Rail, Burton-on-Trent	Darlington 1956

13255–D3255		North Side Works, Leavening	Derby 1956
13261–D3261		Swindon & Cricklade Railway	Derby 1956
13265–D3265–08195		Llangollen & Corwen Railway	Derby 1956
13272–D3272–08202		Avon Valley Railway	Derby 1956
13290–D3290–08220		Great Central Railway (Nottingham)	Derby 1956
13308–D3308–08238		North Yorkshire Moors Railway	Darlington 1956
13336–D3336–08266		Keighley & Worth Valley Railway	Darlington 1957
D3358–08288	"PHOENIX"	Mid Hants Railway	Derby 1957
D3429–08359		Bodmin Railway	Crewe 1958
D3462–08377		Mid Hants Railway	Darlington 1957
D3551–08436 x		Swanage Railway	Derby 1958
D3558–08443		Bo'ness & Kinneil Railway	Derby 1958
D3559–08444		Bodmin Railway	Derby 1958
D3577–08462–08994		Gwendraeth Valley Railway	Crewe 1958
D3586–08471		Severn Valley Railway	Crewe 1958
D3591–08476		Swanage Railway	Crewe 1958
D3594–08479		East Lancashire Railway	Horwich 1958
D3605–08490		Strathspey Railway	Horwich 1958
D3658–08503 x		Barry Tourist Railway	Doncaster 1958
D3690–08528 x		Derwent Valley Railway	Horwich 1959
D3723–08556		North Yorkshire Moors Railway	Darlington 1959
D3757–08590 x	"RED LION"	Midland Railway-Butterley	Crewe 1959
D3759–08592–08993 x§	ASHBURNHAM	Keighley & Worth Valley Railway	Crewe 1959
D3771–08604 x	"PHANTOM"	Didcot Railway Centre	Derby 1959
D3800–08633 x	The Sorter	Churnet Valley Railway	Derby 1959
D3802–08635 x		Severn Valley Railway	Derby 1959
D3830–08663 a	St. Silas	Hitachi, Newton Aycliffe	Horwich 1959
D3854–08687–08995 x§	KIDWELLY	Gwendraeth Valley Railway	Horwich 1959
D3861–08694 x		Great Central Railway (Nottingham)	Horwich 1959
D3873–08706 x		RSS, Rye Farm, Wishaw	Crewe 1960
D3925–08757 x	EAGLE C.U.R.C.	Telford Steam Railway	Horwich 1961
D3935–08767 x		North Norfolk Railway	Horwich 1961
D3937–08769		Dean Forest Railway	Derby 1960
D3940–08772 x	CAMULODUNUM	North Norfolk Railway	Derby 1960
D3941–08773 x		Embsay & Bolton Abbey Railway	Derby 1960
D3952–08784 x		Great Central Railway (Nottingham)	Derby 1960
D3963–08795 x		Chrysalis Rail, Landore Depot	Derby 1960
D3993–08825 x		Chinnor & Princes Risborough Railway	Derby 1960
D3998–08830 a		Peak Rail	Horwich 1960
D4018–08850 x		North Yorkshire Moors Railway	Horwich 1961
D4095–08881 x		Somerset & Dorset Railway Heritage Trust, Midsomer Norton Station	Horwich 1961
D4118–08888 x	Postman's Pride	Kent & East Sussex Railway	Horwich 1962
D4126–08896 x		Severn Valley Railway	Horwich 1962
D4137–08907 x		Great Central Railway	Horwich 1962
D4141–08911 x	"MATEY"	National Railway Museum, Shildon	Horwich 1962
D4145–08915 x		Stephenson Steam Railway	Horwich 1962
D4152–08922 x		Spa Valley Railway	Horwich 1962
D4174–08944 x		East Lancashire Railway	Darlington 1962

D3594–08479 currently carries the number 13594.
D3771–08604 currently carries the number 604.

13190–D3190–08123 currently carries the name "GEORGE MASON CWR".
D3577–08462–08994 also carried the names SPIRIT OF INNOVATION and GWENDRAETH.

13180–D3180–08114 is on loan from the Great Central Railway (Nottingham).
D3429–08359 is on loan from the Kent & East Sussex Railway.
D3802–08635 is being converted into a hydrogen-powered locomotive and is numbered H3802.
D3830–08663 is on loan from the Avon Valley Railway.
D3873–08706 is on loan from the Colne Valley Railway.
D3963–08795 is on loan from the Llanelli & Mynydd Mawr Railway.
D4118–08888 is currently under overhaul at the Avon Valley Railway.
D4152–08922 is on loan from the Great Central Railway (Nottingham).

CLASS 09   0-6-0

Built: 1959–62. Built at Darlington & Horwich. 26 built.
Engine: English Electric 6KT of 298 kW (400 hp) at 680 rpm.
Transmission: Electric: Two EE506 axle-hung traction motors.
Power at Rail: 201 kW (269 hp).
Maximum Tractive Effort: 111 kN (25 000 lbf).   **Weight**: 50 tonnes.
Continuous Tractive Effort: 39 kN (8800 lbf) at 11.6 mph.
Wheel Diameter: 1372 mm.   **Maximum Speed**: 27 mph.

Dual (air/vacuum) braked.

Class 09/0. Built as Class 09.

D 3665–09001		Peak Rail	Darlington 1959
D 3668–09004		Avon Valley Railway	Darlington 1959
D 3721–09010		South Devon Railway	Darlington 1959
D 4100–09012	Dick Hardy	Severn Valley Railway	Horwich 1961
D 4103–09015		Avon Valley Railway	Horwich 1961
D 4105–09017–97806		National Railway Museum, York	Horwich 1961
D 4106–09018		Bluebell Railway	Horwich 1961
D 4107–09019		West Somerset Railway	Horwich 1961
D 4112–09024		East Lancashire Railway	Horwich 1961
D 4113–09025		Lavender Line	Horwich 1962
D 4114–09026	Cedric Wares	Spa Valley Railway	Horwich 1962

Class 09/1. Converted from Class 08 (1992–93) by RFS Industries, Kilnhurst.

D 4013–08845–09107	Severn Valley Railway	Horwich 1961

D 4114–09026 also carried the name William Pearson.

CLASS 10   0-6-0

Built: 1955–62. Built at Darlington & Doncaster. 146 built.
Engine: Lister Blackstone ER6T of 261 kW (350 hp) at 750 rpm.
Transmission: Electric. Two GEC WT 821 axle-hung traction motors.
Power at Rail: 198 kW (265 hp).
Maximum Tractive Effort: 156 kN (35 000 lbf).   **Weight**: 47 tonnes.
Continuous Tractive Effort: 53.4 kN (12 000 lbf) at 8.2 mph.
Wheel Diameter: 1372 mm.   **Maximum Speed**: 20 mph.

D 3452		Bodmin Railway	Darlington 1957
D 3489	"COLONEL TOMLINE"	Helston Railway	Darlington 1958
D 4067	"Margaret Ethel – Thomas Alfred Naylor"	Great Central Railway	Darlington 1961
D 4092		Barrow Hill Roundhouse	Darlington 1962

CLASS 14   0-6-0

Built: 1964–65 at Swindon. 56 built.
Engine: Paxman Ventura 6YJXL of 485 kW (650 hp) at 1500 rpm. Replaced with a Rolls Royce Type DV8T of 336 kW (450 hp) originally fitted to a Class 17 on D 9524 whilst in use with BP.
Transmission: Hydraulic. Voith L217u.
Maximum Tractive Effort: 135 kN (30 910 lbf).
Continuous Tractive Effort: 109 kN (26 690 lbf) at 5.6 mph.
Weight: 51 tonnes.   **Wheel Diameter**: 1219 mm.
Maximum Speed: 40 mph.   **Train Heating**: None.

x   Dual (air/vacuum) braked

BR	Present		
D 9500		Elliott Group, Port Elphinstone, Inverurie	Swindon 1964
D 9502		East Lancashire Railway	Swindon 1964
D 9504 x		Kent & East Sussex Railway	Swindon 1964
D 9513	N.C.B. 38	Wensleydale Railway	Swindon 1964
D 9516 x		Didcot Railway Centre	Swindon 1964
D 9518	NCB No. 7	West Somerset Railway	Swindon 1964

▲ The sole surviving Class 17, D 8568, departs Highley with the Severn Valley Railway's 16.15 service to Bewdley on 21 May 2022. **Robert Pritchard**

▼ Recently having moved to the Embsay & Bolton Abbey Railway, Class 20 D 8110 (20110) departs Holywell Halt on 28 August 2023 with the 15.00 Embsay–Bolton Abbey service. **Jamie Squibbs**

D 9520 x	Mid Norfolk Railway	Swindon 1964
D 9521	Dean Forest Railway	Swindon 1964
D 9523 x	Wensleydale Railway	Swindon 1964
D 9524 x 14901	Andrew Briddon Locomotives, Darley Dale	Swindon 1964
D 9525	Ecclesbourne Valley Railway	Swindon 1965
D 9526	West Somerset Railway	Swindon 1965
D 9529 x	Nene Valley Railway	Swindon 1965
D 9531 x	East Lancashire Railway	Swindon 1965
D 9537	Ecclesbourne Valley Railway	Swindon 1965
D 9539	Ribble Steam Railway	Swindon 1965
D 9551	Severn Valley Railway	Swindon 1965
D 9553 54	Caledonian Railway	Swindon 1965
D 9555	Dean Forest Railway	Swindon 1965

D 9555 is currently under overhaul at the Midland Railway-Butterley.

CLASS 15   Bo-Bo

Built: 1957–60 by BTH/Clayton Equipment Company. 44 built.
Engine: Paxman 16YHXL of 597 kW (800 hp) at 1250 rpm.
Transmission: Electric. Four BTH 137AZ axle-hung traction motors.
Maximum Tractive Effort: 178 kN (40 000 lbf).
Continuous Tractive Effort: 88 kN (19 700 lbf) at 11.3 mph.
Weight: 69 tonnes.   **Wheel Diameter:** 1003 mm.
Maximum Speed: 60 mph.   **Train Heating:** None.

D 8233–ADB 968001	East Lancashire Railway	BTH 1131/1960

CLASS 17   Bo-Bo

Built: 1962–65 by Clayton Equipment Company. 117 built.
Engine: Two Paxman 6ZHXL of 336 kW (450 hp) at 1500 rpm.
Transmission: Electric. Four GEC WT421 axle-hung traction motors.
Power at Rail: 461 kW (618 hp).
Maximum Tractive Effort: 178 kN (40 000 lbf).
Continuous Tractive Effort: 80 kN (18 000 lbf) at 12.8 mph.
Weight: 69 tonnes.   **Wheel Diameter:** 1003 mm.
Maximum Speed: 60 mph.   **Train Heating:** None.

D 8568	Severn Valley Railway	CE 4365U/69 1964

CLASS 20   Bo-Bo

Built: 1957–68 by English Electric at Vulcan Foundry, Newton-le-Willows or Robert Stephenson & Hawthorns, Darlington. 228 built.
Engine: English Electric 8SVT of 746 kW (1000 hp) at 850 rpm.
Transmission: Electric. Four EE 526/5D or EE526/8D axle-hung traction motors.
Power at Rail: 574 kW (770 hp).
Maximum Tractive Effort: 187 kN (42 000 lbf).
Continuous Tractive Effort: 111 kN (25 000 lbf) at 11 mph.
Weight: 74 tonnes.   **Wheel Diameter:** 1092 mm.
Maximum Speed: 75 mph.   **Train Heating:** None.

Dual (air/vacuum) braked except D 8000.

D 8000–20050	National Railway Museum, York (N)	EE/VF 2347/D375 1957
D 8001–20001	Epping Ongar Railway	EE/VF 2348/D376 1957
D 8016–20016	Caledonian Railway	EE/VF 2363/D391 1957
D 8020–20020	Bo'ness & Kinneil Railway	EE/RSH 2742/8052 1959
D 8031–20031	Keighley & Worth Valley Railway	EE/RSH 2753/8063 1960
D 8048–20048	Severn Valley Railway	EE/VF 2770/D495 1959
D 8057–20057	Churnet Valley Railway	EE/RSH 2963/8215 1961
D 8059–20059–20302[1]	Mid Hants Railway	EE/RSH 2965/8217 1961
D 8063–20063	Battlefield Line	EE/RSH 2969/8221 1961
D 8069–20069	HNRC, Worksop	EE/RSH 2975/8227 1961
D 8081–20081	Caledonian Railway	EE/RSH 2987/8239 1961

D 8087–20087	Kent & East Sussex Railway	EE/RSH 2993/8245 1961
D 8088–20088	Caledonian Railway	EE/RSH 2994/8246 1961
D 8098–20098	Great Central Railway	EE/RSH 3003/8255 1961
D 8110–20110	Embsay & Bolton Abbey Railway	EE/RSH 3016/8268 1962
D 8128–20228	Gloucestershire Warwickshire Railway	EE/VF 3599/D998 1966
D 8137–20137 Murray B. Hofmeyr	Gloucestershire Warwickshire Railway	EE/VF 3608/D1007 1966
D 8154–20154	Great Central Railway (Nottingham)	EE/VF 3625/D1024 1966
D 8166–20166	Caledonian Railway	EE/VF 3637/D1036 1966
D 8169–20169	Embsay & Bolton Abbey Railway	EE/VF 3640/D1039 1966
D 8188–20188	Mid Hants Railway	EE/VF 3669/D1064 1967
D 8305–20205	Midland Railway-Butterley	EE/VF 3686/D1081 1967
D 8314–20214	Lakeside & Haverthwaite Railway	EE/VF 3695/D1090 1967
D 8327–20227 "SHERLOCK HOLMES"	North Norfolk Railway	EE/VF 3685/D1080 1968

D 8063–20063 carried the number 2002 and D 8128–20228 carried the number 2004 whilst working for CFD (Compagnie de Chemin de Fer Départementaux) in France.

CLASS 24   Bo-Bo

Built: 1958–61 at Derby, Crewe & Darlington. 151 built.
Engine: Sulzer 6LDA28A of 870 kW (1160 hp) at 750 rpm.
Transmission: Electric. Four BTH 137BY axle-hung traction motors.
Power at Rail: 629 kW (843 hp).
Maximum Tractive Effort: 178 kN (40 000 lbf).
Continuous Tractive Effort: 95 kN (21 300 lbf) at 4.38 mph.
Weight: 81 or 78 tonnes.   **Wheel Diameter:** 1143 mm.
Maximum Speed: 75 mph.   **Train Heating:** Steam.

Class 24/0. 81 tonnes.

D 5032–24032	"HELEN TURNER"	North Yorkshire Moors Railway	Crewe 1959

Class 24/1. 78 tonnes.

D 5054–24054–ADB 968008	"PHIL SOUTHERN"	East Lancashire Railway	Crewe 1959
D 5061–24061–RDB 968007	EXPERIMENT	North Yorkshire Moors Railway	Crewe 1960
D 5081–24081		Gloucestershire Warwickshire Railway	Crewe 1960

D 5061–24061–RDB 968007 also carried the number 97201.

CLASS 25   Bo-Bo

Built: 1961–67. Built at Darlington, Derby & Beyer Peacock, Manchester. 327 built.
Engine: Sulzer 6LDA28B of 930 kW (1250 hp) at 750 rpm.
Transmission: Electric. Four AEI 253AY axle-hung traction motors.
Power at Rail: 708 kW (949 hp).
Maximum Tractive Effort: 200 kN (45 000 lbf).
Continuous Tractive Effort: 93 kN (20 800 lbf) at 17.1 mph.
Weight: 72–76 tonnes.   **Wheel Diameter:** 1143 mm.
Maximum Speed: 90 mph.

Class 25/1. Dual (air/vacuum) braked except D 5217. Train heating: Steam.

D 5185–25035	Great Central Railway	Darlington 1963
D 5207–25057	HNRC, Worksop	Derby 1963
D 5209–25059	Keighley & Worth Valley Railway	Derby 1963
D 5217–25067	Nemesis Rail, Burton-on-Trent	Derby 1963
D 5222–25072	Caledonian Railway	Derby 1963

Class 25/2. Dual (air/vacuum) braked except D 5233. Train heating: Steam: D 5233, D 7585/94. None: D 7523/35/41.

D 5233–25083	Caledonian Railway	Derby 1963
D 7523–25173	Epping Ongar Railway	Derby 1965
D 7535–25185	South Devon Railway	Derby 1965
D 7541–25191	South Devon Railway	Derby 1965
D 7585–25235	Bo'ness & Kinneil Railway	Darlington 1964
D 7594–25244	Kent & East Sussex Railway	Darlington 1964

Class 25/3. Dual (air/vacuum) braked. Train heating: None.

D 7612–25262–25901		South Devon Railway	Derby 1966
D 7615–25265		Nemesis Rail, Burton-on-Trent	Derby 1966
D 7628–25278	"SYBILLA"	North Yorkshire Moors Railway	BP 8038/1965
D 7629–25279		East Lancashire Railway	BP 8039/1965
D 7633–25283–25904		HNRC, Worksop	BP 8043/1965
D 7659–25309–25909		Peak Rail	BP 8069/1966
D 7663–25313		HNRC, Worksop	Derby 1966
D 7671–25321		Midland Railway-Butterley	Derby 1967
D 7672–25322–25912	TAMWORTH CASTLE	Churnet Valley Railway	Derby 1967

D 5209–25059 is currently under overhaul at Barrow Hill Roundhouse.
D 7523–25173 is currently under overhaul at the Battlefield Line.

CLASS 26   Bo-Bo

Built: 1958–59 by the Birmingham Railway Carriage & Wagon Company. 47 built.
Engine: Sulzer 6LDA28A of 870 kW (1160 hp) at 750 rpm.
Transmission: Electric. Four Crompton-Parkinson C171A1 (§ C171D3) axle-hung traction motors.
Power at Rail: 671 kW (900 hp).
Maximum Tractive Effort: 187 kN (42000 lbf).
Continuous Tractive Effort: 133 kN (30000 lbf) at 14 mph.
Weight: 72–75 tonnes.   **Wheel Diameter:** 1092 mm.
Maximum Speed: 75 mph.
Train Heating: Built with steam. Removed from D 5300/01/02/04 in 1967.

Dual (air/vacuum) braked.

Class 26/0.

D 5300–26007	Barrow Hill Roundhouse	BRCW DEL/45/1958
D 5301–26001	Caledonian Railway	BRCW DEL/46/1958
D 5302–26002	Hydrus Group, Brechin	BRCW DEL/47/1958
D 5304–26004	Nemesis Rail, Burton-on-Trent	BRCW DEL/49/1958
D 5310–26010	Llangollen & Corwen Railway	BRCW DEL/55/1959
D 5311–26011	Nemesis Rail, Burton-on-Trent	BRCW DEL/56/1959
D 5314–26014	Caledonian Railway	BRCW DEL/59/1959

Class 26/1. §

D 5324–26024		Bo'ness & Kinneil Railway	BRCW DEL/69/1959
D 5325–26025		Hydrus Group, Brechin	BRCW DEL/69/1959
D 5335–26035		Caledonian Railway	BRCW DEL/80/1959
D 5338–26038	"Tom Clift 1954–2012"	Bo'ness & Kinneil Railway	BRCW DEL/83/1959
D 5340–26040		Waverley Route Heritage Association, Whitrope	BRCW DEL/85/1959
D 5343–26043		Gloucestershire Warwickshire Railway	BRCW DEL/88/1959

CLASS 27   Bo-Bo

Built: 1961–62 by the Birmingham Railway Carriage & Wagon Company, Birmingham. 69 built.
Engine: Sulzer 6LDA28B of 930 kW (1250 hp) at 750 rpm.
Transmission: Electric. Four GEC WT459 axle-hung traction motors.
Power at Rail: 696 kW (933 hp).
Maximum Tractive Effort: 178 kN (40000 lbf).
Continuous Tractive Effort: 111 kN (25000 lbf) at 14 mph.
Weight: 72–75 tonnes.   **Wheel Diameter:** 1092 mm.
Maximum Speed: 90 mph.
Train Heating: Built with steam (except D 5370 – no provision). Replaced with electric on D 5386 and D 5410 but subsequently removed.

Dual (air/vacuum) braked except D 5353.

D 5347–27001	Bo'ness & Kinneil Railway	BRCW DEL/190/1961
D 5351–27005	Bo'ness & Kinneil Railway	BRCW DEL/194/1961
D 5353–27007	Caledonian Railway	BRCW DEL/196/1961
D 5370–27024–ADB 968028	Caledonian Railway	BRCW DEL/213/1962

D 5386–27103–27212–27066 Barrow Hill Roundhouse   BRCW DEL/229/1962
D 5394–27106–27050   Strathspey Railway   BRCW DEL/237/1962
D 5401–27112–27056   Great Central Railway   BRCW DEL/244/1962
D 5410–27123–27205–27059 UK Rail Leasing, Leicester   BRCW DEL/253/1962

CLASS 28 METROVICK Co-Bo

Built: 1958–59 by Metropolitan Vickers, Manchester. 20 built.
Engine: Crossley HSTVee 8 of 896 kW (1200 hp) at 625 rpm.
Transmission: Electric. Five MV 137BZ axle-hung traction motors.
Power at Rail: 671 kW (900 hp).
Maximum Tractive Effort: 223 kN (50 000 lbf). **Weight:** 99 tonnes.
Continuous Tractive Effort: 111 kN (25 000 lbf) at 13.5 mph.
Wheel Diameter: 1003 mm. **Train Heating:** Steam.
Maximum Speed: 75 mph.

D 5705–S 15705–TDB 968006   East Lancashire Railway   MV 1958

CLASS 31 A1A-A1A

Built: 1957–62 by Brush Electrical Engineering Company, Loughborough. 263 built.
Engine: Built with Mirrlees JVS12T of 1020 kW (1365 hp). Re-engined 1964–69 with English Electric 12SVT of 1100 kW (1470 hp) at 850 rpm.
Transmission: Electric. Four Brush TM73-68 axle-hung traction motors.
Power at Rail: 872 kW (1170 hp).
Maximum Tractive Effort: 190 kN (42 800 lbf).
Continuous Tractive Effort: 99 kN (22 250 lbf) at 19.7 mph.
Weight: 106.7–111 tonnes. **Wheel Diameter:** 1092 mm.
Maximum Speed: 90 mph or 80 mph (D 5500). D 5518, D 5522, D 5524, D 5526 and D 5533 were originally 80 mph but were regeared for 90 mph.
Train Heating: Built with steam heating. D 5631–31207 has been restored with steam heating.

D 5500, D 5518, D 5522, D 5524, D 5526 and D 5547 were built without roof-mounted headcode boxes. They were subsequently fitted to D 5518.

Class 31/0. Electro-magnetic control.

D 5500–31018   National Railway Museum, Shildon (N)   BE 71/1957

Class 31/1. Electro-pneumatic control. Dual (air/vacuum) braked. a Air-braked only.

D 5518–31101		Avon Valley Railway	BE 89/1958
D 5523–31105 a	"Radio Caroline"	Mangapps Railway Museum	BE 122/1959
D 5526–31108		Midland Railway-Butterley	BE 125/1959
D 5537–31119		Embsay & Bolton Abbey Railway	BE 136/1959
D 5546–31128	CHARYBDIS	Nemesis Rail, Burton-on-Trent	BE 145/1959
D 5548–31130	Calder Hall Power Station	Avon Valley Railway	BE 147/1959
D 5580–31162		Midland Railway-Butterley	BE 180/1960
D 5581–31163		Chinnor & Princes Risborough Railway	BE 181/1960
D 5613–31190	GRYPHON	Plym Valley Railway	BE 213/1960
D 5627–31203	"Steve Organ G.M."	Pontypool & Blaenavon Railway	BE 227/1960
D 5630–31206		Rushden Transport Museum	BE 230/1960
D 5631–31207		North Norfolk Railway	BE 231/1960
D 5634–31210		Great Central Railway (Nottingham)	BE 234/1960
D 5660–31233 a		Mangapps Railway Museum	BE 260/1960
D 5662–31235		Great Central Railway (Nottingham)	BE 262/1960
D 5683–31255		Mid Norfolk Railway	BE 284/1961
D 5800–31270	"Athena"	Didcot Railway Centre	BE 301/1961
D 5801–31271	"Stratford 1840–2001"	Llangollen & Corwen Railway	BE 302/1961
D 5817–31285 a		Weardale Railway	BE 318/1961
D 5821–31289	"PHOENIX"	Northampton & Lamport Railway	BE 322/1961
D 5862–31327	Phillips-Imperial	Strathspey Railway	BE 398/1962

Class 31/4. Electro-pneumatic control. Dual (air/vacuum) braked. Fitted with Electric Train Supply equipment (steam heating removed when electric supply fitted, except D 5522 and D 5814 from which it was removed later).

D 5522–31418   Midland Railway-Butterley   BE 121/1959

▲ Class 27 D 5394 (27106) arrives at Aviemore with the stock to work the Strathspey Railway's first service of the day on 19 July 2022. **Alisdair Anderson**

▼ Midway through a major restoration, Class 28 D 5705 is seen on display at Bury Bolton Street during a diesel gala at the East Lancashire Railway on 1 July 2022. **Alisdair Anderson**

▲ Whilst on hire to the North Yorkshire Moors Railway, 31128 CHARYBDIS awaits its departure from Grosmont with the 16.40 to Pickering on 9 June 2023. **Andy Chard**

▼ 33108 climbs Eardington bank on 20 May 2023 with the Severn Valley Railway's 14.30 Kidderminster Town–Bridgnorth service. **Brad Joyce**

D 5533–31115–31466		North Yorkshire Moors Railway	BE 132/1959
D 5547–31129–31461		Nemesis Rail, Burton-on-Trent	BE 146/1959
D 5557–31139–31438–31538		Epping Ongar Railway	BE 156/1959
D 5600–31179–31435	Newton Heath TMD	Embsay & Bolton Abbey Railway	BE 200/1960
D 5637–31213–31465 a		Weardale Railway	BE 237/1960
D 5654–31228–31454–31554	THE HEART OF WESSEX	Nemesis Rail, Burton-on-Trent	BE 254/1960
D 5684–31256–31459 a	CERBERUS	Weardale Railway	BE 285/1961
D 5695–31265–31430–31530	Sister Dora	Spa Valley Railway	BE 296/1961
D 5814–31414–31514		Midland Railway-Butterley	BE 315/1961
D 5830–31297–31463–31563		Great Central Railway (Nottingham)	BE 366/1962

Class 31/6. Fitted with Electric Train Supply, through wiring and controls.

D 5609–31186–31601	Devon Diesel Society	Ecclesbourne Valley Railway	BE 209/1960

D 5523–31105 also carried the name Bescot TMD.
D 5581–31163 currently carries the number 97205.
D 5609–31186–31601 also carried the names BLETCHLEY PARK 'STATION X', THE MAYOR OF CASTERBRIDGE and GAUGE 'O' GUILD 1956–2006.
D 5654–31228–31454–31554 also carried the name Immingham.

D 5581–31163 is under repair at Nemesis Rail, Burton-on-Trent.
D 5801–31271 is on loan from the Midland Railway-Butterley.
D 5821–31289 is on loan from Rushden Transport Museum.

CLASS 33 Bo-Bo

Built: 1959–62 by the Birmingham Railway Carriage & Wagon Company, Birmingham. 98 built.
Engine: Sulzer 8LDA28A of 1160 kW (1550 hp) at 750 rpm.
Transmission: Electric. Four Crompton-Parkinson C171C2 axle-hung traction motors.
Power at Rail: 906 kW (1215 hp).
Maximum Tractive Effort: 200 kN (45 000 lbf).
Continuous Tractive Effort: 116 kN (26 000 lbf) at 17.5 mph.
Weight: 78 tonnes. **Wheel Diameter:** 1092 mm.
Maximum Speed: 85 mph. **Train Heating:** Electric.

Dual (air/vacuum) braked.

Class 33/0.

D 6501–33002	Sea King	South Devon Railway	BRCW DEL/93/1960
D 6508–33008	Eastleigh	Battlefield Line	BRCW DEL/100/1960
D 6515–33012	"Lt Jenny Lewis RN"	Swanage Railway	BRCW DEL/107/1960
D 6530–33018		Sonic Rail Services, Burnham-on-Crouch	BRCW DEL/122/1960
D 6534–33019	Griffon	Nemesis Rail, Burton-on-Trent	BRCW DEL/126/1960
D 6539–33021	Eastleigh	Churnet Valley Railway	BRCW DEL/131/1960
D 6553–33035	Spitfire	Wensleydale Railway	BRCW DEL/145/1961
D 6566–33048		West Somerset Railway	BRCW DEL/170/1961
D 6570–33052	Ashford	Bluebell Railway	BRCW DEL/174/1961
D 6571–33053		Battlefield Line	BRCW DEL/175/1961
D 6575–33057	Seagull	West Somerset Railway	BRCW DEL/179/1961
D 6583–33063	"R.J. Mitchell DESIGNER OF THE SPITFIRE"	Spa Valley Railway	BRCW DEL/187/1962
D 6585–33065	Sealion	Spa Valley Railway	BRCW DEL/189/1962

Class 33/1. Fitted for push-pull operation. Triple (vacuum, air and electro-pneumatic) braked.

D 6513–33102	"Sophie"	Churnet Valley Railway	BRCW DEL/105/1960
D 6514–33103	SWORDFISH	Ecclesbourne Valley Railway	BRCW DEL/106/1960
D 6521–33108	VAMPIRE	Severn Valley Railway	BRCW DEL/113/1960
D 6525–33109	Captain Bill Smith RNR	East Lancashire Railway	BRCW DEL/117/1960
D 6527–33110		Sonic Rail Services, Burnham-on-Crouch	BRCW DEL/119/1960
D 6528–33111		Swanage Railway	BRCW DEL/120/1960
D 6535–33116	Hertfordshire Railtours	Great Central Railway (N)	BRCW DEL/127/1960
D 6536–33117		East Lancashire Railway	BRCW DEL/128/1960

Class 33/2. Built to the former loading gauge of the Tonbridge–Battle line.

D 6586–33201		Battlefield Line	BRCW DEL/157/1962
D 6587–33202	"Dennis G. Robinson"	Mid Norfolk Railway	BRCW DEL/158/1962
D 6593–33208		Battlefield Line	BRCW DEL/164/1962

D 6587–33202 also carried the names The Burma Star and METEOR.

D 6514–33103 is on loan from Nemesis Rail, Burton-on-Trent.
D 6571–33053 is on loan from UK Rail Leasing, Leicester.
D 6587–33202 is on loan from Sonic Rail Services, Burnham-on-Crouch.

CLASS 35   HYMEK   B-B

Built: 1961–64 by Beyer Peacock, Manchester. 101 built.
Engine: Bristol Siddeley Maybach MD 870 of 1269 kW (1700 hp) at 1500 rpm.
Transmission: Hydraulic. Mekydro K184U.
Maximum Tractive Effort: 207 kN (46 600 lbf).
Continuous Tractive Effort: 151 kN (33 950 lbf) at 12.5 mph.
Weight: 77 tonnes.   **Wheel Diameter:** 1143 mm.
Maximum Speed: 90 mph.   **Train Heating:** Steam.

D 7017	West Somerset Railway	BP 7911/1962
D 7018	West Somerset Railway	BP 7912/1962
D 7029	Severn Valley Railway	BP 7923/1962
D 7076	East Lancashire Railway	BP 7980/1963

CLASS 37   Co-Co

Built: 1960–66 by English Electric Company at Vulcan Foundry, Newton-le-Willows or Robert Stephenson & Hawthorns, Darlington. 309 built.
Engine: English Electric 12CSVT of 1300 kW (1750 hp) at 850 rpm.
Transmission: Electric. Six English Electric 538/A.
Power at Rail: 932 kW (1250 hp).
Maximum Tractive Effort: 247 kN (55 500 lbf).
Continuous Tractive Effort: 156 kN (35 000 lbf) at 13.6 mph.
Weight: 103–108 tonnes.   **Wheel Diameter:** 1092 mm.
Maximum Speed: 80 mph.
Train heating: Built with steam (* built without heating, but steam later fitted to D 6961, D 6963 and D 6964). Provision of steam heating was removed from D 6823, D 6842, D 6851, D 6852, D 6859, D 6869, D 6905, D 6915, D 6916 and D 6927 soon after delivery and may never have been used. D 6725–37025 and D 6948–37248 have been restored with steam heating.

Dual (air/vacuum) braked.

Class 37/0.

D 6608–37308–37274 *		Severn Valley Railway	EE/VF 3568/D997/1966
D 6703–37003		Mid Norfolk Railway	EE/VF 2866/D582/1960
D 6723–37023	Stratford TMD	Pontypool & Blaenavon Railway	EE/VF 2886 D602/1961
D 6725–37025	Inverness TMD	Bo'ness & Kinneil Railway	EE/VF 2888/D604/1961
D 6729–37029		Epping Ongar Railway	EE/VF 2892/D608/1961
D 6737–37037–37321	Gartcosh	South Devon Railway	EE/VF 2900/D616/1962
D 6742–37042		Eden Valley Railway	EE/VF 3034/D696/1962
D 6775–37075		Keighley & Worth Valley Railway	EE/RSH 3067/8321/1962
D 6797–37097	"Old Fettercairn"	Caledonian Railway	EE/VF 3226/D751/1962
D 6808–37108–37325	Lanarkshire Steel	Crewe Heritage Centre	EE/VF 3237/D762/1963
D 6809–37109		East Lancashire Railway	EE VF 3238/D763/1963
D 6842–37142		Bodmin Railway	EE/VF 3317/D816/1963
D 6852–37152–37310	British Steel Ravenscraig	Peak Rail	EE/VF 3327/D826/1963
D 6890–37190–37314	Dalzell	Locomotive Storage, Margate	EE/RSH 3368/8411/1964
D 6898–37198		Head of Steam, Darlington Railway Museum	EE/RSH 3376/8419/1964
D 6914–37214		Bo'ness & Kinneil Railway	EE/VF 3392/D858/1964
D 6915–37215		Gloucestershire Warwickshire Railway	EE/VF 3393/D859/1964
D 6916–37216	Great Eastern	Pontypool & Blaenavon Railway	EE/VF 3394/D860 1964

D 6927–37227		Chinnor & Princes Risborough Railway	EE/VF 3413/D871/1964
D 6940–37240 *		Tyseley Locomotive Works	EE/VF 3497/D928/1964
D 6948–37248 *	Loch Arkaig	Gloucestershire Warwickshire Railway	EE/VF 3505/D936/1964
D 6950–37250 *		Wensleydale Railway	EE/VF 3507/D938/1964
D 6955–37255 *		Nemesis Rail, Burton-on-Trent	EE/VF 3512/D943/1965
D 6961–37261 *	Caithness	Bo'ness & Kinneil Railway	EE/VF 3521/D950/1965
D 6963–37263 *		Severn Valley Railway	EE/VF 3523/D952/1965
D 6964–37264 *		North Yorkshire Moors Railway	EE/VF 3524/D953/1965
D 6975–37275 *	Oor Wullie	Dartmouth Steam Railway	EE/VF 3535/D964/1965
D 6994–37294 *		Embsay & Bolton Abbey Railway	EE/VF 3554/D983/1965

Class 37/3. Fitted with regeared CP7 bogies. Details as Class 37/0 except:
Maximum Tractive Effort: 250 kN (56 180 lbf).
Continuous Tractive Effort: 184 kN (41 250 lbf) at 11.4 mph.

D 6700–37119–37350	NATIONAL RAILWAY MUSEUM	Great Central Railway (N)	EE/VF 2863/D579/1960
D 6709–37009–37340		Great Central Railway (Nottingham)	EE/VF 2872/D588/1961
D 6732–37032–37353		North Norfolk Railway	EE/VF 2895/D611/1962

Class 37/4. Main generator replaced by alternator. Fitted with Electric Train Supply equipment and regeared CP7 bogies. Details as Class 37/0 except:
Transmission: Electric. Six English Electric 538/5A.
Power at rail: 935 kW (1254 hp).
Maximum Tractive Effort: 256 kN (57 440 lbf).
Continuous Tractive Effort: 184 kN (41 250 lbf) at 11.4 mph.

D 6607–37307–37403 *	Isle of Mull	Bo'ness & Kinneil Railway	EE/VF 3567/D996/1965
D 6971–37271–37418 *	An Comunn Gaidhealach	Railway Technical Centre, Derby	EE/VF 3531/D960/1965
D 6974–37274–37402 *	Stephen Middlemore 23.12.1954–8.6.2013	Barrow Hill Roundhouse	EE/VF 3534/D963/1965

Class 37/5. Main generator replaced by alternator. Fitted with regeared CP7 bogies. Details as Class 37/0 except:
Maximum Tractive Effort: 248 kN (55 590 lbf).
Continuous Tractive Effort: 184 kN (41 250 lbf) at 10.2 mph.

D 6717–37017–37503	British Steel Shelton	The Shires Removal Group, Kinsley	EE/VF 2880/D596/1961
D 6823–37123–37679		RSS, Rye Farm, Wishaw	EE/RSH 3268/8383/1963
D 6869–37169–37674	Saint Blaise Church 1445–1995	Strathspey Railway	EE/VF 3347/D833/1963
D 6905–37205–37688	Great Rocks	LNWR Heritage, Crewe	EE/VF 3383/D849/1963

Class 37/6. Originally refurbished for Nightstar services. Main generator replaced by alternator. Fitted with regeared CP7 bogies and UIC jumpers. Details as Class 37/5 except:
Weight: 106–110 tonnes.
Maximum Speed: 90 mph.

D 6790–37090–37508–37606	Nemesis Rail, Burton-on-Trent	EE/VF 3217/8336/1963

Class 37/7. Main generator replaced by alternator. Regeared CP7 bogies. Ballast weights added. Details as Class 37/0 except:
Weight: 120 tonnes.
Maximum Tractive Effort: 276 kN (62 000 lbf).
Continuous Tractive Effort: 184 kN (41 250 lbf) at 10.2 mph.

D 6724–37024–37714	"Cardiff Canton"	Great Central Railway	EE/VF 2887/D603/1961
D 6767–37067–37703		Dartmouth Steam Railway	EE/VF 3059/D721/1962

D 6607–37307–37403 also carried the names Glendarroch and Ben Cruachan.
D 6703–37003 carried the name First East Anglian Regiment for a short time in 1963 but was never officially named.
D 6724–37024–37714 also carried the name Thornaby TMD.
D 6905–37205–37688 also carried the name Kingmoor TMD.
D 6948–37248 also carried the name Midland Railway Centre.
D 6971–37271–37418 also carried the names Pectinidae, Gordon Grigg and East Lancashire Railway.
D 6974–37274–37402 also carried the names Oor Wullie and Bont Y Bermo.
D 6975–37275 also carried the name Stainless Pioneer.

D6703–37003 is currently under overhaul at UK Rail Leasing, Leicester Depot.
D6905–37205–37688 is on long-term hire to main line operator Locomotive Services.
D6963–37263 is on loan from the Telford Steam Railway.
D6971–37271–37418 is on long-term hire to main line operator Loram.

CLASS 40   1Co-Co1

Built: 1958–62 by English Electric at Vulcan Foundry, Newton-le-Willows & Robert Stephenson & Hawthorns, Darlington. 200 built.
Engine: English Electric 16SVT MkII of 1492 kW (2000 hp) at 850 rpm.
Transmission: Electric. Six EE 526/5D axle-hung traction motors.
Power at Rail: 1156 kW (1550 hp).
Maximum Tractive Effort: 231 kN (52000 lbf).
Continuous Tractive Effort: 137 kN (30900 lbf) at 18.8 mph.
Weight: 132 tonnes.   **Wheel Diameters:** 914/1143 mm.
Maximum Speed: 90 mph.
Train Heating: Steam. D306–40106 has been restored with steam heating.

Dual (air/vacuum) braked except D306.

D200–40122		National Railway Museum, Shildon (N)	
			EE/VF 2367/D395 1958
D212–40012–97407	AUREOL	East Lancashire Railway	EE/VF 2667/D429 1959
D213–40013	ANDANIA	LNWR Heritage, Crewe	EE/VF 2668/D430 1959
D306–40106	"ATLANTIC CONVEYOR"	East Lancashire Railway	EE/RSH 2726/8136 1960
D318–40118–97408		Battlefield Line	EE/RSH 2853/8148 1961
D335–40135–97406		East Lancashire Railway	EE/VF 3081/D631 1961
D345–40145		East Lancashire Railway	EE/VF 3091/D641 1961

D212–40012–97407 is on loan from the Midland Railway-Butterley.
D213–40013 is on long-term hire to main line operator Locomotive Services.
D306–40106 is on loan from the East Lancashire Railway.

CLASS 41   PROTOTYPE HST POWER CAR   Bo-Bo

Built: 1972 at Crewe. 2 built. Two prototype High Speed Diesel Train (HSDT) power cars (41001/002) were constructed to a locomotive lot (No. 1501) whilst the intermediate vehicles (10000, 10100, 11000–002 and 12000–002) were constructed to coaching stock lots. On 10 July 1974, the power cars were reclassified as coaching stock and issued with a coaching stock lot number. All prototype HSDT vehicles were thus categorised as multiple unit stock and renumbered into the 4xxxx series, Class 252 being allocated for the complete set. 41001 has been restored to original Class 41 condition and is used as a conventional locomotive.
Engine: Paxman Valenta 12RP200L of 1680 kW (2250 hp) at 1500 rpm.
Transmission: Electric. Four Brush TMH 68-46 frame-mounted traction motors.
Power at Rail: 1320 kW (1770 hp).
Maximum Tractive Effort: 80 kN (17980 lbf).
Continuous Tractive Effort: 46 kN (10340 lbf) at 64.5 mph.
Weight: 67 tonnes.   **Wheel Diameter:** 1020 mm.
Maximum Speed: 125 mph.   **Train Heating:** Electric.

Air braked.

41001–43000–ADB975812	National Railway Museum, Shildon (N)	Crewe 1972

CLASS 42   WARSHIP   B-B

Built: 1958–61 at Swindon. 38 built.
Engines: Two Bristol Siddeley Maybach MD650 of 821 kW (1100 hp) at 1530 rpm.
Transmission: Hydraulic. Mekydro K 104U.
Maximum Tractive Effort: 223 kN (52400 lbf).
Continuous Tractive Effort: 209 kN (46900 lbf) at 11.5 mph.
Weight: 80 tonnes.   **Wheel Diameter:** 1033 mm.
Maximum Speed: 90 mph.   **Train Heating:** Steam.

D821	GREYHOUND	Severn Valley Railway	Swindon 1960
D832	ONSLAUGHT	East Lancashire Railway	Swindon 1961

▲ 37264 climbs past Beckhole with the North Yorkshire Moors Railway's 12.35 Whitby–Pickering on 8 August 2023 . **Anthony Hicks**

▼ Currently on hire to Locomotive Services, 47712 Lady Diana Spencer stands at Carrbridge on 25 February 2023 with an Intercity railtour from Edinburgh to Inverness. **Ian Beardsley**

▲ Recently repainted into BR blue, Class 42 D821 GREYHOUND heads away from Hay Bridge with one of the Severn Valley Railway's services to Bridgnorth on 29 May 2023. **Martyn Tattam**

▼ Joint holder of the world speed record for diesel traction, 43159 RIO WARRIOR leads a railtour from Ilkeston to St Pancras through Luton on 28 October 2023. **Timara Easter**

CLASS 43   PRODUCTION HST POWER CAR   Bo-Bo

Built: 1975-82 by BREL Crewe. 197 built. Originally categorised as multiple unit stock, with complete sets classified as Classes 253/254, but later separated and used as conventional locomotives swapping between sets.
Engines: Built with Paxman Valenta 12RP200L of 1680 kW (2250 hp) at 1500 rpm. Some re-engined 1994–2003 with Paxman 12VP185 of 1680 kW (2250 hp) at 1500 rpm and some re-engined 2004–10 with MTU 16V4000R41R of 1680 kW (2250 hp) at 1500 rpm.
Transmission: Electric. Four Brush TMH68-46 frame-mounted traction motors.
Power at Rail: 1320 kW (1770 hp).
Maximum Tractive Effort: 80 kN (17 980 lbf).
Continuous Tractive Effort: 46 kN (10 340 lbf) at 64.5 mph.
Weight: 70.25–75 tonnes.   **Wheel Diameter:** 1020 mm.
Maximum Speed: 125 mph.   **Train Supply:** Three-phase electric.
Air braked.

Number	Name	Location	Built
43002 (ex-unit 253 001)	Sir Kenneth Grange	National Railway Museum, York (N)	Crewe 1975
43018 (ex-unit 253 009)	The Red Cross	Crewe Heritage Centre	Crewe 1976
43023 (ex-unit 253 011)	SQN LEADER HAROLD STARR ONE OF THE FEW	Colne Valley Railway	Crewe 1976
43025 (ex-unit 253 012)	Exeter	Great Central Railway (Nottingham)	Crewe 1976
43044 (ex-unit 253 022)	"Edward Paxman"	Great Central Railway (Nottingham)	Crewe 1977
43045 (ex-unit 253 022)	The Grammar School Doncaster A.D. 1350	Nene Valley Railway	Crewe 1977
43048 (ex-unit 253 024)	T.C.B. Miller MBE	Midland Railway-Butterley	Crewe 1977
43056 (ex-unit 254 001)	The Royal British Legion	Gwili Railway	Crewe 1977
43060 (ex-unit 254 003)	County of Leicestershire	Nene Valley Railway	Crewe 1977
43071 (ex-unit 254 008)	Rio Explorer	Colne Valley Railway	Crewe 1977
43073 (ex-unit 254 009)	Neville Hill HST Depot 42 Years	Colne Valley Railway	Crewe 1978
43081 (ex-unit 254 013)		Crewe Heritage Centre	Crewe 1978
43082 (ex-unit 254 014)	RAILWAY children Fighting for street children	Colne Valley Railway	Crewe 1978
43083 (ex-unit 254 014)		Arlington Fleet Services, Eastleigh Works	Crewe 1978
43089 (ex-unit 254 017)	HAYABUSA	Midland Railway-Butterley	Crewe 1978
43102 (ex-unit 254 024)	The Journey Shrinker	National Railway Museum, Shildon (N)	Crewe 1978
43159 (ex-unit 254 036)	Rio Warrior	Midland Railway-Butterley	Crewe 1981
43165 (ex-unit 253 042)	Prince Michael of Kent	Colne Valley Railway	Crewe 1981

43102 was also numbered 43302 for a time.

43002 also carried the names Top of the Pops and TECHNIQUEST.
43023 also carried the name County of Cornwall.
43025 also carried the name The Institution of Railway Operators 2000–2010 TEN YEARS PROMOTING OPERATIONAL EXCELLENCE.
43044 also carried the name Borough of Kettering.
43056 also carried the name University of Bradford.
43071 also carried the name Forward Birmingham.
43082 also carried the name DERBYSHIRE FIRST and originally carried a revised version of its existing name – RAILWAY children THE VOICE FOR STREET CHILDREN WORLDWIDE.
43089 also carried the name Rio Thunderer.
43102 also carried the names City of Wakefield and HST Silver Jubilee, Diocese of Newcastle and World Speed Record – HST. The full name currently carried is The Journey Shrinker 148.5 MPH The Worlds Fastest Diesel Train.

CLASS 44   PEAK   1Co-Co1

Built: 1959–60 at Derby. 10 built.
Engine: Sulzer 12LDA28A of 1720 kW (2300 hp) at 750 rpm.
Transmission: Electric. Six Crompton Parkinson C171B1 axle-hung traction motors.
Power at Rail: 1342 kW (1800 hp).
Maximum Tractive Effort: 222 kN (50 000 lbf).
Continuous Tractive Effort: 129 kN (29 100 lbf) at 23.2 mph.
Weight: 135 tonnes.   **Wheel Diameters:** 914/1143 mm.
Maximum Speed: 90 mph.
Train Heating: Built with steam but facility removed in 1962.

D 4–44004	GREAT GABLE	Midland Railway-Butterley	Derby 1959
D 8–44008	PENYGHENT	Peak Rail	Derby 1959

CLASS 45   1Co-Co1

Built: 1960–63 at Crewe and Derby. 127 built.
Engine: Sulzer 12LDA28B of 1860 kW (2500 hp) at 750 rpm.
Transmission: Electric. Six Crompton Parkinson C172A1 axle-hung traction motors.
Power at Rail: 1491 kW (2000 hp).
Maximum Tractive Effort: 245 kN (55 000 lbf).
Continuous Tractive Effort: 133 kN (30 000 lbf) at 25 mph.
Weight: 135 or 138 tonnes.   **Wheel Diameters:** 914/1143 mm.
Maximum Speed: 90 mph.   **Train Heating:** Built with steam.

Dual (air/vacuum) braked.

Class 45/0. Weight 138 tonnes.

D 14–45015		Battlefield Line	Derby 1960
D 53–45041	ROYAL TANK REGIMENT	Nene Valley Railway	Crewe 1962
D 100–45060	SHERWOOD FORESTER	Barrow Hill Roundhouse	Crewe 1961

Class 45/1. Steam heating replaced with Electric Train Supply equipment. Weight 135 tonnes.

D 22–45132		Epping Ongar Railway	Derby 1961
D 40–45133		Midland Railway-Butterley	Derby 1961
D 61–45112	THE ROYAL ARMY ORDNANCE CORPS	Nemesis Rail, Burton-on-Trent	Crewe 1962
D 67–45118	THE ROYAL ARTILLERYMAN	LNWR Heritage, Crewe	Crewe 1962
D 86–45105		Barrow Hill Roundhouse	Crewe 1961
D 99–45135	3RD CARABINIER	East Lancashire Railway	Crewe 1961
D 120–45108		East Lancashire Railway	Crewe 1961
D 123–45125	"LEICESTERSHIRE AND DERBYSHIRE YEOMANRY"	Great Central Railway	Crewe 1961
D 135–45149		Gloucestershire Warwickshire Railway	Crewe 1961

D 53–45041 is on loan from the Midland Railway-Butterley.
D 67–45118 is currently under overhaul at Barrow Hill Roundhouse.
D 120–45108 is on loan from the Midland Railway-Butterley.

CLASS 46   1Co-Co1

Built: 1961–63 at Derby. 56 built.
Engine: Sulzer 12LDA28B of 1860 kW (2500 hp) at 750 rpm.
Transmission: Electric. Six Brush TM73-68 MkIII axle-hung traction motors.
Power at Rail: 1460 kW (1960 hp).
Maximum Tractive Effort: 245 kN (55 000 lbf).
Continuous Tractive Effort: 141 kN (31 600 lbf) at 22.3 mph.
Weight: 141 tonnes.   **Wheel Diameters:** 914/1143 mm.
Maximum Speed: 90 mph.
Train Heating: Built with steam. D 182–46045–97404 has been restored with steam heating.

Dual (air/vacuum) braked.

D 147–46010	Barrow Hill Roundhouse	Derby 1961

D 172–46035–97403	Ixion	Peak Rail	Derby 1962
D 182–46045–97404		Severn Valley Railway	Derby 1962

D 182–46045–97404 is on loan from the Midland Railway-Butterley.

CLASS 47   Co-Co

Built: 1963–67 at Crewe and Brush Electrical Engineering Company, Loughborough. 512 built.
Engine: Sulzer 12LDA28C of 1920 kW (2580 hp) at 750 rpm. D 1705 was built with a Sulzer 12LVA24 of 1976 kW (2650 hp) engine but this was replaced with a 12LDA28C in 1972.
Transmission: Electric. Six Brush TG 160-60 axle-hung traction motors.
Power at Rail: 1550 kW (2080 hp).
Maximum Tractive Effort: 267 kN (60 000 lbf). (§ 245 kN (55 000 lbf)).
Continuous Tractive Effort: 133 kN (33 000 lbf) at 26 mph.
Weight: 119–121 tonnes.   **Wheel Diameter:** 1143 mm.
Maximum Speed: 95 mph.
Train Heating: Built with steam (except Class 47/3).

Dual (air/vacuum) braked.

Class 47/0.

D 1524–47004	Old Oak Common Traction & Rolling Stock Depot	Embsay & Bolton Abbey Railway	BE 419/1963
D 1693–47105		Gloucestershire Warwickshire Railway	BE 455/1963
D 1705–47117	"SPARROWHAWK"	Great Central Railway	BE 467/1965
D 1842–47192		Ecclesbourne Valley Railway	Crewe 1965
D 1855–47205–47395		Northampton & Lamport Railway	Crewe 1965
D 1994–47292		Churnet Valley Railway	Crewe 1966

Class 47/3. Built with no train heating.

D 1787–47306	The Sapper	Bodmin Railway	BE 549/1964
D 1886–47367		Mid Norfolk Railway	BE 648/1965
D 1895–47376	Freightliner 1995	Gloucestershire Warwickshire Railway	BE 657/1965

Class 47/4. Fitted with Electric Train Supply equipment. D 1500, D 1501 & D 1516 built with dual heat. Steam heating removed from others when Electric Train Supply equipment fitted.

D 1500–47401 §	North Eastern	Midland Railway-Butterley	BE 342/1962
D 1501–47402 §	Gateshead	Peak Rail	BE 343/1962
D 1516–47417 §		Midland Railway-Butterley	BE 358/1963
D 1566–47449		Llangollen & Corwen Railway	Crewe 1964
D 1606–47029–47635	Jimmy Milne	Epping Ongar Railway	Crewe 1964
D 1619–47038–47564–47761	COLOSSUS	Midland Railway-Butterley	Crewe 1964
D 1643–47059–47631–47765	Ressaldar	East Lancashire Railway	Crewe 1965
D 1654–47070–47620–47749	Prince Henry	Eden Valley Railway	Crewe 1965
D 1656–47072–47609–47798	Prince William	National Railway Museum, York (N)	Crewe 1965
D 1661–47077–47613–47840	NORTH STAR	North Yorkshire Moors Railway	Crewe 1965
D 1662–47484	ISAMBARD KINGDOM BRUNEL	RSS, Rye Farm, Wishaw	Crewe 1965
D 1713–47488	Rail Riders	Nemesis Rail, Burton-on-Trent	BE 475/1964
D 1755–47541–47773	The Queen Mother	Tyseley Locomotive Works	BE 483/1964
D 1762–47167–47580–47732	County of Essex	Mid Norfolk Railway	BE 524/1964
D 1778–47183–47579–47793	James Nightall G.C.	Mid Hants Railway	BE 540/1964
D 1909–47232–47665–47785	Fiona Castle	Wensleydale Railway	BE 671/1965
D 1921–47244–47640	University of Strathclyde	Nemesis Rail, Burton-on-Trent	BE 683/1965
D 1927–47250–47600–47744	Royal Mail Cheltenham	Nemesis Rail, Burton-on-Trent	BE 689/1966
D 1933–47255–47596	Aldeburgh Festival	Mid Norfolk Railway	BE 695/1966
D 1946–47503–47771	Heaton Traincare Depot	Arlington Fleet Services, Eastleigh Works	BE 708/1966
D 1966–47266–47629–47828	Severn Valley Railway	LNWR Heritage, Crewe	Crewe 1965
D 1970–47269–47643		Bo'ness & Kinneil Railway	Crewe 1965

Class 47/7. Fitted with push-pull equipment. Electric Train Supply equipment fitted & steam heating removed. Maximum Speed 100 mph.

D 1932–47493–47701	Waverley	Nemesis Rail, Burton-on-Trent	BE 694/1966
D 1948–47505–47712	Lady Diana Spencer	LNWR Heritage, Crewe	BE 610/1966

D 1654–47070–47620–47799 was also numbered 47835 for a time.
D 1656–47072–47609–47798 was also numbered 47834 for a time.
D 1909–47232–47665–47785 was also numbered 47820 for a time.

D 1500–47401 also carried the name Star of the East.
D 1606–47029–47635 also carried the name The Lass O' Ballochmyle.
D 1654–47070–47620–47799 also carried the name Windsor Castle.
D 1656–47072–47609–47798 also carried the name FIRE FLY.
D 1713–47488 also carried the name DAVIES THE OCEAN.
D 1755–47541–47773 also carried the name Reservist.
D 1762–47167–47580–47732 also carried the name Restormel.
D 1778–47183–47579–47793 also carried the names Saint Augustine and Christopher Wren.
D 1909–47232–47665–47785 also carried the name The Statesman.
D 1927–47250–47600–47744 also carried the names Saint David/Dewi Sant, Saint Edwin and The Cornish Experience.
D 1932–47493–47701 also carried the names Saint Andrew and Old Oak Common Traction & Rolling Stock Depot.
D 1946–47503–47771 also carried the name The Geordie.
D 1948–47505–47712 also carried the names Dick Whittington, ARTEMIS and Pride of Carlisle.
D 1966–47266–47629–47828 also carried the name Joe Strummer.

D 1661–47077–47613–47840 is on loan from the West Somerset Railway.
D 1778–47183–47579–47793 is on loan from the Mangapps Railway Museum.
D 1842–47192 is on loan from Crewe Heritage Centre.
D 1948–47505–47712 is on long-term hire to main line operator Locomotive Services.
D 1966–47266–47629–47828 is on long-term hire to main line operator Locomotive Services.

CLASS 50   Co-Co

Built: 1967–68 by English Electric at Vulcan Foundry, Newton-le-Willows. 50 built.
Engine: English Electric 16CVST of 2010 kW (2700 hp) at 850 rpm.
Transmission: Electric. Six EE 538/5A axle-hung traction motors.
Power at Rail: 1540 kW (2070 hp).
Maximum Tractive Effort: 216 kN (48500 lbf).
Continuous Tractive Effort: 147 kN (33000 lbf) at 18.8 mph.
Weight: 117 tonnes.   **Wheel Diameter:** 1092 mm.
Maximum Speed: 100 mph.   **Train Heating:** Electric.

Dual (air/vacuum) braked except 50008 (air only).

D 400–50050	Fearless	LNWR Heritage, Crewe	EE/VF 3770/D1141	1967
D 402–50002	Superb	South Devon Railway	EE/VF 3772/D1143	1967
D 407–50007	Hercules	Severn Valley Railway	EE/VF 3777/D1148	1968
D 408–50008	Thunderer	Knottingley Depot	EE/VF 3778/D1149	1968
D 415–50015	Valiant	East Lancashire Railway	EE/VF 3785/D1156	1968
D 417–50017	Royal Oak	Great Central Railway	EE/VF 3787/D1158	1968
D 419–50019	Ramillies	Mid Norfolk Railway	EE/VF 3789/D1160	1968
D 421–50021	Rodney	Arlington Fleet Services, Eastleigh Works	EE/VF 3791/D1162	1968
D 426–50026	Indomitable	Arlington Fleet Services, Eastleigh Works	EE/VF 3796/D1167	1968
D 427–50027	Lion	Mid Hants Railway	EE/VF 3797/D1168	1968
D 429–50029	Renown	Peak Rail	EE/VF 3799/D1170	1968
D 430–50030	Repulse	Peak Rail	EE/VF 3800/D1171	1968
D 431–50031	Hood	Severn Valley Railway	EE/VF 3801/D1172	1968
D 433–50033	Glorious	Severn Valley Railway	EE/VF 3803/D1174	1968
D 435–50035	Ark Royal	Severn Valley Railway	EE/VF 3805/D1176	1968
D 442–50042	Triumph	Bodmin Railway	EE/VF 3812/D1183	1968
D 444–50044	Exeter	Severn Valley Railway	EE/VF 3814/D1185	1968
D 449–50049–50149	Defiance	Severn Valley Railway	EE/VF 3819/D1190	1968

D 407–50007 currently carries the identity of long-scrapped classmate 50034 Furious on one side. It also carried the name SIR EDWARD ELGAR.

▲ Class 47/4 D1501 (47402) approaches Darley Dale with Peak Rail's 14.20 Rowsley South–Matlock service on 15 April 2023. **Andy Chard**

▼ Class 52 D1062 WESTERN COURIER, one of four Westerns based at the Severn Valley Railway, is pictured on display outside of Kidderminster carriage shed on 7 October 2023. **Tom McAtee**

D 407–50007 is on long-term hire to main line operator GB Railfreight.
D 433–50033 is on loan from Tyseley Locomotive Works.
D 449–50049 is on long-term hire to main line operator GB Railfreight.

CLASS 52   WESTERN   C-C

Built: 1961–64 at Crewe and Swindon. 74 built.
Engines: Two Bristol Siddeley Maybach MD655 of 1007 kW (1350 hp) at 1500 rpm.
Transmission: Hydraulic. Voith L630rV.
Maximum Tractive Effort: 297.3 kN (66 770 lbf).
Continuous Tractive Effort: 201.2 kN (45 200 lbf) at 14.5 mph.
Weight: 111 tonnes.   **Wheel Diameter:** 1092 mm.
Maximum Speed: 90 mph.   **Train Heating:** Steam.

Dual (air/vacuum) braked.

D 1010	WESTERN CAMPAIGNER	West Somerset Railway	Swindon 1962
D 1013	WESTERN RANGER	Severn Valley Railway	Swindon 1962
D 1015	WESTERN CHAMPION	Severn Valley Railway	Swindon 1963
D 1023	WESTERN FUSILIER	Didcot Railway Centre (N)	Swindon 1963
D 1041	WESTERN PRINCE	East Lancashire Railway	Crewe 1962
D 1048	WESTERN LADY	Severn Valley Railway	Crewe 1962
D 1062	WESTERN COURIER	Severn Valley Railway	Crewe 1963

CLASS 55   DELTIC   Co-Co

Built: 1961–62 by English Electric at Vulcan Foundry, Newton-le-Willows. 22 built.
Engine: Two Napier Deltic T18-25 of 1230 kW (1650 hp) at 1500 rpm.
Transmission: Electric. Six EE 538 axle-hung traction motors.
Power at Rail: 1969 kW (2640 hp).
Maximum Tractive Effort: 222 kN (50 000 lbf).
Continuous Tractive Effort: 136 kN (30 500 lbf) at 32.5 mph.
Weight: 105 tonnes.   **Wheel Diameter:** 1092 mm.
Maximum Speed: 100 mph.
Train Heating: Built with steam, electric subsequently fitted.

Dual (air/vacuum) braked.

D 9000–55022	ROYAL SCOTS GREY	LNWR Heritage, Crewe	EE/VF 2905/D557 1961
D 9002–55002	THE KING'S OWN YORKSHIRE LIGHT INFANTRY	National Railway Museum, York (N)	EE/VF 2907/D559 1961
D 9009–55009	ALYCIDON	Barrow Hill Roundhouse	EE/VF 2914/D566 1961
D 9015–55015	TULYAR	Barrow Hill Roundhouse	EE/VF 2920/D572 1961
D 9016–55016	GORDON HIGHLANDER	Locomotive Storage, Margate	EE/VF 2921/D573 1961
D 9019–55019	ROYAL HIGHLAND FUSILIER	Barrow Hill Roundhouse	EE/VF 2924/D576 1961

CLASS 56   Co-Co

Built: 1976–84 by Electroputere, Craiova, Romania and BREL Doncaster & Crewe. 135 built.
Engine: Ruston-Paxman 16RK3CT of 2424 kW (3250 hp) at 900 rpm.
Transmission: Electric. Six Brush TM73-62 axle-hung traction motors.
Power at Rail: 1790 kW (2400 hp).
Maximum Tractive Effort: 275 kN (61 800 lbf).
Continuous Tractive Effort: 240 kN (53 950 lbf) at 32.5 mph.
Weight: 125 tonnes.   **Wheel Diameter:** 1143 mm.
Maximum Speed: 80 mph.   **Train Heating:** None.

Air braked.

56006		East Lancashire Railway	EP 755/1977
56045–56301	British Steel Shelton	UK Rail Leasing, Leicester Depot	Doncaster 1978

56045–56301 is on hire to main line operator DC Rail.

CLASS 58 — Co-Co

Built: 1982–87 by BREL Doncaster. 50 built.
Engine: Ruston-Paxman 12RK3ACT of 2460 kW (3300 hp) at 1000 rpm.
Transmission: Electric. Brush TM73-62 traction motors.
Power at Rail: 1780 kW (2387 hp).
Maximum Tractive Effort: 275 kN (61 800 lbf).
Continuous Tractive Effort: 240 kN (53 950 lbf) at 32.5 mph.
Weight: 130 tonnes.   **Wheel Diameter:** 1120 mm.
Maximum Speed: 80 mph.   **Train Heating:** None.

Air braked.

58012		Battlefield Line	Doncaster 1984
58016		UK Rail Leasing, Leicester Depot	Doncaster 1984
58023	Peterborough Depot	UK Rail Leasing, Leicester Depot	Doncaster 1985
58048	Coventry Colliery	Battlefield Line	Doncaster 1986

CLASS 60 — Co-Co

Built: 1989–93 by Brush Traction at Loughborough. 100 built.
Engine: Mirrlees 8MB275T of 2310 kW (3100 hp) at 1000 rpm.
Transmission: Electric. Six axle-hung Brush TM2161A traction motors.
Power at Rail: 1800 kW (2415 hp).
Maximum Tractive Effort: 500 kN (106 500 lbf).
Continuous Tractive Effort: 336 kN (71 570 lbf) at 17.4 mph.
Weight: 129 tonnes (+ 131 tonnes).   **Wheel Diameter:** 1118 mm.
Maximum Speed: 60 mph.   **Train Heating:** None.

Air braked.

60050	Roseberry Topping	The Shires Removal Group, Kinsley	BE 952/1991
60081 +	ISAMBARD KINGDOM BRUNEL	Locomotive Storage, Margate	BE 983/1991
60086	Schiehallion	The Shires Removal Group, Kinsley	BE 988/1992

CLASS 98/1 — 0-6-0

Built: 1987 by Brecon Mountain Railway. 1 built for use on Aberystwyth–Devil's Bridge line.
Engine: Caterpillar 3304T of 105 kW (140 hp).
Transmission: Hydraulic. Twin Disc torque converter.
Gauge: 1' 11½".   **Weight:** 12.75 tonnes.
Maximum Speed: 15 mph.   **Wheel Diameter:** 610 mm.

Air braked.

Vale of Rheidol Railway   BMR 1987

2.4. EXPERIMENTAL DIESEL LOCOMOTIVES

PROTOTYPE DELTIC   Co-Co

Built: 1955 by English Electric. Used by BR 1959–61.
Engine: Two Napier Deltic T18-25 of 1230 kW (1650 hp) at 1500 rpm.
Transmission: Electric. Six EE 526A axle-hung traction motors.
Power at Rail: 1976 kW (2650 hp).
Maximum Tractive Effort: 267 kN (60000 lbf).
Continuous Tractive Effort: 104 kN (23400 lbf) at 43.5 mph.
Weight: 107.7 tonnes.   **Wheel Diameter**: 1092 mm.
Maximum Speed: 105 mph.   **Train Heating**: Steam.

DELTIC   National Railway Museum, Shildon (N)   EE 2003/1955

PROTOTYPE ENGLISH ELECTRIC SHUNTER   0-6-0

Built: 1957 by English Electric at Vulcan Foundry, Newton-le-Willows. Used by BR 1957–60.
Engine: English Electric 6RKT of 373 kW (500 hp) at 750 rpm.
Transmission: Electric.
Power at Rail:
Maximum Tractive Effort: 147 kN (33 000 lbf).
Continuous Tractive Effort: (lbf) at   mph.
Weight: 48 tonnes.   **Wheel Diameter**: 1219 mm.
Maximum Speed: 35 mph.

D 226–D 0226   "VULCAN"   Keighley & Worth Valley Railway   EE/VF 2345/D226 1956

PROTOTYPE NORTH BRITISH SHUNTER   0-4-0

Built: 1954 by North British Locomotive Company, Glasgow. Used by BR Western Region (27414) and BR London Midland & Southern regions (27415). Subsequently sold for industrial use.
Engine: Paxman 6 VRPHXL of 160 kW (225 hp) at 1250 rpm. Replaced with Rolls Royce C8TFL of   kW (hp) at   rpm on 27414.
Transmission: Hydraulic. Voith L24V.   **Weight**:   tonnes.
Maximum Tractive Effort: 112 kN (22850 lbf). **Maximum Speed**: 12 mph.
Wheel Diameter: 1016 mm.

Built without brakes, but vacuum brakes now fitted to 27414.

BR	Present		
–	TOM	Telford Steam Railway	NBL 27414/1954
–	TIGER	Bo'ness & Kinneil Railway	NBL 27415/1954

PROTOTYPE NORTH BRITISH SHUNTER   0-4-0

Built: 1958 by North British Locomotive Company, Glasgow. Used by BR Western Region at Old Oak Common in 1958. Subsequently sold for industrial use.
Engine: MAN W6V 17.5/22 of 168 kW (225 hp).
Transmission: Hydraulic. Voith L24V.   **Weight**:
Maximum Tractive Effort: 112 kN (22850 lbf). **Maximum Speed**: 12 mph.
Wheel Diameter: 940 mm.

No train brakes.

BR	Present		
–	D1	Pallot Steam, Motor & General Museum, Jersey	NBL 27734/1958

2.5. CIVIL ENGINEERS' DIESEL LOCOMOTIVES

CLASS 97/6   0-6-0

Built: 1952–59 by Ruston & Hornsby at Lincoln for BR Western Region Civil Engineers. 5 built.
Engine: Ruston 6VPH of 123 kW (165 hp).
Transmission: Electric. One British Thomson Houston RTA5041 traction motor.
Maximum Tractive Effort: 75 kN (17000 lbf).   **Weight:** 31 tonnes.
Maximum Speed: 20 mph.   **Wheel Diameter:** 978 mm.

PWM 650–97650	Peak Rail	RH 312990/1952
PWM 651–97651	Swindon & Cricklade Railway	RH 431758/1959
PWM 654–97654	Peak Rail	RH 431761/1959

▲ D0226 "VULCAN" departs Keighley with the 09.20 to Ingrow West on 23 June 2023, the first day of the Keighley & Worth Valley Railway's 2023 diesel gala.   **Tony Christie**

2.6 NEW BUILD DIESEL LOCOMOTIVES

GENERAL

The following is a list of new build diesel locomotive projects that are expected to be completed within the next two years or at least have frames in place. Technical details refer to the original locomotives: new build locomotives may differ from these.

2.6.1. NEW BUILD DIESEL LOCOMOTIVES UNDER CONSTRUCTION

BR CLASS 23 BABY DELTIC Bo-Bo

Original Class Built: 1959 by English Electric at Vulcan Foundry, Newton-le-Willows. 10 built (D5901–09). This new build locomotive is being rebuilt from Class 37 Co-Co 37372 using a set of bogies from a Class 20.
Engine: Napier Deltic T9-29 of 820 kW (1100 hp) at 1600 rpm.
Transmission: Electric. Four EE 533A axle-hung traction motors.
Power at Rail: 565 kW (768 hp).
Maximum Tractive Effort: 47 000 lbf.
Continuous Tractive Effort: (lbf) at   mph.
Weight: 75.2 tonnes. **Wheel Diameter:** 1092 mm.
Maximum Speed: 75 mph. **Train Heating:** Steam.

D5910   Barrow Hill Roundhouse   Under construction

2.7 REPLICA DIESEL LOCOMOTIVES

GENERAL

The following is a list of diesel locomotives which would have been included in the preceding chapters had the originals survived. Only locomotives that work, previously worked or can be relatively easily made to work are included. Technical details refer to the original locomotives: details of the replicas may differ from these.

2.7.1. REPLICA DIESEL LOCOMOTIVES UNDER CONSTRUCTION

LMS CLASS D16/1 Co-Co

Original Class Built: 1947–48 at Derby. 2 built (10000–001). This replica locomotive is being built using the frames from BR Class 58 58022 and a set of bogies from a BR Class EM2 (77).
Engine: English Electric 16SVT MkI of 1190 kW (1600 hp) at 750 rpm.
Transmission: Electric. Six EE 519/1B axle-hung traction motors.
Power at Rail: kW (hp).
Maximum Tractive Effort: 41 400 lbf.
Continuous Tractive Effort: (lbf) at   mph.
Weight: 115 tonnes. **Wheel Diameter:** 1067 mm.
Maximum Speed: 93 mph. **Train Heating:** Steam.

10000   Ecclesbourne Valley Railway   Under construction

3. ELECTRIC LOCOMOTIVES

GENERAL

Electric railways have existed in Great Britain for more than 120 years. Several early railway companies pioneered this form of traction, most notably the North Eastern Railway with a small fleet of electric locomotives for hauling heavy coal and steel trains in County Durham using overhead wires to supply the electric, but it was the need for mass movement of passengers into and around metropolitan areas that led to the rapid growth of electrification in the inter-war years. Early systems employed direct current normally supplied from a third rail; several different voltages were trialled but the 750 V DC favoured by the Southern Railway, at the time Britain's largest electrified network, eventually became the standard. After World War II, technological advances led to alternating current supplied from overhead wires becoming the norm; several suburban networks and all of Britain's electrified main lines away from the former Southern Region now operate from 25 kV AC overhead supply.

For further information about wheel arrangement, dimensions, tractive effort and brakes please refer to Section 2: Diesel Locomotives.

NUMBERING SYSTEMS

Prior to nationalisation, each railway company allocated locomotive numbers in accordance with its own policy. However, after nationalisation in 1948, a common system was devised and electric locomotives were allocated five-figure numbers in the series 20000–29999.

Numbering of electric locomotives from 1957 was similar to that of diesel locomotives, except that the numbers were prefixed with an "E" instead of a "D". Locomotives of pre-nationalisation design continued to be numbered in the 2xxxx series, although LNER design Classes EM1 and EM2 (see Section 3.3) later acquired an "E" prefix to their existing numbers. As with diesels, electric locomotives were allocated a two-digit class number followed by a three-digit serial number in 1968.

3.1. PRE-GROUPING DESIGN ELECTRIC LOCOMOTIVES

LSWR   Bo

Built: 1898. Siemens design for operation on the Waterloo & City line.
System: 750 V DC third rail.   **Train Heating:** None.
Traction Motors: Two Siemens 45 kW (60 hp).   **Weight:**
Maximum Speed: **Wheel Diameter:** 3′ 4″.

BR	SR		
DS75	75S	National Railway Museum, Shildon (N)	SM 6/1898

NORTH EASTERN RAILWAY CLASS ES1   Bo-Bo

Built: 1905. Used on Newcastle Quay branch. 2 built.
System: 600 V DC overhead or third rail.   **Train Heating:** None.
Traction Motors: 4 BTH design.   **Weight:** 56 tons.
Maximum Speed: 25 mph.   **Wheel Diameter:** 915 mm.

BR	LNER	NER		
26500	1–4075–6480	1	National Railway Museum, Shildon (N)	BE 1905

3.2. PRE-GROUPING DESIGN BATTERY-ELECTRIC LOCOMOTIVE

NORTH STAFFORDSHIRE RAILWAY　　　　　　　　　　　　　　　　2-A

Built: 1917. This is an electric shunting locomotive with batteries powering its two electric motors. It was used for 46 years to shunt wagons at the T Bolton & Son Works and adjacent station at Oakamoor.
Battery: 108 cells giving an output of 61 kW (82 hp).
Transmission: Wilson four-speed gearbox driving a rear jackshaft.
Maximum Tractive Effort: 50 kN (15300 lbf).　　**Wheel Diameter:** 940 mm.

NSR	LMS		
1	BEL 2	National Railway Museum, Shildon (N)	Stoke 1917

3.3. LNER DESIGN ELECTRIC LOCOMOTIVES

LNER/BR CLASS EM1 (BR CLASS 76)　　　　　　　　　　　　　　Bo+Bo

Built: 1941–53 at Doncaster (26000) and Gorton (others) for Manchester–Sheffield/Wath-upon-Dearne. 58 built.
System: 1500 V DC overhead.
Traction Motors: 4 MV 186 axle-hung.
Maximum Rail Power: 2460 kW (3300 hp).
Continuous Rating: 970 kW (1300 hp).
Maximum Tractive Effort: 200 kN (45000 lbf).
Continuous Tractive Effort: 39 kN (8800 lbf) at 56 mph.
Weight: 88 tonnes.　　　　　　　　　　**Wheel Diameter:** 1270 mm.
Maximum Speed: 65 mph.　　　　　　　**Train Heating:** Steam.

26020–E 26020–76020　　　　National Railway Museum, York (N)　　Gorton 1027/1951

BR CLASS EM2 (BR CLASS 77)　　　　　　　　　　　　　　　　　Co-Co

Built: 1953–55 at Gorton for BR to LNER design for Manchester–Sheffield/Wath-upon-Dearne. 7 built. Sold to NS (Netherlands Railways) 1969.
System: 1500 V DC overhead.
Traction Motors: 6 MV 146 axle-hung.
Maximum Rail Power: 1716 kW (2300 hp).
Maximum Tractive Effort: 200 kN (45000 lbf).
Continuous Tractive Effort: 78 kN (15600 lbf) at 23 mph.
Weight: 102 tonnes.　　　　　　　　　**Wheel Diameter:** 1092 mm.
Maximum Speed: 90 mph.
Train Heating: Steam whilst on BR, electric fitted by NS.

Vacuum whilst on BR. Air fitted by NS.

BR	NS			
27000–E 27000	1502	ELECTRA	Midland Railway-Butterley	Gorton 1065/1953
27001–E 27001	1505	ARIADNE	Science & Industry Museum, Manchester	Gorton 1066/1954
27003–E 27003	1501	DIANA	Netherlands National Railway Museum, Utrecht	Gorton 1068/1954

3.4. BRITISH RAILWAYS ELECTRIC LOCOMOTIVES

In 1957, British Railways introduced a new numbering system, which applied to all electric locomotives except those built to pre-nationalisation designs. Each locomotive was allocated a number of up to four digits prefixed with a "E", as follows:

Type	Number Range
AC Electric	E1000–E4999
DC Electric	E5000–E6999

In this section, locomotives are listed in 1968 two-digit class number order. Within each class, locomotives are listed in 1957 number order.

CLASS 71   Bo-Bo

Built: 1958–60 at Doncaster. 24 built.
System: 660–750 V DC third rail or overhead.   **Traction Motors:** English Electric 532.
Continuous Rating: 1715 kW (2300 hp).   **Maximum Tractive Effort:** 191 kN (43000 lbf).
Continuous Tractive Effort: 55 kN (12400 lbf) at 69.6 mph.
Weight: 76.2 tonnes.   **Wheel Diameter:** 1219 mm.
Maximum Speed: 90 mph.   **Train Heating:** Electric.

Dual (air/vacuum) braked.

E5001–71001	National Railway Museum, Shildon (N)	Doncaster 1959

CLASS 73/0 ELECTRO-DIESEL   Bo-Bo

Built: 1962 at Eastleigh. 6 built.   **System:** 660–750 V DC third rail.
Engine: English Electric 4SRKT of 447 kW (600 hp) at 850 rpm.
Traction Motors: English Electric 546/1B.
Continuous Rating: Electric 1060 kW (1420 hp).
Maximum Tractive Effort: Electric 187 kN (42000 lbf). Diesel 152 kN (34100 lbf).
Continuous Tractive Effort: Diesel 72 kN (16100 lbf) at 10 mph.
Weight: 76.3 tonnes.   **Wheel Diameter:** 1016 mm.
Maximum Speed: 80 mph.   **Train Heating:** Electric.

Fitted for push-pull operation. Triple (vacuum, air and electro-pneumatic) braked.

E6001–73001–73901		Ecclesbourne Valley Railway	Eastleigh 1962
E6002–73002		Arlington Fleet Services, Eastleigh Works	Eastleigh 1962
E6003–73003	Sir Herbert Walker	Swindon & Cricklade Railway	Eastleigh 1962

E6001–73001–73901 is on loan from LNWR Heritage, Crewe.

CLASS 73/1 ELECTRO-DIESEL   Bo-Bo

Built: 1965–67 by English Electric at Vulcan Foundry, Newton-le-Willows. 43 built.
System: 660–750 V DC third rail.
Engine: English Electric 4SRKT of 447 kW (600 hp) at 850 rpm.
Traction Motors: English Electric 546/1B.
Continuous Rating: Electric 1060 kW (1420 hp).
Maximum Tractive Effort: Electric 179 kN (40000 lbf). Diesel 152 kN (34100 lbf).
Continuous Tractive Effort: Diesel 60 kN (13600 lbf) at 11.5 mph.
Weight: 76.8 tonnes.   **Wheel Diameter:** 1016 mm.
Maximum Speed: 90 mph.   **Train Heating:** Electric.

Fitted for push-pull operation. Triple (vacuum, air and electro-pneumatic) braked.

E6020–73114	Stewarts Lane Traction & Maintenance Depot	Nemesis Rail, Burton-upon-Trent	EE/VF 3582/E352 1966
E6022–73116–73210	Selhurst	Ecclesbourne Valley Railway	EE/VF 3584/E354 1966
E6024–73118	The Romney, Hythe and Dymchurch Railway	Barry Tourist Railway	EE/VF 3586/E356 1966

E6036–73129	City of Winchester	Cambrian Heritage Railways, Oswestry	EE/VF 3598/E368 1966
E6037–73130	City of Portsmouth	East Kent Railway	EE/VF 3709/E369 1966
E6040–73133	The Bluebell Railway	Bluebell Railway	EE/VF 3712/E372 1966
E6047–73140		Spa Valley Railway	EE/VF 3719/E379 1966

E6037–73130 is on loan from the Llanelli & Mynydd Mawr Railway.

CLASS 81   Bo-Bo

Built: 1959–64 by the Birmingham Railway Carriage & Wagon Company, Birmingham. 25 built.
System: 25 kV AC overhead.
Traction Motors: AEI 189 frame mounted.
Continuous Rating: 2390 kW (3200 hp).
Maximum Tractive Effort: 222 kN (50000 lbf).
Continuous Tractive Effort: 76 kN (17000 lbf) at 71 mph.
Weight: 79 tonnes.   **Wheel Diameter:** 1219 mm.
Maximum Speed: 100 mph.   **Train Heating:** Electric.

Dual (air/vacuum) braked.

E3003–81002   Barrow Hill Roundhouse   BRCW 1085/1960

CLASS 82   Bo-Bo

Built: 1960–62 by Beyer Peacock, Manchester. 10 built.
System: 25 kV AC overhead.
Traction Motors: AEI 189 frame mounted.
Continuous Rating: 2460 kW (3300 hp).
Maximum Tractive Effort: 222 kN (50000 lbf).
Continuous Tractive Effort: 76 kN (17000 lbf) at 73 mph.
Weight: 80 tonnes.   **Wheel Diameter:** 1219 mm.
Maximum Speed: 100 mph.   **Train Heating:** Electric.

Dual (air/vacuum) braked.

E3054–82008   Barrow Hill Roundhouse   BP 7893/1961

CLASS 83   Bo-Bo

Built: 1960–62 by English Electric at Vulcan Foundry, Newton-le-Willows. 15 built.
System: 25 kV AC overhead.
Traction Motors: English Electric 532A frame mounted.
Continuous Rating: 2200 kW (2950 hp).
Maximum Tractive Effort: 169 kN (38000 lbf).
Continuous Tractive Effort: 68 kN (15260 lbf) at 73 mph.
Weight: 76 tonnes.   **Wheel Diameter:** 1219 mm.
Maximum Speed: 100 mph.   **Train Heating:** Electric.

Dual (air/vacuum) braked.

E3035–83012   Barrow Hill Roundhouse   EE 2941/VF E277/1961

CLASS 84   Bo-Bo

Built: 1960–61 by North British Locomotive Company, Glasgow. 10 built.
System: 25 kV AC overhead.
Traction Motors: GEC WT501 frame mounted.
Continuous Rating: 2312 kW (3100 hp).
Maximum Tractive Effort: 222 kN (50000 lbf).
Continuous Tractive Effort: 78 kN (17600 lbf) at 66 mph.
Weight: 76.6 tonnes.   **Wheel Diameter:** 1219 mm.
Maximum Speed: 100 mph.   **Train Heating:** Electric.

Dual (air/vacuum) braked.

E3036–84001   National Railway Museum, York (N)   NBL 27793/1960

▲ With 82008 visible in the background, Class 83 E3035 makes a rare appearance outdoors as it is displayed in the shed yard at Barrow Hill Roundhouse on 27 August 2022. **Ian Beardsley**

▼ One of only two Class 87s to survive in preservation, 87035 Robert Burns stands on display at Crewe Heritage Centre on 16 April 2022. **Brad Joyce**

CLASS 85 — Bo-Bo

Built: 1961–65 at Doncaster. 40 built.
System: 25 kV AC overhead.
Traction Motors: AEI 189 frame mounted.
Continuous Rating: 2390 kW (3200 hp).
Maximum Tractive Effort: 222 kN (50 000 lbf).
Continuous Tractive Effort: 76 kN (17 000 lbf) at 71 mph.
Weight: 82.5 tonnes.
Maximum Speed: 100 mph.
Wheel Diameter: 1219 mm.
Train Heating: Electric.

Dual (air/vacuum) braked.

E 3061–85006–85101   Barrow Hill Roundhouse   Doncaster 1961

CLASS 86/2 — Bo-Bo

Built: 1965–66 at Doncaster or English Electric at Vulcan Foundry, Newton-le-Willows. 58 converted from Class 86/0s, which were rebuilt with resilient wheels and Flexicoil suspension.
System: 25 kV AC overhead.
Traction Motors: AEI 282BZ axle hung.
Continuous Rating: 3010 kW (4040 hp).
Maximum Tractive Effort: 207 kN (46 500 lbf).
Continuous Tractive Effort: 85 kN (19 200 lbf).
Weight: 85 tonnes.
Maximum Speed: 100 mph.
Wheel Diameter: 1156 mm.
Train Heating: Electric.

Fitted for push-pull operation. Dual (air/vacuum) braked.

E 3137–86045–86259   Les Ross/Peter Pan   Nemesis Rail, Burton-upon-Trent   Doncaster 1966

Also carried the name Greater MANCHESTER THE LIFE & SOUL OF BRITAIN.

CLASS 87 — Bo-Bo

Built: 1973–75 by BREL at Crewe. 36 built.
System: 25 kV AC overhead.
Traction motors: GEC G412Az frame mounted.
Continuous Rating: 3730 kW (5000 hp).
Maximum Tractive Effort: 258 kN (58 000 lbf).
Continuous Tractive Effort: 95 kN (21 300 lbf) at 87 mph.
Weight: 83.5 tonnes.
Maximum Speed: 110 mph.
Wheel Diameter: 1150 mm.
Train Heating: Electric.

Fitted for push-pull operation. Air braked.

87001	Royal Scot/STEPHENSON	National Railway Museum, York (N)	Crewe 1973
87035	Robert Burns	Crewe Heritage Centre	Crewe 1974

CLASS 89 — Co-Co

Built: 1987 by BREL at Crewe. 1 built.
System: 25 kV AC overhead.
Traction motors: Brush TM 2201A frame mounted.
Continuous Rating: 4350 kW (6550 hp).
Maximum Tractive Effort: 205 kN (46000 lbf).
Continuous Tractive Effort: 105 kN (23600 lbf) at 92 mph.
Weight: 104 tonnes. **Wheel Diameter:** 1150 mm.
Maximum Speed: 125 mph. **Train Heating:** Electric.

Fitted for push-pull operation. Air braked.

89001	Avocet	UK Rail Leasing, Loughborough	Crewe 1987

CLASS 91 — Bo-Bo

Built: 1988–91 by BREL at Crewe (as subcontractors for GEC). 31 built.
System: 25 kV AC overhead.
Traction motors: GEC G426AZ.
Continuous Rating: 4540 kW (6090 hp).
Maximum Tractive Effort: 190 kN (43000 lbf).
Continuous Tractive Effort: 170 kN (38500 lbf) at 96 mph.
Weight: 84 tonnes. **Wheel Diameter:** 1000 mm.
Maximum Speed: 125 mph. **Train Heating:** Electric.

Fitted for push-pull operation. Air braked.

91031–91131	County of Northumbeland	Bo'ness & Kinneil Railway	Crewe 1991

Also carried the name Sir Henry Royce.

▲ The first and so far only member of its class to enter preservation, 91131 stands on display in the Museum of Scottish Railways at the Bo'ness & Kinneil Railway on 14 October 2023. **Chris Curtis**

4. GAS TURBINE VEHICLES

GENERAL

The potential for gas turbines as a source of propulsion for railway vehicles was first explored in the immediate post-war period, but the trials were not successful and the idea was dropped. The oil crisis of the early 1970s led to a re-examination of the concept for the ill-fated Experimental Advanced Passenger Train project. Again, the trials were unsuccessful and the idea of using gas-turbines for railways in the UK has yet to be revisited.

LOCOMOTIVE   A1A-A1A

Built: 1950 by Brown Boveri in Switzerland. 1 built. Offered to International Union of Railways' Office of Research & Experiments following withdrawal for use in researching how traction design parameters affect wheel-rail contact. Rebuilt by SBB (Swiss Federal Railways) as 1A1-3.
Power Unit: Brown Boveri gas turbine of 1828 kW (2450 hp).
Transmission: Electric. Four traction motors.
Maximum Tractive Effort: 140 kN (31 500 lbf).
Continuous Tractive Effort: 55 kN (12 400 lbf) at 64 mph.
Weight: 117.1 tonnes.   **Wheel Diameter:** 1232 mm.
Maximum Speed: 90 mph.   **Train Heating:** Steam.

18000   Didcot Railway Centre   BBC 4559/1950

EXPERIMENTAL ADVANCED PASSENGER TRAIN (APT-E)

Built: 1972 at Derby Litchurch Lane.
Power Units: Eight Leyland 350 automotive gas turbines of 222 kW (298 hp).
Traction Motors: Four GEC 253AY. Articulated unit.

PC1	National Railway Museum, Shildon (N)	Derby 1972
PC2	National Railway Museum, Shildon (N)	Derby 1972
TC1	National Railway Museum, Shildon (N)	Derby 1972
TC2	National Railway Museum, Shildon (N)	Derby 1972

PLATFORM 5 MAIL ORDER
www.platform5.com

BRITAIN'S HERITAGE RAILWAYS

Britain's Heritage Railways contains detailed information on every standard gauge heritage railway in Britain. More than 100 railways are listed in directory format, giving historical details, fleet lists and useful visitor information, including:

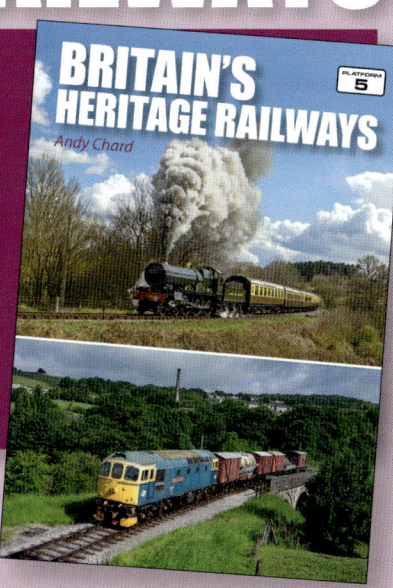

- Contact Details and Website Addresses
- Journey Times
- Public Transport Directions
- Special Events
- Rolling Stock Fleet Lists
- Opening/Operating Times
- Line Mileages

The book describes interesting features and attractions at each site and includes a stock list of all main line locomotives, industrial locomotives and multiple units at each site – a total of over 2,000 vehicles. Well-illustrated. 192 pages. Published 2023.

Cover Price £22.95. Mail Order Price £20.95 plus P&P.

If ordering at www.platform5.com use the promotion code **BHR** at the basket.

ORDER BY POST, TELEPHONE OR AT www.platform5.com

POSTAGE & PACKING: 10% UK; 30% Europe; 50% Rest of World. Cheques payable to Platform 5 Publishing Ltd.

**Mail Order Department (PL), Platform 5 Publishing Ltd,
52 Broadfield Road, SHEFFIELD, S8 0XJ, ENGLAND. Tel: 0114 255 8000**

5. MULTIPLE UNIT VEHICLES

GENERAL

During the early years of the 20th century, attempts were made to develop what can best be described as self-propelled carriages, which paved the way for the multiple units that operate the majority of services on the national rail network in Britain today.

The GWR and GNSR produced Steam Rail Motors, which were a combination of steam locomotive and carriage. These were powerful enough to move themselves as well as an additional carriage, referred to as a Trailer. They did not prove successful, though, and many were subsequently converted to Auto-Trailers for use with conventional locomotives.

More successful was the development by the NER of the Petrol-Electric Railcar. This was one of several schemes to transfer bus technology to rail vehicles that took place prior to nationalisation, the most successful being on the GWR, where the concept was developed and the result was a fleet of distinctive diesel railcars. During the 1950s, BR developed the idea of Diesel Railcars as part of its search for cheaper vehicles to operate on lightly-used lines. Numerous new designs appeared, with examples of almost all of these having made it into preservation after being replaced by the second generation Diesel Multiple Units that were introduced during the 1980s and 1990s, at least some of which have also now been preserved.

The earliest Electric Multiple Units were introduced in the late 19th century, their development largely driven by the difficulties associated with operating steam traction underground. The early 20th century saw rapid development of the technology and upon the 1923 grouping the SR, LMS and LNER each inherited sections of electrified lines. Further expansion, particularly by the SR, saw vast quantities of EMUs constructed, and a growing number of vehicles are finding their way into preservation, albeit often for use as hauled coaching stock or as static exhibits.

The sub-sections within this section are arranged by means of propulsion in the order that such means was first introduced or became most commonly in use. Where appropriate, multiple sub-sections are provided for common means of propulsion, further divided between pre-grouping companies, the "Big Four", British Railways and post-privatisation companies. Within each sub-section, multiple units are listed in numerical order of the owning company, unless otherwise stated in the sub-section introduction.

PREFIXES AND SUFFIXES

Coaching stock vehicles used to carry regional prefix letters to denote the owning region. These were removed in the 1980s. These are not shown. Pre-nationalisation number series vehicles carried both prefix and suffix letters, the suffix denoting the pre-nationalisation number series. The prefixes and suffixes are shown for these vehicles.

DIMENSIONS

Dimensions are shown as length (over buffers or couplers) x width (over bodysides including door handles).

SEATING CAPACITIES

These are shown as nF/nS nT relating to First and Second Class seats and lavatories respectively, eg a car with 12 First Class seats, 51 Second Class seats and one lavatory would be shown as 12/51 1T. Prior to 3 June 1956, Second Class was referred to as "Third" Class. It is now referred to as "Standard" Class. Certain old vehicles are thus shown as Third Class.

BOGIES

All vehicles are assumed to have two four-wheeled bogies unless otherwise stated.

5.1. STEAM RAIL MOTOR

GWR STEAM RAIL MOTOR

Original Class Built: 1905–08. 35 built. Converted to Auto Trailer 212 in 1935. Converted back to Steam Rail Motor in 2011 using a replica steam propulsion unit. Sometimes operates with GWR Auto Trailer 92, which was returned to service in 2013.
Boiler Pressure: 160 lbf/sq in. **Weight:** 45.55 tons.
Wheel Diameters: 4' 0" (driving), 3' 7½". **Valve Gear:** Walschaerts.
Cylinders: 12" x 16" (O). **Tractive Effort:** 6530 lbf.
Seats: –/61.

93   Didcot Railway Centre   Rebuilt Llangollen 2011

5.2. PETROL ELECTRIC RAILCAR

NER PETROL ELECTRIC AUTOCAR

Built: 1903 at York. 2 built. Single cars with two driving cabs. This vehicle survived as a grounded body and has been restored to its 1923 form (but as a diesel railcar) using the chassis from GNR B 2391 and mechanical parts from a BR Class 416 EMU, including the power bogie. It will operate with NER trailer autocoach 3453, currently under restoration.
Engine: Built with Napier of 68 kW (85 hp). Re-engined firstly with Wolseley of 67 kW (90 hp) and then with ex-War Department engine of 168 kW (225 hp). Rebuilt with Cummins QSL9 diesel engine of 250 kW (340 hp) at 1800 rpm.
Transmission: Electric. Rebuilt with two English Electric EE507 traction motors of 185 kW.
Body: 55' 10" x 8' 9¾". **Weight:** 35 tons.
Seats: –/44 (–/52 as built).
Maximum speed: 36 mph.

Rebuild has dual (vacuum/air) brakes.

3170   Embsay & Bolton Abbey Railway   Rebuilt Embsay 2018

5.3. SR PETROL RAILCAR

DREWERY CAR CO. RYDE PIER TRAM

Original Class Built: 1927 by Drewery Car Co. 2 built for the Ryde Pier Tramway, Isle of Wight. Single cars with one driving cab. This replica has been built using some components from SR Petrol Railcar 2 but has two driving cabs. It has assumed the identity of a former member of the class. It will operate with a new build trailer car, currently under construction.
Engine: Built with Baguley of 18 kW (25 hp). Re-engined in 1958–59 with Bedford diesel engine of 19 kW (26 hp). Rebuilt with Perkins P6 diesel engine of 22.07 kW (30 hp).
Transmission: Mechanical.
Body: 26' 8" x 7' 5". **Weight:** 5.26 tons.
Seats: –/20 (–/22 as built).
Maximum Speed: 20 mph.

Air brakes.

BR	SR		
2	2	Isle of Wight Steam Railway	A J Lowther & Sons/Alan Keef 2021

▲ Normally based at the Embsay & Bolton Abbey Railway, NER Petrol Electric Autocar 3170 arrives at Quorn & Woodhouse during a visit to the Great Central on 29 December 2023. **Paul Biggs**

▼ The Isle of Wight Steam Railway's replica of SR Ryde Pier Tram 2 stands on static display in its Train Story discovery centre at Havenstreet on 12 July 2022. **Ian Beardsley**

5.4. GWR DIESEL RAILCARS

UNCLASSIFIED   PARK ROYAL

Built: 1934 by Park Royal. Single cars with two driving cabs.
Engines: Two AEC 90 kW (121 hp).   **Transmission:** Mechanical.
Body: 19.58 x 2.70 m.   **Weight:** 26.6 tons.
Seats: –/44.   **Maximum Speed:** 75 mph.

BR	GWR		
W 4	W 4	National Railway Museum, York (N)	PR 1934

UNCLASSIFIED   GWR

Built: 1940 at Swindon. Single cars with two driving cabs.
Engines: Two AEC 78 kW (105 hp).   **Transmission:** Mechanical.
Body: 20.21 x 2.70 m.   **Weight:** 36.2 tons.
Seats: –/48.
Maximum Speed: 40 mph.

BR	GWR		
W 20	W 20	Kent & East Sussex Railway	Swindon 1940
W 22	W 22	Didcot Railway Centre	Swindon 1941

5.5. BRITISH RAILWAYS DIESEL MULTIPLE UNITS

NUMBERING SYSTEM

Early BR Diesel Multiple Units were numbered in the 79xxx series, but when it was evident that this series did not contain enough numbers the 5xxxx series was allocated to this type of vehicle and the few locomotive-hauled non-corridor coaches that were in the 5xxxx series were renumbered into the 4xxxx series. Power cars in the 50xxx series and driving trailers in the 56xxx series were eventually renumbered into the 53xxx and 54xxx series respectively to avoid conflicting numbers with Class 50 and 56 diesel locomotives.

Diesel Electric Multiple Unit power cars were numbered in the 60000–60499 series, trailers in the 60500–60799 series and driving trailers in the 60800–60999 series.

A few notes on "Pacer" preservation: Since the 19th edition of this book was published, a large number of Pacer Railbuses of Classes 142, 143 and 144 have entered preservation across Britain. Inexpensive to operate and relatively easy to maintain, these were obtained cheaply by a number of different heritage railways and prove particularly useful on off-peak services.

A number of Pacer vehicles are best classed as being "in industrial service", rather than "preserved", and these are listed in our "British Railways Pocket Book 3: Diesel Multiple Units" and the bound volume "British Railways Locomotives & Coaching Stock". Located at emergency services training centres, schools, hospitals and the like, these vehicles are also listed here but with a † symbol after the number to differentiate them from their "preserved" classmates.

The former BR operating departments used a series of Type Codes to describe the various types of multiple unit in service. For details of Type Codes used in this section see Appendix IV.

Some DMU vehicles are usually used only as hauled stock and these are denoted by a letter "h" after the number.

5.5.1. DIESEL MECHANICAL/HYDRAULIC MULTIPLE UNITS

Unless otherwise stated, all vehicles in this section have a Maximum Speed of 70 mph and mechanical transmission, while multiple units are gangwayed within each set with seating in open saloons.

In this section, classes are listed in three-digit class number order. Multiple unit vehicles are listed in original five-digit number order within each class. Unclassified multiple units are listed at the beginning of each sub-section.

UNCLASSIFIED — DERBY LIGHTWEIGHT 2-CAR UNIT

Built: 1955. Original formation: DMBS–DTCL.
Engines: Two BUT (AEC) of 112 kW (150 hp).

DMBS	18.49 x 2.82 m	27.4 tonnes	–/61
DTCL	18.49 x 2.82 m	21.3 tonnes	9/53 1T

79018–DB 975007	DMBS	Ecclesbourne Valley Railway	Derby 1955
79612–DB 975008	DTCL	Ecclesbourne Valley Railway	Derby 1955

UNCLASSIFIED — DERBY LIGHTWEIGHT SINGLE-CAR UNIT

Built: 1956. Non-gangwayed single car with two driving cabs.
Engines: Two AEC of 112 kW (150 hp).

DMBS	18.49 x 2.82 m	27 tonnes	–/57

79900–DB 975010 IRIS	DMBS	Great Central Railway	Derby 1956

79900–DB 975010 is on loan from the Ecclesbourne Valley Railway.

CLASS 100 — GRCW 2-CAR UNITS

Built: 1957–58.
Original formation: DMBS–DTCL.
Engines: Two AEC 220 of 112 kW (150 hp).

DMBS	18.49 x 2.82 m	30.5 tonnes	–/52
DTCL	18.49 x 2.82 m	25.5 tonnes	12/54 1T

51118	DMBS	Midland Railway-Butterley	GRCW 1957
56097	DTCL	Midland Railway-Butterley	GRCW 1957
56301	DTCL	Mid Norfolk Railway	GRCW 1957

CLASS 101 — METRO-CAMMELL UNITS

Built: 1958–59. Various formations.
Engines: Two AEC 220 of 112 kW (150 hp).

DMBS	18.49 x 2.82 m	32.5 tonnes	–/52 or –/49.
DMCL	18.49 x 2.82 m	32.5 tonnes	12/53 or 12/46 1T.
DMSL	18.49 x 2.82 m	32.5 tonnes	–/72 1T (originally DMCL 12/53 1T)
DTCL	18.49 x 2.82 m	25.5 tonnes	12/53 1T
DTSL	18.49 x 2.82 m	25.5 tonnes	–/71 1T (originally DTCL 12/53 1T)
TSL	18.49 x 2.82 m	25.5 tonnes	–/71 1T (§ –/58 1T, † –/72 1T) (§† originally TCL 12/53 1T)

50160–53160 Daisy 1956–2003	DMSL	North Yorkshire Moors Railway	MC 1956
50164–53164 Daisy 1956–2003	DMBS	North Yorkshire Moors Railway	MC 1956
50170–53170	DMSL	Ecclesbourne Valley Railway	MC 1957
50193–53193–977898	DMCL	Great Central Railway	MC 1957
50203–53203–977897	DMBS	Great Central Railway	MC 1957
50204–53204	DMBS	North Yorkshire Moors Railway	MC 1957
50222–53222–977693	DMBS	Plym Valley Railway	MC 1957
50253–53253	DMBS	Ecclesbourne Valley Railway	MC 1957
50256–53256	DMBS	Wensleydale Railway	MC 1957
50266–53266	DMCL	Great Central Railway	MC 1957

50321–53321–977900	DMCL	Great Central Railway	MC 1958
50338–53338–977694	DMCL	Plym Valley Railway	MC 1958
50746–53746	DMSL	Wensleydale Railway	MC 1957
51187	DMBS	Cambrian Heritage Railways, Llynclys	MC 1958
51188	DMBS	North Norfolk Railway	MC 1958
51189	DMBS	Keighley & Worth Valley Railway	MC 1958
51192	DMBS	North Norfolk Railway (N)	MC 1958
51205	DMBS	Cambrian Heritage Railways, Llynclys	MC 1958
51210	DMBS	Wensleydale Railway	MC 1958
51213	DMBS	East Anglian Railway Museum	MC 1958
51226	DMBS	Mid Norfolk Railway	MC 1958
51228	DMBS	North Norfolk Railway	MC 1958
51427–977899	DMBS	Great Central Railway	MC 1959
51434 "MATTHEW SMITH 1974–2002"	DMBS	Mid Norfolk Railway	MC 1959
51499	DMCL	Mid Norfolk Railway	MC 1959
51503	DMCL	Mid Norfolk Railway	MC 1959
51505	DMCL	Ecclesbourne Valley Railway	MC 1959
51511	DMSL	North Yorkshire Moors Railway	MC 1959
51512	DMSL	Cambrian Heritage Railways, Llynclys	MC 1959
51803	DMSL	Keighley & Worth Valley Railway	MC 1959
56055–54055	DTSL	Cambrian Heritage Railways, Llynclys	MC 1957
56062–54062	DTSL	North Norfolk Railway	MC 1957
56342–54342–042222	DTCL	Great Central Railway	MC 1958
56343–54343	DTSL	Wensleydale Railway	MC 1958
56347–54347	DTSL	Mid Norfolk Railway	MC 1958
56352–54352	DTCL	North Norfolk Railway (N)	MC 1958
56356–54356–6300 h HEBRIDEAN	DTCL	LNWR Heritage, Crewe	MC 1959
56358–54358	DTCL	East Anglian Railway Museum	MC 1959
56408–54408 h	DTSL	Lavender Line	MC 1958
59117§	TSL	Mid Norfolk Railway	MC 1958
59303	TSL	Ecclesbourne Valley Railway	MC 1957
59539†	TSL	North Yorkshire Moors Railway	MC 1959

51188 is on loan from the Ecclesbourne Valley Railway.

CLASS 103   PARK ROYAL 2-CAR UNITS

Built: 1958.
Original formation: DMBS–DTCL.
Engines: Two AEC 220 of 112 kW (150 hp).

DMBS	18.49 x 2.82 m	34 tonnes	–/52
DTCL	18.49 x 2.82 m	27 tonnes	16/48 1T

50413	DMBS	Helston Railway	PR 1958
56160–DB 975228	DTCL	Denbigh & Mold Junction Railway	PR 1958
56169	DTCL	Helston Railway	PR 1958

CLASS 104   BRCW UNITS

Built: 1957–58. Various formations.
Engines: Two BUT (Leyland) of 112 kW (150 hp).

DMBS	18.49 x 2.82 m	31.5 tonnes	–/52
TCL	18.49 x 2.82 m	24.5 tonnes	12/54 1T
TBSL	18.49 x 2.82 m	25.5 tonnes	–/51 1T
DMCL	18.49 x 2.82 m	31.5 tonnes	12/54 1T
DTCL	18.49 x 2.82 m	24.5 tonnes	12/54 1T

50437–53437	DMBS	East Lancashire Railway	BRCW 1957
50447–53447	DMBS	Llangollen & Corwen Railway	BRCW 1957
50454–53454	DMBS	Llangollen & Corwen Railway	BRCW 1957
50455–53455	DMBS	East Lancashire Railway	BRCW 1957
50479–53479	DMBS	North Norfolk Railway	BRCW 1958
50494–53494	DMCL	East Lancashire Railway	BRCW 1957
50517–53517	DMCL	East Lancashire Railway	BRCW 1957

50528–53528	DMCL	Llangollen & Corwen Railway		BRCW 1958
50531–53531	DMCL	East Lancashire Railway		BRCW 1958
56182–54182–977554	DTCL	North Norfolk Railway		BRCW 1958
59137	TCL	East Lancashire Railway		BRCW 1957
59228	TBSL	East Lancashire Railway		BRCW 1958

CLASS 105   CRAVENS 2-CAR UNITS

Built: 1957–59.
Original formation: DMBS–DTCL or DMCL.
Engines: Two AEC 220 of 112 kW (150 hp).

DMBS	18.49 x 2.82 m	29.5 tonnes	–/52
DTCL	18.49 x 2.82 m	23.5 tonnes	12/51 1T

51485	DMBS	East Lancashire Railway	Cravens 1959
56121	DTCL	East Lancashire Railway	Cravens 1957
56456–54456	DTCL	Llangollen & Corwen Railway	Cravens 1959

CLASS 107   DERBY HEAVYWEIGHT 3-CAR UNITS

Built: 1960–61.
Original formation: DMBS–TSL–DMCL.
Engines: Two BUT (Leyland) of 112 kW (150 hp).

DMBS	18.49 x 2.82 m	35 tonnes	–/52
DMCL	18.49 x 2.82 m	35.5 tonnes	12/53 1T
TSL	18.49 x 2.82 m	28.5 tonnes	–/71 1T

51990–977830	DMBS	Strathspey Railway	Derby 1960
51993–977834	DMBS	Nemesis Rail, Burton-on-Trent	Derby 1961
52005–977832	DMBS	Nemesis Rail, Burton-on-Trent	Derby 1961
52006	DMBS	Somerset & Dorset Railway Heritage Trust, Midsomer Norton Station	Derby 1961
52008	DMBS	Keith & Dufftown Railway	Derby 1961
52012–977835	DMCL	Nemesis Rail, Burton-on-Trent	Derby 1960
52025–977833	DMCL	Somerset & Dorset Railway Heritage Trust, Midsomer Norton Station	Derby 1961
52029	DMCL	Fife Heritage Railway	Derby 1961
52030–977831	DMCL	Keith & Dufftown Railway	Derby 1961
52031	DMCL	Nemesis Rail, Burton-on-Trent	Derby 1961
59791	TSL	Nemesis Rail, Burton-on-Trent	Derby 1961

CLASS 108   DERBY LIGHTWEIGHT UNITS

Built: 1958–61. Various formations.
Engines: Two Leyland of 112 kW (150 hp).

DMBS	18.49 x 2.79 m	29.5 tonnes	–/52
TBSL	18.49 x 2.79 m	21.5 tonnes	–/50 1T
TSL	18.49 x 2.79 m	21.5 tonnes	–/68 1T
DMCL	18.49 x 2.79 m	28.5 tonnes	12/53 1T
DTCL	18.49 x 2.79 m	21.5 tonnes	12/53 1T

51566 has been converted into a DMS with a bar seating –/63.

50599–53599	DMBS	Ecclesbourne Valley Railway	Derby 1958
50619–53619	DMBS	Dean Forest Railway	Derby 1958
50628–53628	DMBS	Keith & Dufftown Railway	Derby 1958

50645–53645	DMCL	Great Central Railway (Nottingham)	Derby 1958
50926–53926–977814	DMBS	Great Central Railway (Nottingham)	Derby 1959
50928–53928	DMBS	Keighley & Worth Valley Railway	Derby 1959
50933–53933	DMBS	Severn Valley Railway	Derby 1960
50971–53971	DMBS	Kent & East Sussex Railway	Derby 1959
50980–53980	DMBS	Weardale Railway	Derby 1959
51562	DMCL	National Railway Museum, York (N)	Derby 1959
51565	DMCL	Keighley & Worth Valley Railway	Derby 1959
51566	DMCL	Dean Forest Railway	Derby 1959
51567–977854	DMCL	Ecclesbourne Valley Railway	Derby 1959
51568	DMCL	Keith & Dufftown Railway	Derby 1959
51571	DMCL	Kent & East Sussex Railway	Derby 1960
51572	DMCL	Weardale Railway	Derby 1960
51907	DMBS	Midland Railway-Butterley	Derby 1960
51909	DMBS	East Somerset Railway	Derby 1960
51914	DMBS	Dean Forest Railway	Derby 1960
51919	DMBS	Garw Valley Railway	Derby 1960
51922	DMBS	National Railway Museum, York (N)	Derby 1960
51933	DMBS	Llangollen & Corwen Railway	Derby 1960
51937–977806	DMBS	Poulton & Wyre Railway	Derby 1960
51941	DMBS	Severn Valley Railway	Derby 1960
51942	DMBS	Mid Norfolk Railway	Derby 1961
51947	DMBS	East Somerset Railway	Derby 1961
51950	DMBS	Peak Rail	Derby 1961
52048	DMCL	Garw Valley Railway	Derby 1960
52053–977807	DMCL	Keith & Dufftown Railway	Derby 1960
52054	DMCL	Weardale Railway	Derby 1960
52062	DMCL	Peak Rail	Derby 1961
52064	DMCL	Severn Valley Railway	Derby 1961
56207–54207 h	DTCL	Appleby-Frodingham RPS, Scunthorpe	Derby 1958
56208–54208	DTCL	Severn Valley Railway	Derby 1958
56223–54223	DTCL	Llangollen & Corwen Railway	Derby 1959
56224–54224	DTCL	Keith & Dufftown Railway	Derby 1959
56270–54270	DTCL	Mid Norfolk Railway	Derby 1959
56271–54271	DTCL	East Somerset Railway	Derby 1960
56274–54274	DTCL	Weardale Railway	Derby 1960
56279–54279	DTCL	Oaklands, Toprow, Norfolk	Derby 1960
56484–54484	DTCL	Poulton & Wyre Railway	Derby 1960
56490–54490	DTCL	Midland Railway-Butterley	Derby 1960
56491–54491	DTCL	Keith & Dufftown Railway	Derby 1960
56492–54492	DTCL	Dean Forest Railway	Derby 1960
56495–54495	DTCL	Whistlestop Valley Railway	Derby 1960
56504–54504	DTCL	Llangollen & Corwen Railway	Derby 1960
59245 h	TBSL	Appleby-Frodingham RPS, Scunthorpe	Derby 1958
59250	TBSL	Severn Valley Railway	Derby 1958
59387	TSL	Dean Forest Railway	Derby 1958

50628 and 56224 are named "Spirit of Speyside".
51568 and 52053 are named "Spirit of Banffshire".

51947 survives as a grounded body.

CLASS 109   D WICKHAM 2-CAR UNITS

Built: 1957.
Original formation: DMBS–DTCL.
Engines: Two BUT (Leyland) of 112 kW (150 hp).

DMBS	18.49 x 2.82 m	27.5 tonnes	–/52	
DTCL	18.49 x 2.82 m	20.5 tonnes	16/50 1T	

50416–DB 975005	DMBS	Llangollen & Corwen Railway	Wkm 1957
56171–DB 975006	DTCL	Llangollen & Corwen Railway	Wkm 1957

▲ One of six Class 117 vehicles based at the Dartmouth Steam Railway, TSL 59513 "JEAN" is seen stabled in the sidings at Kingswear on 19 October 2022. **Ian Beardsley**

▼ Made up of DMBS 51591, TSL 59609 and DMBS 51625, the Midland Railway-Butterley's Class 127 stands at Butterley on 2 April 2022. **Ian Beardsley**

CLASS 110 — BRCW CALDER VALLEY 3-CAR UNITS

Built: 1961–62.
Original formation: DMBC–TSL–DMCL.
Engines: Two Rolls-Royce C6NFLH38D of 134 kW (180 hp).

DMBC	18.48 x 2.82 m	32.5 tonnes	12/33
DMCL	18.48 x 2.82 m	32.5 tonnes	12/54 1T
TSL	18.48 x 2.82 m	24.5 tonnes	–/72 1T

51813	DMBC	East Lancashire Railway	BRCW 1961
51842	DMCL	East Lancashire Railway	BRCW 1961
52071	DMBC	Lakeside & Haverthwaite Railway	BRCW 1962
52077	DMCL	Lakeside & Haverthwaite Railway	BRCW 1961
59701	TSL	East Lancashire Railway	BRCW 1961

CLASS 111 — METRO-CAMMELL TRAILER BUFFET

Built: 1960. Used to augment other units as required.

TRSBL	18.49 x 2.82 m	25.5 tonnes	–/53 1T

59575	TRSBL	Great Central Railway	MC 1960

CLASS 114 — DERBY HEAVYWEIGHT 2-CAR UNITS

Built: 1956–57.
Original formation: DMBS–DTCL. Some rebuilt for parcels use, formation DMPMV–DTPMV.
Engines: Two Leyland Albion of 149 kW (200 hp).

DMBS	20.45 x 2.82 m	38 tonnes	–/62
DMPMV	20.45 x 2.82 m	41.5 tonnes	–
DTCL	20.45 x 2.82 m	30 tonnes	12/62 1T
DTPMV	20.45 x 2.82 m	30 tonnes	–

50015–53015–55929–977775	DMPMV	Midland Railway-Butterley	Derby 1957
50019–53019	DMBS	Midland Railway-Butterley	Derby 1957
56006–54006	DTCL	Midland Railway-Butterley	Derby 1956
56015–54015–54904–977776	DTPMV	Midland Railway-Butterley	Derby 1957
56047–54047	DTCL	Strathspey Railway	Derby 1957

55929 and 54904 were allocated departmental numbers 977715 and 977716 but these were never carried and they subsequently became 977775 and 977776.

CLASS 115 — DERBY SUBURBAN 4-CAR UNITS

Built: 1960. Non-gangwayed when built, but gangways subsequently fitted.
Original formation: DMBS–TSso–TCL–DMBS.
Engines: Two Leyland Albion of 149 kW (200 hp).

DMBS	20.45 x 2.82 m	38.5 tonnes	–/74 (originally –/78)
TCL	20.45 x 2.82 m	30.5 tonnes	28/38 (originally 30/40) 2T
TSso	20.45 x 2.82 m	29.5 tonnes	–/98 (originally –/106)

59678 has been converted to TRCBL seating 28/32 by the West Somerset Railway.

51655	DMBS	Thomas Muir (Rosyth), Port of Rosyth	Derby 1960
51669	DMBS	Midland Railway-Butterley	Derby 1960
51849	DMBS	Midland Railway-Butterley	Derby 1960
51859	DMBS	West Somerset Railway	Derby 1960
51880	DMBS	West Somerset Railway	Derby 1960
51886	DMBS	Buckinghamshire Railway Centre	Derby 1960
51887	DMBS	West Somerset Railway	Derby 1960
51899	DMBS	Buckinghamshire Railway Centre	Derby 1960

59659	TSso	Midland Railway-Butterley	Derby 1960
59664	TCL	The Old Station Hub, Talybont-on-Usk	Derby 1960
59678	TCL	West Somerset Railway	Derby 1960
59719	TCL	Dartmouth Steam Railway	Derby 1960
59740	TSso	South Devon Railway	Derby 1960
59761	TCL	Buckinghamshire Railway Centre	Derby 1960

59719 has been converted to a mess room at Churston.
59740 has been converted to a static cafe at Staverton.

CLASS 116   DERBY SUBURBAN 3-CAR UNITS

Built: 1957–58. Non-gangwayed when built, but gangways subsequently fitted.
Original formation: DMBS–TS or TC–DMS.
Engines: Two Leyland of 112 kW (150 hp).

DMBS	20.45 x 2.82 m	36.5 tonnes	–/65
DMS	20.45 x 2.82 m	36.5 tonnes	–/89 (originally –/95)
TS§	20.45 x 2.82 m	29 tonnes	–/98 (originally –/102)
TC	20.45 x 2.82 m	29 tonnes	20/68 (originally 28/74)

§   converted from TC seating 28/74.

51131	DMBS	Battlefield Line	Derby 1958
51138	DMBS	Great Central Railway (Nottingham)	Derby 1958
51151	DMS	Great Central Railway (Nottingham)	Derby 1958
59003 h "LILY"	TS	Dartmouth Steam Railway	Derby 1957
59004 h "EMMA"	TS	Dartmouth Steam Railway	Derby 1957
59444 h	TC	Chasewater Railway	Derby 1958

51138 was allocated departmental number 977921 but this was never carried.

CLASS 117   PRESSED STEEL SUBURBAN 3-CAR UNITS

Built: 1960. Non-gangwayed when built, but gangways subsequently fitted.
Original formation: DMBS–TCL–DMS.
Engines: Two Leyland of 112 kW (150 hp).

DMBS	20.45 x 2.82 m	36.5 tonnes	–/65
TCL	20.45 x 2.82 m	30.5 tonnes	22/48 (originally 24/50) 2T
DMS	20.45 x 2.82 m	36.5 tonnes	–/89 (originally –/91)

59494, 59503 and 59507 have been converted to TSs by the Dartmouth Steam Railway.
59513 and 59517 have been converted to TSLs by the Dartmouth Steam Railway.

51339	DMBS	Colne Valley Railway	PS 1960
51342	DMBS	Epping Ongar Railway	PS 1960
51347	DMBS	Gwili Railway	PS 1960
51351	DMBS	Pontypool & Blaenavon Railway	PS 1960
51352	DMBS	South Devon Railway	PS 1960
51353	DMBS	Wensleydale Railway	PS 1960
51354	DMBS	West Somerset Railway	PS 1960
51356	DMBS	Swanage Railway	PS 1960
51360	DMBS	Gloucestershire Warwickshire Railway	PS 1960
51363	DMBS	Gloucestershire Warwickshire Railway	PS 1960
51365	DMBS	Plym Valley Railway	PS 1960
51367	DMBS	Strathspey Railway	PS 1960
51370	DMBS	Mid Norfolk Railway	PS 1960
51371–977987	DMBS	Arlington Fleet Services, Eastleigh Works	PS 1960
51372	DMBS	Gloucestershire Warwickshire Railway	PS 1960
51375–977992	DMS	Chinnor & Princes Risborough Railway	PS 1960
51376	DMS	South Devon Railway	PS 1960
51381	DMS	Mangapps Railway Museum	PS 1960
51382	DMS	Colne Valley Railway	PS 1960

51384	DMS	Epping Ongar Railway	PS 1960
51388	DMS	Swanage Railway	PS 1960
51392	DMS	Swanage Railway	PS 1960
51396	DMS	Great Central Railway	PS 1960
51397	DMS	Pontypool & Blaenavon Railway	PS 1960
51400	DMS	Wensleydale Railway	PS 1960
51401	DMS	Gwili Railway	PS 1960
51402	DMS	Strathspey Railway	PS 1960
51405	DMS	Gloucestershire Warwickshire Railway	PS 1960
51407	DMS	Plym Valley Railway	PS 1960
51412	DMS	Mid Norfolk Railway	PS 1960
51413–977988	DMS	Arlington Fleet Services, Eastleigh Works	PS 1960
59486	TCL	Swanage Railway	PS 1960
59488	TCL	Dartmouth Steam Railway	PS 1960
59492	TCL	Arlington Fleet Services, Eastleigh Works	PS 1960
59493 h	TCL	South Devon Railway	PS 1960
59494 h "CHLOE"	TCL	Dartmouth Steam Railway	PS 1960
59500	TCL	Wensleydale Railway	PS 1960
59501	TCL	Great Central Railway (Nottingham)	PS 1960
59503 h "NINA"	TCL	Dartmouth Steam Railway	PS 1960
59505	TCL	Gloucestershire Warwickshire Railway	PS 1960
59506	TCL	Great Central Railway	PS 1960
59507 h "ANNA"	TCL	Dartmouth Steam Railway	PS 1960
59508	TCL	Gwili Railway	PS 1960
59509	TCL	Wensleydale Railway	PS 1960
59510	TCL	Gloucestershire Warwickshire Railway	PS 1960
59511	TCL	Strathspey Railway	PS 1960
59513 h "JEAN"	TCL	Dartmouth Steam Railway	PS 1960
59514	TCL	Swindon & Cricklade Railway	PS 1960
59515 h	TCL	Yeovil Railway Centre	PS 1960
59517 h "POPPY"	TCL	Dartmouth Steam Railway	PS 1960
59520	TCL	Mid Norfolk Railway	PS 1960
59521 h	TCL	Helston Railway	PS 1960

51353 has been converted into a community centre at Leeming Bar.
51371–977987, 51413–977988 and 59492 are undergoing overhaul for use on the North Somerset Railway at Arlington Fleet Services, Eastleigh Works.
59488 has been converted into a static visitor centre at Kingswear station.

CLASS 118 — BRCW SUBURBAN 3-CAR UNITS

Built: 1960. Non-gangwayed when built, but gangways subsequently fitted.
Original formation: DMBS–TCL–DMS.
Engines: Two Leyland of 112 kW (150 hp).

DMS	20.45 x 2.82 m	36.5 tonnes	–/89 (originally –/91)

51321–977753	DMS	Battlefield Line	BRCW 1960

CLASS 119 — GRCW CROSS-COUNTRY 3-CAR UNITS

Built: 1959.
Original formation: DMBC–TRSBL–DMSL.
Engines: Two Leyland of 112 kW (150 hp).

DMBC	20.45 x 2.82 m	37.5 tonnes	18/16
DMSL	20.45 x 2.82 m	38.5 tonnes	–/68 2T

51073	DMBC	Ecclesbourne Valley Railway	GRCW 1959
51074	DMBC	Swindon & Cricklade Railway	GRCW 1959
51104	DMSL	Swindon & Cricklade Railway	GRCW 1959

CLASS 120   SWINDON CROSS-COUNTRY 3-CAR UNITS
Built: 1958.
Original formation: DMBC–TRSBL–DMSL.

TRSBL	20.45 x 2.82 m	31.5 tonnes	–/60 2T

59276	TRSBL	Great Central Railway	Swindon 1958

CLASS 121   PRESSED STEEL SINGLE UNITS & DRIVING TRAILERS
Built: 1960–61. Non-gangwayed single cars with two driving cabs plus driving trailers used for augmentation. The driving trailers were latterly fitted with gangways for coupling to power cars of other classes.
Engines: Two Leyland of 112 kW (150 hp).

DMBS	20.45 x 2.82 m	38 tonnes	–/65
DTS	20.45 x 2.82 m	30 tonnes	–/89 (originally –/91)

55020–977722	DMBS	Bodmin Railway	PS 1960
55023	DMBS	Chinnor & Princes Risborough Railway	PS 1960
55024–977858	DMBS	Chinnor & Princes Risborough Railway	PS 1960
55025–977859	DMBS	Honeybourne Airfield Industrial Estate	PS 1960
55027–977975	DMBS	Ecclesbourne Valley Railway	PS 1960
55028–977860 John Cameron	DMBS	Swanage Railway	PS 1960
55029–977968	DMBS	Rushden Transport Museum	PS 1960
55031–977976	DMBS	Ecclesbourne Valley Railway	PS 1960
55032–977842	DMBS	Wensleydale Railway	PS 1960
55033–977826	DMBS	Colne Valley Railway	PS 1960
55034–977828	DMBS	Ecclesbourne Valley Railway	PS 1961
56287–54287	DTS	Epping Ongar Railway	PS 1961
56289–54289	DTS	East Lancashire Railway	PS 1961

CLASS 122   GRCW SINGLE-CAR UNITS
Built: 1958. Non-gangwayed single cars with two driving cabs.
Engines: Two AEC 220 of 112 kW (150 hp).

DMBS	20.45 x 2.82 m	36.5 tonnes	–/65

55000	DMBS	South Devon Railway	GRCW 1958
55001–DB975023	DMBS	East Lancashire Railway	GRCW 1958
55003	DMBS	Gloucestershire Warwickshire Railway	GRCW 1958
55005	DMBS	Battlefield Line	GRCW 1958
55006	DMBS	Ecclesbourne Valley Railway	GRCW 1958
55009	DMBS	Great Central Railway	GRCW 1958
55012	DMBS	Weardale Railway	GRCW 1958
55019–DB975042	DMBS	Llanelli & Mynydd Mawr Railway	GRCW 1958

CLASS 126   SWINDON INTER-CITY UNITS

Built: 1956–59. 51017, 51043 and 59404 for Ayrshire services and 79443 for Glasgow–Edinburgh services. Various formations.
Engines: Two AEC 220 of 112 kW (150 hp).

DMBSL	20.45 × 2.82 m	38.5 tonnes	–/52 1T
DMSL	20.45 × 2.82 m	38.5 tonnes	–/64 1T
TCK	20.45 × 2.82 m	32.3 tonnes	18/32 2T
TRCsoBL	20.45 × 2.82 m	34 tonnes	18/12 1T (First Class seating in compartments)

51017	DMSL	Bo'ness & Kinneil Railway	Swindon 1959
51043	DMBSL	Bo'ness & Kinneil Railway	Swindon 1959
59404	TCK	Bo'ness & Kinneil Railway	Swindon 1959
79443	TRCsoBL	Bo'ness & Kinneil Railway	Swindon 1957

59404 was converted by BR to a TSK –/56 but has been restored as a TCK.

CLASS 127   DERBY SUBURBAN 4-CAR UNITS

Built: 1959. Non-gangwayed.
Original formation: DMBS–TSL–TS–DMBS. Some DMBS cars were rebuilt as DMPMV cars, normal formation DMPMV(A)–DMPMV(B).
Engines: Two Rolls-Royce C8 of 177 kW (238 hp).
Transmission: Hydraulic.

DMBS	20.45 × 2.82 m	40.6 tonnes	–/76
DMPMV (A)	20.45 × 2.82 m	40 tonnes	–
DMPMV (B)	20.45 × 2.82 m	40 tonnes	–
TSL	20.45 × 2.82 m	30.5 tonnes	–/86 2T

51591–55966		DMBS	Midland Railway-Butterley	Derby 1959
51610–55967		DMPMV(B)	Midland Railway-Butterley	Derby 1959
51616 h	"ALF BENNEY"	DMBS	Helston Railway	Derby 1959
51618		DMBS	Llangollen & Corwen Railway	Derby 1959
51622		DMBS	Vincent Engineering, Henstridge	Derby 1959
51625–55976		DMBS	Midland Railway-Butterley	Derby 1959
59603 h		TSL	Chasewater Railway	Derby 1959
59609		TSL	Midland Railway-Butterley	Derby 1959

51591–55966 and 51625–55976 were converted by BR to DMPMV(A)s but have been restored as DMBSs.
51622 is due to be moved to the Helston Railway.

CLASS 153   SUPER SPRINTER   LEYLAND BUS SINGLE UNITS

Built: 1987–88 as 2-car Class 155 units. Converted to single-car units with two driving cabs by Hunslet-Barclay, Kilmarnock 1991–92.
Formation: DMSL.
Engines: One Cummins NT855R5 of 213 kW (285 hp) at 2100 rpm.
Transmission: Hydraulic, Voith T211r.
Maximum Speed: 75 mph.

Air braked.

DMSL	23.21 × 2.70 m		41.2 tonnes	–/72 1T

52308	DMSL	(ex-unit 153 308)	Great Central Railway	Leyland 1987 reb 1991
57371	DMSL	(ex-unit 153 371)	Great Central Railway	Leyland 1988 reb 1992
57374	DMSL	(ex-unit 153 374)	Llanelli & Mynydd Mawr Railway	Leyland 1988 reb 1992

57374 survives as a grounded body.

5.5.2. FOUR-WHEELED DIESEL RAILBUSES

A small number of diesel railbuses appeared in the 1950s as a result of the Modernisation Plan. These were intended for use on very lightly loaded branch line services. Within a few years of their introduction, many of the services for which they were designed ceased and they were withdrawn.

Faced with the need to find replacements for the ageing DMU fleet in the late 1970s, the concept was again investigated. As a result, a number of prototypes emerged, which it was hoped would lead to substantial orders from both BR and overseas railways. Although BR purchased large numbers of 2- and 3-car railbuses, no significant overseas orders materialised.

In this section, 1950s vehicles are listed first, followed by 1970s and 1980s prototypes and finally 1980s 2-car units, many of which have recently been preserved.

UNCLASSIFIED — WAGGON UND MASCHINENBAU

Built: 1958. 5 built.
Engine: Buessing of 112 kW (150 hp) at 1900 rpm (§ AEC 220 of 112 kW (150 hp)).
Transmission: Mechanical.
Maximum Speed: 70 mph.

DMS   13.95 x 2.67 m   15 tonnes   –/56

79960	Ribble Steam Railway	WMD 1265/1958
79962	Keighley & Worth Valley Railway	WMD 1267/1958
79963	East Anglian Railway Museum	WMD 1268/1958
79964§	Keighley & Worth Valley Railway	WMD 1298/1958

79960 is on loan from the North Norfolk Railway.

UNCLASSIFIED — AC CARS

Built: 1958. 5 built.
Engine: AEC 220 of 112 kW (150 hp) (§ engine removed).
Transmission: Mechanical.
Maximum Speed: 70 mph.

DMS   11.33 x 2.82 m   11 tonnes   –/46

79976§	Nemesis Rail, Burton-on-Trent	AC 1958
79978	Swindon & Cricklade Railway	AC 1958

UNCLASSIFIED — WICKHAM TRACK RECORDING CAR

Built: 1958 for BR Research. Later known as the Wickham Self-Propelled Laboratory. Preserved as passenger-carrying Railbus and fitted with 28 seats.
Engine: Meadows 6HDC500 of 71 kW (97 hp) at 1800 rpm.
Transmission: Mechanical, to one axle only. 4 speed epicyclic gearbox Type R11.
Maximum Speed: 55 mph.

999507–RDB 999507   Lavender Line   Wkm 8025/1958

UNCLASSIFIED — BR DERBY/LEYLAND

Built: 1977. Used by BR and in the USA.
Engine: Leyland 510 of 149 kW (200 hp) (fitted 1979).
Transmission: Mechanical. Self Changing Gears.
Maximum Speed: 75 mph.

Air braked.

DMS   12.32 x 2.50 m   16.67 tonnes   –/40
R1–RDB 975874   Wensleydale Railway (N)   RTC Derby 1977

▲ Making up one of only two Class 141 units in preservation, DMS 55513 and DMSL 55533 (unit 141 113) are seen stabled at the Midland Railway-Butterley on 2 April 2022. **Ian Beardsley**

▼ With Class 142 DMSL 55614 and DMS 55564 (142 023) on the left, Class 143 DMSL 55684 and DMS 55659 (143 618) stand at Marsh Mills on the Plym Valley Railway on 31 July 2022. **Tony Christie**

UNCLASSIFIED — BREL DERBY/LEYLAND

Built: 1981. Used by BR. Subsequently sold to Northern Ireland Railways.
Engine: Leyland 690 of 149 kW (200 hp).
Transmission: Mechanical. Self Changing Gears SE4 epicyclic gearbox and cardan shafts to SCG RF28 final drive.
Maximum Speed: 75 mph.
Gauge: Built as 1435 mm but converted to 1600 mm when sold to Northern Ireland Railways.

Air braked.

DMS	15.30 x 2.50 m	19.96 tonnes	–/56

R3.03–RDB 977020	RB3	Downpatrick Steam Railway, NI	RTC Derby 1981

UNCLASSIFIED — BREL-LEYLAND

Built: 1984. Built for demonstration purposes. RE 002 used in mainland Europe. RE 004 used in the USA.
Engine: Leyland TL11 of 152 kW (205 hp).
Transmission: Mechanical.
Maximum Speed: 75 mph.

Air braked.

DMS	x 2.50 m	37.5 tonnes	–/64 (* –/40)

RE 002		Carlingford Brewing Company, Dundalk, Ireland	BREL Leyland 1984
RE 004*	RB 004	Waverley Route Heritage Association, Whitrope	BREL Leyland 1984

CLASS 140 — DERBY/LEYLAND BUS 2-CAR PACER RAILBUS

Built: 1981. Prototype
Formation: DMSL–DMS.
Engine: Leyland TL11 of 152 kW (205 hp)
Transmission: Mechanical. Self-Changing Gears 4-speed gearbox.
Maximum Speed: 75 mph.

Air braked.

DMSL	16.20 x 2.50 m	23.2 tonnes	–/50 1T
DMS	16.20 x 2.50 m	23.0 tonnes	–/52

55500	DMS	(ex-unit 140 001)	Keith & Dufftown Railway	Derby 1981
55501	DMSL	(ex-unit 140 001)	Keith & Dufftown Railway	Derby 1981

CLASS 141 — BREL/LEYLAND BUS 2-CAR PACER RAILBUS

Built: 1983–84. Modified by Andrew Barclay 1988–89.
Formation: DMS–DMSL.
Engine: Leyland TL11 of 152 kW (205 hp) (* Cummins L10 of 165 kW (225 hp)).
Transmission: Mechanical, Self Changing Gears (* Hydraulic, Voith T211r).
Maximum Speed: 75 mph.

Air braked.

DMS	15.45 x 2.50 m	26.0 tonnes	–/50
DMSL	15.45 x 2.50 m	26.5 tonnes	–/44 1T

55508	DMS	(ex-unit 141 007–141 108)	Arlington Fleet Services, Eastleigh	BREL Leyland 1984
55513 *	DMS	(ex-unit 141 012–141 113)	Midland Railway-Butterley	BREL Leyland 1984
55528	DMSL	(ex-unit 141 007–141 108)	Arlington Fleet Services, Eastleigh	BREL Leyland 1984
55533 *	DMSL	(ex-unit 141 012–141 113)	Midland Railway-Butterley	BREL Leyland 1984

In addition, a further 28 Class 141 vehicles were exported for use abroad:

55502, 55505, 55507, 55509, 55511, 55514, 55515, 55516, 55517, 55518, 55519, 55520, 55522, 55525, 55527, 55529, 55531, 55534, 55535, 55536, 55537, 55538, 55539 and 55540 were sold to Iranian Islamic Republic Railways: .

55506, 55512, 55526 and 55532 were sold to Connexion, Utrecht, Netherlands: .

CLASS 142   BREL/LEYLAND BUS 2-CAR PACER RAILBUS

Built: 1985–87.
Formation: DMS–DMSL.
Engine: Built with Leyland T11 of 152 kW (205 hp). Re-engined 1994–96 with Cummins LT10-R of 165 kW (225 hp) at 1950 rpm.
Transmission: Built with Mechanical, Self Changing Gears. Fitted with Hydraulic, Voith T211r post 1991.
Maximum Speed: 75 mph.

Air braked.

DMS	15.45 x 2.80 m	24.5 tonnes	–/62, c –/46, s –/56, t –/53 or 55, u –/52 or –/54
DMSL	15.45 x 2.80 m	25.0 tonnes	–/59 1T, c –/44 1T, s –/50 1T, u –/60 1T

† Vehicles classed as "in industrial service" rather than "preserved".

55542 t	DMS	(ex-unit 142001)	National Railway Museum, Shildon (N)	Derby 1985
55545 t	DMS	(ex-unit 142004)	Telford Steam Railway	Derby 1985
55547 c	DMS	(ex-unit 142006)	Llanelli & Mynydd Mawr Railway	Derby 1985
55552 t	DMS	(ex-unit 142011)	Midland Railway-Butterley	Derby 1985
55554	DMS	(ex-unit 142013)	Midland Railway-Butterley	Derby 1985
55558 s	DMS	(ex-unit 142017)	East Kent Railway	Derby 1985
55559 s	DMS	(ex-unit 142018–142518)	Wensleydale Railway	Derby 1985
55560 s	DMS	(ex-unit 142019–142519)	Waverley Route Heritage Association, Whitrope	Derby 1985
55561 s	DMS	(ex-unit 142020–142520)	Waverley Route Heritage Association, Whitrope	Derby 1985
55564 t	DMS	(ex-unit 142023)	Plym Valley Railway	Derby 1985
55568 t	DMS	(ex-unit 142027)	Chasewater Railway	Derby 1986
55569 t	DMS	(ex-unit 142028)	Wensleydale Railway	Derby 1985
55570	DMS	(ex-unit 142029)	Chasewater Railway	Derby 1985
55571	DMS	(ex-unit 142030)	Chasewater Railway	Derby 1985
55574 t†	DMS	(ex-unit 142033)	South Wales Police Training Centre, Bridgend	Derby 1986
55576 t	DMS	(ex-unit 142035)	Wensleydale Railway	Derby 1986
55577 t	DMS	(ex-unit 142036)	East Kent Railway	Derby 1986
55579 t	DMS	(ex-unit 142038)	Mid Norfolk Railway	Derby 1986
55582 u	DMS	(ex-unit 142041)	Wensleydale Railway	Derby 1986
55584 u†DMS		(ex-unit 142043)	Sussex Police Training Centre, Kingstanding	Derby 1986
55586 u†DMS		(ex-unit 142045)	Kirk Merrington Primary School, Spennymoor	Derby 1986
55592 t	DMSL	(ex-unit 142001)	National Railway Museum, Shildon (N)	Derby 1985
55595 t	DMSL	(ex-unit 142004)	Telford Steam Railway	Derby 1985
55597 c	DMSL	(ex-unit 142006)	Llanelli & Mynydd Mawr Railway	Derby 1985
55602 t	DMSL	(ex-unit 142011)	Midland Railway-Butterley	Derby 1985
55604	DMSL	(ex-unit 142013)	Midland Railway-Butterley	Derby 1985
55608 s	DMSL	(ex-unit 142017)	East Kent Railway	Derby 1985
55609 s	DMSL	(ex-unit 142018–142518)	Wensleydale Railway	Derby 1985
55610 s	DMSL	(ex-unit 142019–142519)	Waverley Route Heritage Association, Whitrope	Derby 1985
55611 s	DMSL	(ex-unit 142020–142520)	Waverley Route Heritage Association, Whitrope	Derby 1985
55614 t	DMSL	(ex-unit 142023)	Plym Valley Railway	Derby 1985
55618 t	DMSL	(ex-unit 142027)	Chasewater Railway	Derby 1986
55619 t	DMSL	(ex-unit 142028)	Wensleydale Railway	Derby 1985
55620	DMSL	(ex-unit 142029)	Chasewater Railway	Derby 1985
55621	DMSL	(ex-unit 142030)	Chasewater Railway	Derby 1985
55624 t†	DMSL	(ex-unit 142033)	South Wales Police Training Centre, Bridgend	Derby 1986
55626 t	DMSL	(ex-unit 142035)	Wensleydale Railway	Derby 1986
55627 t	DMSL	(ex-unit 142036)	East Kent Railway	Derby 1986
55629 t	DMSL	(ex-unit 142038)	Mid Norfolk Railway	Derby 1986
55632 u	DMSL	(ex-unit 142041)	Wensleydale Railway	Derby 1986
55634 u†DMSL		(ex-unit 142043)	Sussex Police Training Centre, Kingstanding	Derby 1986
55636 u†DMSL		(ex-unit 142045)	Kirk Merrington Primary School, Spennymoor	Derby 1986
55638 u	DMSL	(ex-unit 142047)	Station Yard, Stow Bridge	Derby 1986
55705 u	DMS	(ex-unit 142055)	Foxfield Railway	Derby 1986
55708 u	DMS	(ex-unit 142058)	Telford Steam Railway	Derby 1986
55710 t	DMS	(ex-unit 142060)	Wensleydale Railway	Derby 1986
55711 t	DMS	(ex-unit 142061)	Mid Norfolk Railway	Derby 1986
55728 s	DMS	(ex-unit 142078)	Weardale Railway	Derby 1987

55734 s	DMS	(ex-unit 142084)	Rushden Transport Museum	Derby 1987
55737 s†DMS		(ex-unit 142087)	Wensleydale Railway	Derby 1987
55740 s†DMS		(ex-unit 142090)	Wensleydale Railway	Derby 1987
55741 s	DMS	(ex-unit 142091)	Rushden Transport Museum	Derby 1987
55744 s	DMS	(ex-unit 142094)	Embsay & Bolton Abbey Steam Railway	Derby 1987
55751 u	DMSL	(ex-unit 142055)	Foxfield Railway	Derby 1986
55754 u	DMSL	(ex-unit 142058)	Telford Steam Railway	Derby 1986
55756 t	DMSL	(ex-unit 142060)	Wensleydale Railway	Derby 1986
55757 t	DMSL	(ex-unit 142061)	Mid Norfolk Railway	Derby 1986
55774 s	DMSL	(ex-unit 142078)	Weardale Railway	Derby 1987
55780 s	DMSL	(ex-unit 142084)	Rushden Transport Museum	Derby 1987
55783 s†DMSL		(ex-unit 142087)	Wensleydale Railway	Derby 1987
55786 s†DMSL		(ex-unit 142090)	Wensleydale Railway	Derby 1987
55787 s	DMSL	(ex-unit 142091)	Rushden Transport Museum	Derby 1987
55790 s	DMSL	(ex-unit 142094)	Embsay & Bolton Abbey Steam Railway	Derby 1987

CLASS 143   ALEXANDER/BARCLAY 2-CAR PACER RAILBUS

Built: 1985–86.
Formation: DMS–DMSL.
Engine: Built with Leyland TL11 of 152 kW (205 hp). Re-engined with Cummins LT10-R of 165 kW (225 hp) at 1950 rpm.
Transmission: Built with Mechanical, Self Changing Gears. Fitted with Hydraulic, Voith T211r post 1990.
Maximum Speed: 75 mph.

Air braked.

DMS	15.45 x 2.80 m	24.0 tonnes	–/48 2W
DMSL	15.45 x 2.80 m	24.5 tonnes	–/44 1T 2W

55642	DMS	(ex-unit 143001–143601)	Tanat Valley Light Railway	AB 1985
55644	DMS	(ex-unit 143017–143617)	Tarka Valley Railway	AB 1985
55647	DMS	(ex-unit 143006–143606)	Llanelli & Mynydd Mawr Railway	AB 1985
55648	DMS	(ex-unit 143007–143607)	Llanelli & Mynydd Mawr Railway	AB 1985
55651	DMS	(ex-unit 143002–143602)	Nene Valley Railway	AB 1985
55653	DMS	(ex-unit 143012–143612)	Llanelli & Mynydd Mawr Railway	AB 1985
55657	DMS	(ex-unit 143016–143616)	Tanat Valley Light Railway	AB 1985
55658	DMS	(ex-unit 143003–143603)	RSS, Rye Farm, Wishaw	AB 1985
55659	DMS	(ex-unit 143018–143618)	Plym Valley Railway	AB 1985
55660	DMS	(ex-unit 143019–143619)	Tanat Valley Light Railway	AB 1986
55663	DMS	(ex-unit 143022–143622)	Llanelli Railway Goods Shed	AB 1986
55664	DMS	(ex-unit 143023–143623)	Wensleydale Railway	AB 1986
55666	DMS	(ex-unit 143025–143625)	Keighley & Worth Valley Railway	AB 1986
55667	DMSL	(ex-unit 143001–143601)	Tanat Valley Light Railway	AB 1985
55668	DMSL	(ex-unit 143002–143602)	Nene Valley Railway	AB 1985
55669	DMSL	(ex-unit 143003–143603)	RSS, Rye Farm, Wishaw	AB 1985
55672	DMSL	(ex-unit 143006–143606)	Llanelli & Mynydd Mawr Railway	AB 1985
55673	DMSL	(ex-unit 143007–143607)	Llanelli & Mynydd Mawr Railway	AB 1985
55678	DMSL	(ex-unit 143012–143612)	Llanelli & Mynydd Mawr Railway	AB 1985
55682	DMSL	(ex-unit 143016–143616)	Tanat Valley Light Railway	AB 1985
55683	DMSL	(ex-unit 143017–143617)	Tarka Valley Railway	AB 1985
55684	DMSL	(ex-unit 143018–143618)	Plym Valley Railway	AB 1986
55685	DMSL	(ex-unit 143019–143619)	Tanat Valley Light Railway	AB 1986
55688	DMSL	(ex-unit 143022–143622)	Llanelli Railway Goods Shed	AB 1986
55689	DMSL	(ex-unit 143023–143623)	Wensleydale Railway	AB 1986
55691	DMSL	(ex-unit 143025–143625)	Keighley & Worth Valley Railway	AB 1986

55644 was originally formed in unit 143003 until 1989.
55651 was originally formed in unit 143010 until 1989.
55658 was originally formed in unit 143017 until 1989.

Unit 143622 (including 55663 and 55688) was also numbered 143322 for a time.
Unit 143623 (including 55664 and 55689) was also numbered 143323 for a time.
Unit 143625 (including 55666 and 55691) was also numbered 143325 for a time.

55683 is named "Founder Member & Chairman Rod Garner 1943–2020".

CLASS 144   ALEXANDER/BREL DERBY PACER RAILBUS

Built: 1986–87.
Formation: DMS–DMSL or DMS–MS–DMSL.
Engine: Built with Leyland T11 of 152 kW (205 hp). Re-engined 1994–96 with Cummins LT10-R of 165 kW (225 hp) at 1950 rpm.
Transmission: Built with Mechanical, Self Changing Gears. Fitted with Hydraulic, Voith T211r post 1991.
Maximum Speed: 75 mph.

Air braked.

DMS	15.45 x 2.80 m	24.0 tonnes	–/45
MS	15.43 x 2.80 m	23.5 tonnes	–/58
DMSL	15.45 x 2.80 m	24.5 tonnes	–/41 1T

† Vehicles classed as "in industrial service" rather than "preserved".

55801 †	DMS	(ex-unit 144 001)	Airedale General Hospital, Steeton	Derby 1986
55802 †	DMS	(ex-unit 144 002)	The Dales School – Blythedale, Blythe	Derby 1986
55803	DMS	(ex-unit 144 003)	Great Central Railway (Nottingham)	Derby 1986
55804	DMS	(ex-unit 144 004)	Aln Valley Railway	Derby 1986
55806	DMS	(ex-unit 144 006)	Cambrian Heritage Railways, Oswestry	Derby 1986
55807	DMS	(ex-unit 144 007)	Cambrian Heritage Railways, Oswestry	Derby 1986
55808 †	DMS	(ex-unit 144 008)	Fagley Primary School, Bradford	Derby 1986
55809	DMS	(ex-unit 144 009)	East Lancashire Railway	Derby 1987
55810 †	DMS	(ex-unit 144 010)	East Lancashire Railway	Derby 1987
55811	DMS	(ex-unit 144 011)	Keighley & Worth Valley Railway	Derby 1987
55813	DMS	(ex-unit 144 013)	Telford Steam Railway	Derby 1987
55816	DMS	(ex-unit 144 016)	Aln Valley Railway	Derby 1987
55817	DMS	(ex-unit 144 017)	Appleby-Frodingham RPS, Scunthorpe	Derby 1987
55818	DMS	(ex-unit 144 018)	Mid Norfolk Railway	Derby 1987
55819	DMS	(ex-unit 144 019)	Tyseley Locomotive Works	Derby 1987
55820	DMS	(ex-unit 144 020)	Wensleydale Railway	Derby 1987
55822	DMS	(ex-unit 144 022)	Keith & Dufftown Railway	Derby 1987
55824 †	DMSL	(ex-unit 144 001)	Platform 1, Huddersfield Station	Derby 1986
55825 †	DMSL	(ex-unit 144 002)	The Dales School – Blythedale, Blythe	Derby 1986
55826	DMSL	(ex-unit 144 003)	Great Central Railway (Nottingham)	Derby 1986
55827	DMSL	(ex-unit 144 004)	Aln Valley Railway	Derby 1986
55829	DMSL	(ex-unit 144 006)	Cambrian Heritage Railways, Oswestry	Derby 1986
55830	DMSL	(ex-unit 144 007)	Cambrian Heritage Railways, Oswestry	Derby 1986
55831	DMSL	(ex-unit 144 008)	Corby & District Model Railway Society, Corby	Derby 1986
55832	DMSL	(ex-unit 144 009)	East Lancashire Railway	Derby 1987
55833 †	DMSL	(ex-unit 144 010)	East Lancashire Railway	Derby 1987
55834	DMSL	(ex-unit 144 011)	Keighley & Worth Valley Railway	Derby 1987
55836	DMSL	(ex-unit 144 013)	Telford Steam Railway	Derby 1987
55839	DMSL	(ex-unit 144 016)	Aln Valley Railway	Derby 1987
55840	DMSL	(ex-unit 144 017)	Appleby Frodingham RPS, Scunthorpe	Derby 1987
55841	DMSL	(ex-unit 144 018)	Mid Norfolk Railway	Derby 1987
55842	DMSL	(ex-unit 144 019)	Tyseley Locomotive Works	Derby 1987
55843	DMSL	(ex-unit 144 020)	Wensleydale Railway	Derby 1987
55845	DMSL	(ex-unit 144 022)	Keith & Dufftown Railway	Derby 1987
55846	DMSL	(ex-unit 144 023)	Tyseley Locomotive Works	Derby 1987
55852	MS	(ex-unit 144 016)	Aln Valley Railway	Derby 1988
55853	MS	(ex-unit 144 017)	Appleby Frodingham RPS, Scunthorpe	Derby 1988
55854	MS	(ex-unit 144 018)	Mid Norfolk Railway	Derby 1988
55855	MS	(ex-unit 144 019)	Tyseley Locomotive Works	Derby 1988
55856	MS	(ex-unit 144 020)	Wensleydale Railway	Derby 1988
55858	MS	(ex-unit 144 022)	Keith & Dufftown Railway	Derby 1988
55859	MS	(ex-unit 144 023)	Tyseley Locomotive Works	Derby 1988

55801 and 55824 carried the name THE PENISTONE LINE PARTNERSHIP.

55810 and 55833 are reserved for Greater Manchester Fire & Rescue.

55824 survives as a grounded body.

5.5.3. DIESEL ELECTRIC MULTIPLE UNITS

At the time of the 1955 Modernisation Plan, much of the then Southern Region was already operating from third rail electric supply, with just a handful of lines not so equipped. Complete electrification was out of the question, so much thought was given to how to replace steam traction on these lines. The solution was the Diesel Electric Multiple Unit, which was essentially an Electric Multiple Unit fitted with a diesel engine to enable operation on non-electrified lines.

In the early 1980s, BR desperately needed to replace its ageing fleet of Diesel Multiple Units and returned to the DEMU concept as a possible solution. Two prototype units were built but the high cost of the vehicles proved to be too expensive and the project was dropped. One of these units was later used to trial three-phase traction equipment, and one of the vehicles from this survives in preservation; it can be found in the Electric Multiple Units section.

Most of the Southern Region lines for which DEMUs had originally been acquired either closed or were the subject of a later electrification programme.

In this section, classes are listed in three-digit class number order. Multiple unit vehicles are listed in original five-digit number order within each class.

CLASS 201 "HASTINGS" 6-CAR DIESEL-ELECTRIC UNITS

Built: 1957 by BR Eastleigh Works on frames constructed at Ashford. Special narrow-bodied units built to the former loading gauge of the Tonbridge–Battle line. Gangwayed within set.
Original formation: DMBSO–TSOL–TSOL–TFK–TSOL–DMBSO.
Engines: English Electric 4SRKT of 370 kW (500 hp).
Transmission: Two EE 507 traction motors on the power car inner bogie.
Maximum Speed: 75 mph.

DMBSO	18.35 x 2.50 m	54 tonnes	–/22
TSOL	18.35 x 2.50 m	29 tonnes	–/52 2T
TFK	18.36 x 2.50 m	30 tonnes	42/– 2T

60000	"Hastings"	DMBSO	(ex-unit 1001)	St Leonards Railway Engineering	Eastleigh 1957
60001		DMBSO	(ex-unit 1001)	St Leonards Railway Engineering	Eastleigh 1957
60500		TSOL	(ex-unit 1001)	St Leonards Railway Engineering	Eastleigh 1957
60501		TSOL	(ex-unit 1001)	St Leonards Railway Engineering	Eastleigh 1957
60502		TSOL	(ex-unit 1001)	St Leonards Railway Engineering	Eastleigh 1957
60700		TFK	(ex-unit 1001)	St Leonards Railway Engineering	Eastleigh 1957

CLASS 202 "HASTINGS" 6-CAR DIESEL-ELECTRIC UNITS

Built: 1957–58 by BR Eastleigh Works on frames constructed at Ashford. Special narrow-bodied units built to the former loading gauge of the Tonbridge–Battle line. Gangwayed within set.
Original formation: DMBSO–TSOL–TSOL(or TRSKB)–TFK–TSOL–DMBSO.
Engines: English Electric 4SRKT of 370 kW (500 hp).
Transmission: Two EE 507 traction motors on the power car inner bogie.
Maximum Speed: 75 mph.

DMBSO	20.34 x 2.50 m	55 tonnes	–/30
TSOL	20.34 x 2.50 m	29 tonnes	–/60 2T
TFK	20.34 x 2.50 m	31 tonnes	48/– 2T
TRSKB	20.34 x 2.50 m	34 tonnes	–/21

60016–60116	DMBSO	(ex-unit 1012)	St Leonards Railway Engineering	Eastleigh 1957
60018–60118	DMBSO	(ex-unit 1013–203 101)	St Leonards Railway Engineering	Eastleigh 1957
60019–60119	DMBSO	(ex-unit 1013–203 101)	St Leonards Railway Engineering	Eastleigh 1957
60527	TSOL	(ex-unit 1013–203 101)	St Leonards Railway Engineering	Eastleigh 1957
60528	TSOL	(ex-unit 1013–202 001)	St Leonards Railway Engineering	Eastleigh 1957
60529	TSOL	(ex-unit 1013–202 001)	St Leonards Railway Engineering	Eastleigh 1957
60708	TFK	(ex-unit 1012)	St Leonards Railway Engineering	Eastleigh 1957
60709	TFK	(ex-unit 1013–203 101)	St Leonards Railway Engineering	Eastleigh 1957
60750–RDB 975386	TRSKB	(ex-unit 1032)	Battlefield Line	Eastleigh 1958

60018, 60019, 60527, 60709 were also formed in unit 202 001.

60116 carries the name "Mountfield" and 60118 carries the name "Tunbridge Wells".

CLASS 205 "HAMPSHIRE" 2- & 3-CAR DIESEL-ELECTRIC UNITS

Built: 1957–59 by BR Eastleigh Works on frames constructed at Ashford. Non-gangwayed (* subsequently fitted with gangways).
Original formation: DMBSO–TSO–DTCsoL or DMBSO–DTCsoL.
Engines: English Electric 4SRKT of 450 kW (600 hp).
Transmission: Two EE 507 traction motors on the power car inner bogie.
Maximum Speed: 75 mph.

DMBSO	20.34 x 2.82 m	56 tonnes	–/52 (* –/39)	
TSO	20.28 x 2.82 m	30 tonnes	–/104	
DTCsoL	20.34 x 2.82 m	32 tonnes	19/50 2T (§ 13/50 2T) (originally 13/62 2T)	
DTSOL	20.34 x 2.82 m	32 tonnes	–/76 2T (originally DTCsoL 13/62 2T)	

60100–60154	DMBSO	(ex-unit 1101–205 001)	East Kent Railway	Eastleigh 1957
60108	DMBSO	(ex-unit 1109–205 009)	Eden Valley Railway	Eastleigh 1957
60110*	DMBSO	(ex-unit 1111–205 205)	Epping Ongar Railway	Eastleigh 1957
60117	DMBSO	(ex-unit 1118–205 018)	Lavender Line	Eastleigh 1957
60122	DMBSO	(ex-unit 1123–205 023)	Lavender Line	Eastleigh 1959
60124	DMBSO	(ex-unit 1125–205 025)	Mid Hants Railway	Eastleigh 1959
60658	TSO	(ex-unit 1109–205 009)	Eden Valley Railway	Eastleigh 1959
60800§	DTCsoL	(ex-unit 1101–205 001)	East Kent Railway	Eastleigh 1957
60808	DTCsoL	(ex-unit 1109–205 009)	Eden Valley Railway	Eastleigh 1957
60810*	DTSOL	(ex-unit 1111–205 205)	Epping Ongar Railway	Eastleigh 1957
60820	DTCsoL	(ex-unit 1108–205 008)	Lavender Line	Eastleigh 1958
60824§	DTCsoL	(ex-unit 1125–205 025)	Mid Hants Railway	Eastleigh 1959

Unit 205 205 (including 60110 and 60810) was also numbered 205 101 for a time.

60820 was originally part of unit 1121. It was reformed into unit 1108 (later 205 008) in 1974. Originally used on the Hastings–Ashford line and the Bexhill West and New Romney branches. The four units 1119–1122 originally used on these services were referred to as "HASTINGS" when based at St Leonards depot. On loan from St Leonards Railway Engineering.

▲ Class 202 DMBSO 60116 "MOUNTFIELD" leads Hastings Diesels' "Cambridge Clipper" railtour away from Ely on 3 September 2023. **Aubrey Evans**

CLASS 205   "BERKSHIRE"   3-CAR DIESEL-ELECTRIC UNITS

Built: 1960–62 by BR Eastleigh Works on frames constructed at Ashford. Non-gangwayed.
Original formation: DMBSO–TSO–DTCsoL.
Engines: English Electric 4SRKT of 450 kW (600 hp).
Transmission: Two EE 507 traction motors on the power car inner bogie.
Maximum Speed: 75 mph.

DMBSO	20.34 x 2.82 m	56 tonnes	–/42
TSO	20.28 x 2.82 m	30 tonnes	–/104
DTCsoL	20.34 x 2.82 m	32 tonnes	13/62 2T

60145–977939	DMBSO	(ex-unit 1127–205 027)	St Leonards Railway Engineering	Eastleigh 1962
60146	DMBSO	(ex-unit 1128–205 028)	Caledonian Railway	Eastleigh 1962
60149–977940	DMBSO	(ex-unit 1131–205 031)	St Leonards Railway Engineering	Eastleigh 1962
60150	DMBSO	(ex-unit 1132–205 032)	Caledonian Railway	Eastleigh 1962
60151	DMBSO	(ex-unit 1133–205 033)	Lavender Line	Eastleigh 1962
60673	TSO	(ex-unit 1128–205 028)	Caledonian Railway	Eastleigh 1962
60677	TSO	(ex-unit 1132–205 032)	Caledonian Railway	Eastleigh 1962
60827	DTCsoL	(ex-unit 1128–205 028)	Caledonian Railway	Eastleigh 1962
60828	DTCsoL	(ex-unit 1129–205 018)	Lavender Line	Eastleigh 1962
60831	DTCsoL	(ex-unit 1132–205 032)	Caledonian Railway	Eastleigh 1962
60832	DTCsoL	(ex-unit 1133–205 033)	Lavender Line	Eastleigh 1962

60828 was also formed in unit 205 018 for a time.

CLASS 207   "OXTED"   3-CAR DIESEL-ELECTRIC UNITS

Built: 1962 by BR Eastleigh Works on frames constructed at Ashford. Reduced body width to allow operation through Somerhill Tunnel. Non-gangwayed (* subsequently fitted with gangways).
Original formation: DMBSO–TCsoL–DTSO.
Engines: English Electric 4SRKT of 370 kW (500 hp).
Transmission: Two EE 507 traction motors on the power car inner bogie.
Maximum Speed: 75 mph.

DMBSO	20.34 x 2.74 m	56 tonnes	–/42 (* –/40)
DTSO	20.32 x 2.74 m	32 tonnes	–/76 (* –/75)
TCsoL	20.34 x 2.74 m	31 tonnes	24/42

60127*	DMBSO	(ex-unit 1302–207 203)	Swindon & Cricklade Railway	Eastleigh 1962
60130*	DMBSO	(ex-unit 1305–207 202)	Bluebell Railway	Eastleigh 1962
60142	DMBSO	(ex-unit 1317–207 017)	Spa Valley Railway	Eastleigh 1962
60616	TCsoL	(ex-unit 1317–207 017)	Spa Valley Railway	Eastleigh 1962
60904*	DTSO	(ex-unit 1305–207 202)	Bluebell Railway	Eastleigh 1962
60916	DTSO	(ex-unit 1317–207 017)	Spa Valley Railway	Eastleigh 1962

Unit 207 202 (including 60130 and 60904) was also numbered 207 005 and 207 102 for a time.
Unit 207 203 (including 60127) was also numbered 207 002 and 207 103 for a time.

60130 is named Brighton Royal Pavilion.

_# 5.6. SOUTHERN RAILWAY ELECTRIC MULTIPLE UNITS

In this section, classes are listed in order of the lowest numbered example of the class to be still in existence. Within classes, vehicles are listed in numerical order of original number.

For details of type codes see Appendix IV.

CLASS 487 — WATERLOO & CITY LINE UNITS

Built: 1940. No permanent formations.
System: 630 V DC third rail.
Traction Motors: Two EE 500 of 140 kW (185 hp). **Maximum Speed:** 35 mph.

DMBSO	14.33 x 2.64 m	29 tons	–/40

BR	SR		
S 61 S	61	DMBSO	London Transport Depot Museum, Acton (N) EE 1940

1285 CLASS (later 3 Sub) — SUBURBAN UNITS

Built: 1925. Non-gangwayed.
Original Formation: DMBS–TS–DMBS.
System: 630 V DC third rail.
Traction Motors: Two MV 167 kW (225 hp). **Maximum Speed:** 75 mph.

DMBS	18.90 x 2.44 m	39 tons	–/70

BR	SR		
S 8143 S	8143	DMBS (ex-unit 1293, later 4308)	National Railway Museum, York (N) MC 1925

4 Cor   "NELSONS"   PORTSMOUTH EXPRESS STOCK

Built: 1937–38. Gangwayed throughout.
Original Formation: DMBSO–TSK–TCK–DMBSO.
System: 630 V DC third rail.
Traction Motors: Two EE 167 kW (225 hp) per power car.
Maximum Speed: 75 mph.

DMBSO	19.54 x 2.88 m	46.5 tons	–/52
TSK	19.54 x 2.85 m	32.65 tons	–/68
TCK	19.54 x 2.85 m	32.6 tons	30/24

BR	SR				
S 10096 S	10096	TSK	(ex-unit 3142)	Hope Farm, Sellindge	Eastleigh 1937
S 11161 S	11161	DMBSO	(ex-unit 3142)	East Kent Railway	Eastleigh 1937
S 11179 S	11179	DMBSO	(ex-unit 3131)	National Railway Museum, Shildon (N)	Eastleigh 1937
S 11187 S	11187	DMBSO	(ex-unit 3135)	East Kent Railway	Eastleigh 1937
S 11201 S	11201	DMBSO	(ex-unit 3142)	Hope Farm, Sellindge	Eastleigh 1937
S 11825 S	11825	TCK	(ex-unit 3142)	Hope Farm, Sellindge	Eastleigh 1937

S 11161 S was originally in unit 3065 and S 11825 S in unit 3135.

4 Sub (later Class 405) — SUBURBAN UNITS

Built: 1941–51. Non-gangwayed.
Original Formation: DMBSO–TS–TSO–DMBSO.
System: 630 V DC third rail.
Traction Motors: Two EE507 of 185 kW (250 hp). **Maximum Speed:** 75 mph.

DMBSO	19.05 x 2.82 m	42 tons	–/82
TS	18.90 x 2.82 m	27 tons	–/120
TSO	18.90 x 2.82 m	26 tons	–/102

S 10239 S	TS	(ex-units 4413–4732)	Locomotive Storage, Margate	Eastleigh 1947
S 12354 S	TSO	(ex-units 4381–4732)	Locomotive Storage, Margate	Eastleigh 1948

| S 12795 S | DMBSO (ex-unit 4732) | Locomotive Storage, Margate | Eastleigh 1951 |
| S 12796 S | DMBSO (ex-unit 4732) | Locomotive Storage, Margate | Eastleigh 1951 |

2 Bil — SEMI-FAST UNITS

Built: 1937. Non-gangwayed.
Original Formation: DMBSK–DTCK.
System: 630 V DC third rail.
Traction Motors: Two EE of 205 kW (275 hp).   **Maximum Speed**: 75 mph.

DMBSK	19.24 x 2.85 m	43.5 tons	–/52
DTCK	19.24 x 2.85 m	31.25 tons	24/30

BR	SR				
S 10656 S	10656	DMBSK	(ex-unit 1890–2090)	National Railway Museum, Shildon (N)	Eastleigh 1937
S 12123 S	12123	DTCK	(ex-unit 1890–2090)	National Railway Museum, Shildon (N)	Eastleigh 1937

4 DD — DOUBLE-DECK SUBURBAN UNITS

Built: 1949. Non-gangwayed.
Original Formation: DMBS–TS–TS–DMBS.
System: 630 V DC third rail.
Traction Motors: Two EE of 185 kW (250 hp).   **Maximum Speed**: 75 mph.

DMBS	19.24 x 2.85 m	39 tons	–/121

S 13003 S	DMBS	(ex-unit 4002–4902)	Hope Farm, Sellindge	Lancing 1949
S 13004 S	DMBS	(ex-unit 4002–4902)	Hope Farm, Sellindge	Lancing 1949

4 EPB (later Class 415) — SUBURBAN UNITS

Built: 1951–57. Non-gangwayed.
Original Formation: DMBSO–TS–TSO–DMBSO.
System: 630 V DC third rail.
Traction Motors: Two EE507 of 185 kW (250 hp).   **Maximum Speed**: 75 mph.

DMBSO	19.05 x 2.82 m	42 tons	–/82
TSO	18.90 x 2.82 m	26 tons	–/102

S 14351 S	DMBSO	(ex-unit 5176)	Northamptonshire Ironstone Railway	Eastleigh 1955
S 14352 S	DMBSO	(ex-unit 5176)	Hope Farm, Sellindge	Eastleigh 1955
S 15354 S	TSO	(ex-unit 5176)	Hope Farm, Sellindge	Eastleigh 1955

2 EPB (later Class 416/1) — SUBURBAN UNITS

Built: 1959. Non-gangwayed.
Original Formation: DMBSO–DTSO.
System: 630 V DC third rail.
Traction Motors: Two EE of 185 kW (250 hp).   **Maximum Speed**: 75 mph.

DMBSO	19.05 x 2.82 m	40 tons	–/82
DTSO	18.90 x 2.82 m	30 tons	–/92

S 14573 S	DMBSO	(ex-unit 5667–6307)	Hope Farm, Sellindge	Eastleigh 1959
S 16117 S	DTSO	(ex-unit 5667–6307)	Hope Farm, Sellindge	Eastleigh 1959

5.7. PULLMAN CAR COMPANY ELECTRIC MULTIPLE UNITS

In this section, classes and vehicles within classes are listed in Pullman Car Company schedule number order.

For details of Type Codes see Appendix IV.

GENERAL

Pullman cars owned by the Pullman Car Company operated as parts of EMU formations on the Southern Railway (later BR Southern Region). In addition, the three Brighton Belle EMU sets were composed entirely of Pullman vehicles.

All vehicles are used as hauled stock except * – static exhibits.

6 Pul

Built: 1932. 6-car sets incorporating one Pullman kitchen composite. Gangwayed within set.
Original Formation: DMBSO–TSK–TCK–TPCK–TCK–DMBSO.

TPCK   20.40 x 2.77 m   43 tons   12/16 2T

RUTH	S 264 S	TPCK	(ex-unit 2017–3042)	Stewarts Lane Depot, London	MC 1932
BERTHA	S 278 S	TPCK	(ex-unit 2012–3001)	West Coast Railway Company, Carnforth	MC 1932

5 BEL   BRIGHTON BELLE UNITS

Built: 1932. 5-car all Pullman sets. Gangwayed within set.
Original Formation: DMPBSOL–TPSOL–TPFKOL–TPFKOL–DMPBSOL.
System: 630 V DC third rail.
Traction Motors: Four BTH of 167 kW (225 hp).

TPFKOL	20.40 x 2.77 m	42 tons	20/–
TPSOL	20.40 x 2.77 m	41 tons	–/56
DMPBSOL	20.62 x 2.77 m	62 tons	–/48

HAZEL	S279S	TPFKOL	(ex-unit 2051–3051) Peak Rail	MC 1932
AUDREY	S280S	TPFKOL	(ex-unit 2052–3052) Stewarts Lane Depot, London	MC 1932
GWEN	S281S	TPFKOL	(ex-unit 2053–3053) Stewarts Lane Depot, London	MC 1932
DORIS	S282S	TPFKOL	(ex-unit 2051–3051) LNWR Heritage, Crewe	MC 1932
MONA	S283S	TPFKOL	(ex-unit 2053–3053) Stewarts Lane Depot, London	MC 1932
VERA	S284S	TPFKOL	(ex-unit 2052–3052) Stewarts Lane Depot, London	MC 1932
CAR No. 85	S285S	TPSOL	(ex-unit 2053–3053) LNWR Heritage, Crewe	MC 1932
CAR No. 86	S286S	TPSOL	(ex-unit 2051–3051) Stewarts Lane Depot, London	MC 1932
CAR No. 87	S287S	TPSOL	(ex-unit 2052–3052) Peak Rail	MC 1932
CAR No. 88	S288S	DMPBSOL	(ex-unit 2051–3051) LNWR Heritage, Crewe	MC 1932
CAR No. 89*	S289S	DMPBSOL	(ex-unit 2051–3051) Carriages of Cambridge	MC 1932
CAR No. 91	S291S	DMPBSOL	(ex-unit 2052–3052) LNWR Heritage, Crewe	MC 1932
CAR No. 92	S292S	DMPBSOL	(ex-unit 2053–3053) Stewarts Lane Depot, London	MC 1932
CAR No. 93	S293S	DMPBSOL	(ex-unit 2053–3053) Stewarts Lane Depot, London	MC 1932

The following vehicles are part of the Brighton Belle project: Nos. S279S, S282S, S285S, S287S, S288S, S291S. These are being comprehensively rebuilt using the frames, bogies and traction equipment from 400 Series Electric Multiple Units to return them to use as an EMU.

CAR No. 85 is now named "GRAVETYE MANOR", Car No. 88 is now named "BERYL" and Car No. 91 is now named "MABEL".

5.8. LMS & CONSTITUENT COMPANIES' ELECTRIC MULTIPLE UNITS

In this section, classes and vehicles within classes are listed in LMS number order.

For details of Type Codes see Appendix IV.

LNWR — EUSTON–WATFORD STOCK

Built: 1915. Oerlikon design. Non-gangwayed.
Original Formation: DMBSO–TSO–DTSO.
System: 630 V DC third rail. Used on Euston–Watford line.
Traction Motors: Four Oerlikon 179 kW (240 hp).
Maximum Speed:

DMBSO	17.60 x 2.73 m		54.75 tonnes	–/48	

BR	LMS	LNWR			
M 28249 M	5751–28249	31 E	DMBSO	National Railway Museum, York (N)	MC 1915

CLASS 502 — LIVERPOOL–SOUTHPORT STOCK

Built: 1939. Non-gangwayed.
Original Formation: DMBSO–TSO–DTSO (originally DTCO).
System: 630 V DC third rail.
Traction Motors: Four EE 175 kW. **Maximum Speed:** 65 mph.

DMBSO	21.18 x 2.90 m	42.5 tonnes	–/88
DTSO	21.18 x 2.90 m	25.5 tonnes	–/79 (built as DTCO 53/25)

BR	LMS			
M 28361 M	28361	DMBSO	Merseyside Transport Trust, Burscough	Derby 1939
M 29896 M	29896	DTSO	Merseyside Transport Trust, Burscough	Derby 1939

▲ LNWR DMBSO 28249 stands on display in the Great Hall of the National Railway Museum, York on 29 January 2024. **Robert Pritchard**

CLASS 503 — MERSEY WIRRAL STOCK

Built: 1938. Non-gangwayed.
Original Formation: DMBSO–TSO (originally TCO)–DTSO.
System: 630 V DC third rail.
Traction Motors: 4 BTH 100 kW. **Maximum Speed:** 65 mph.

DMBSO	18.48 x 2.77 m	36.5 tonnes	–/56
TSO	17.77 x 2.77 m	20.5 tonnes	–/58 (built as TCO 40/19)

BR	LMS			
M 28690 M	28690	DMBSO	Cambrian Heritage Railways, Llynclys	MC 1938

MSJ&A STOCK

Built: 1931. Non-gangwayed.
Original Formation: DMBS–TC–DTS.
System: 1500 V DC overhead. Used on Manchester South Junction and Altrincham line until it was converted to 25 kV AC. This line is now part of the Manchester Metrolink system.
Traction Motors: **Maximum Speed:** 65 mph.

TC	17.60 x 2.85 m	31 tonnes.	24/72	

BR	LMS	MSJ&A			
M 29666 M	29666	117	TC	Midland Railway-Butterley	MC 1931
M 29670 M	29670	121	TC	Midland Railway-Butterley	MC 1931

5.9. LNER & CONSTITUENT COMPANIES' ELECTRIC MULTIPLE UNITS

In this section, classes and vehicles within classes are listed in LNER number order. For details of Type Codes see Appendix IV.

NORTH EASTERN RAILWAY — DMLV

Built: 1904. Driving motor luggage van for North Tyneside line. After withdrawal from capital stock, this vehicle was used as a rail de-icing car.
System: 675 V DC third rail.
Traction Motors: **Maximum Speed:**

DMLV	17.40 x 2.77 m	46.5 tonnes	

BR	LNER	NER			
DE 900730	23267	3267	DMLV	Stephenson Steam Railway (N)	MC 1904

CLASS 306 — LIVERPOOL STREET–SHENFIELD STOCK

Built: 1949. Non-gangwayed.
Original Formation: DMSO–TBSO–DTSO.
System: 25 kV AC overhead (originally 1500 V DC overhead).
Traction Motors: Four Crompton Parkinson of 155 kW.
Maximum Speed: 65 mph.

DMSO	18.41 x 2.90 m	51.7 tonnes	–/62
TBSO	16.78 x 2.90 m	26.4 tonnes	–/46
DTSO	16.87 x 2.90 m	27.9 tonnes	–/60

E 65217 E	DMSO	(ex-unit 306 017)	National Railway Museum, Shildon (N)	MC 1949
E 65417 E	TBSO	(ex-unit 306 017)	National Railway Museum, Shildon (N)	MC 1949
E 65617 E	DTSO	(ex-unit 306 017)	National Railway Museum, Shildon (N)	BRCW 1949

5.10. BRITISH RAILWAYS & POST PRIVATISATION ELECTRIC MULTIPLE UNITS

NUMBERING SYSTEM

BR EMU power cars were usually numbered in the 6xxxx series, beginning with 61000, whilst trailer cars were numbered in the 7xxxx series. Exceptions to this rule are the APT-P and battery EMU vehicles.

In this section, classes are listed in three-digit class number order. Multiple unit vehicles are listed in original five-digit number order within each class. Unclassified battery EMUs are listed at the end of the section.

For details of type codes see Appendix IV.

CLASS 302   BR

Built: 1958–60 for London Fenchurch Street–Shoeburyness services.
System: 25 kV AC overhead.
Original Formation: BDTSOL–MBS–TCsoL–DTS. Non-gangwayed.
Formation as Rebuilt: BDTCOL–MBSO–TSOL–DTSO. Gangwayed within set.
Traction Motors: Four English Electric EE 536A of 143.5 kW.
Maximum Speed: 75 mph.

DTSO   20.36 x 2.83 m   33.4 tonnes   –/88

| 75033 | DTSO | (ex-unit 302 201) | Mangapps Railway Museum | York 1958 |
| 75250 | DTSO | (ex-unit 302 277) | Mangapps Railway Museum | York 1959 |

CLASS 303   PRESSED STEEL

Built: 1959–61 for Glasgow area services. Gangwayed within set (originally non-gangwayed).
System: 25 kV AC overhead.
Original Formation: DTSO–MBSO–BDTSO.
Traction Motors: Four MV of 155 kW.
Maximum Speed: 75 mph.

DTSO	20.18 x 2.83 m	34.4 tonnes	–/56 (originally –/83)
MBSO	20.18 x 2.83 m	56.4 tonnes	–/48 (originally –/70)
BDTSO	20.18 x 2.83 m	38.4 tonnes	–/56 (originally –/83)

61503	MBSO	(ex-unit 303 023)	Bo'ness & Kinneil Railway	PS 1960
75597	DTSO	(ex-unit 303 032)	Bo'ness & Kinneil Railway	PS 1960
75613	BDTSO	(ex-unit 303 013)	Metropolitan Police Specialist Training Centre, Gravesend	PS 1960
75632	BDTSO	(ex-unit 303 032)	Bo'ness & Kinneil Railway	PS 1960

CLASS 307   BR

Built: 1954–56 for London Liverpool Street–Southend Victoria services.
System: 1500 V DC overhead. Converted 1960–61 to 25 kV AC overhead.
Original Formation: BDTBS–MS–TCsoL–DTSOL. Non-gangwayed.
Formation as Rebuilt: BDTBSO–MSO–TSOL–DTCOL. Gangwayed within set.
Traction Motors: Four GEC WT344 of 130 kW.
Maximum Speed: 75 mph.

| BDTBSO | 20.18 x 2.83 m | 43 tonnes | –/66 |
| DTCOL | 20.18 x 2.83 m | 33 tonnes | 24/48 1T |

| 75023 | BDTBSO | (ex-unit 307 123) | Colne Valley Railway | Eastleigh 1956 |
| 75102–95301 | DTCOL | (ex-unit 307 102) | Reid Freight Services, Cockshute Sidings, Stoke-on-Trent | Eastleigh 1956 |

75110–94323	DTCOL	(ex-unit 307 110)	Embsay & Bolton Abbey Railway		Eastleigh 1956
75112–94306	DTCOL	(ex-unit 307 112)	Embsay & Bolton Abbey Railway		Eastleigh 1956
75120–94320	DTCOL	(ex-unit 307 120)	Mid Norfolk Railway		Eastleigh 1956
75123–94326	DTCOL	(ex-unit 307 123)	Embsay & Bolton Abbey Railway		Eastleigh 1956
75124–94302	DTCOL	(ex-unit 307 124)	Embsay & Bolton Abbey Railway		Eastleigh 1956

75102 also carried the number 94301.

75102, 75110, 75112, 75120, 75123 and 75124 were rebuilt as propelling control vehicles.

CLASS 308   BR

Built: 1961 for London Liverpool Street–Clacton stopping services.
System: 25 kV AC overhead.
Original Formation: BDTCOL–MBS–TCSoL–DTS. Non-gangwayed.
Formation as Rebuilt: BDTCOL–MBSO–TSOL–DTSO. Gangwayed within set.
Traction Motors: Four English Electric EE 536A of 143.5 kW.
Maximum Speed: 75 mph.

BDTCOL	20.18 x 2.82 m	36.3 tonnes	24/52 1T

75881	BDTCOL	(ex-unit 308 136)	Colne Valley Railway	York 1961

CLASS 309   BR

Built: 1962–63 for London Liverpool Street–Clacton express services. Gangwayed throughout.
System: 25 kV AC overhead.
Original Formation: BDTCsoL–MBSK–TSOL or TRUB–DTCOL or DTCsoL.
Formation as Rebuilt: BDTCsoL–MBSOL–TSOL–DTSOL.
Traction Motors: Four GEC WT401 of 210 kW.
Maximum Speed: 100 mph.

MBSOL	20.18 x 2.82 m	57.7 tonnes	–/52 2T
BDTCsoL	20.18 x 2.82 m	40.0 tonnes	18/32 2T
DTSOL	20.18 x 2.82 m	36.6 tonnes	–/56 2T

61928–977966	MBSOL	(ex-unit 309 624)	Lavender Line	York 1962
61937–977963	MBSOL	(ex-unit 309 616)	Tanat Valley Light Railway	York 1962
75642–977962	BDTCsoL	(ex-unit 309 616)	Tanat Valley Light Railway	York 1962
75965–977965	BDTCsoL	(ex-unit 309 624)	Lavender Line	York 1962
75972–977967	DTSOL	(ex-unit 309 624)	Lavender Line	York 1962
75981–977964	DTSOL	(ex-unit 309 616)	Tanat Valley Light Railway	York 1963

Unit 309 616 also carries the unit number 960 101.
Unit 309 624 also carries the unit number 960 102.

61928 is named NEW DALBY.

CLASS 311   CRAVENS

Built: 1967 for Glasgow "South Side electrification" extension to Gourock and Wemyss Bay. Non-gangwayed.
System: 25 kV AC overhead.
Original Formation: DTSO(A)–MBSO–DTSO(B).
Traction Motors: Four AEI of 165 kW.   **Maximum Speed**: 75 mph.

MBSO	20.18 x 2.83 m	56.4 tonnes	–/70
DTSO(B)	20.18 x 2.83 m	38.4 tonnes	–/83

62174–977845	MBSO	(ex-unit 311 103)	Summerlee Museum of Scottish Industrial Life	Cravens 1967
76433–977844	DTSO(B)	(ex-unit 311 103)	Summerlee Museum of Scottish Industrial Life	Cravens 1967

CLASS 312　　　　　　　　　　　　　　　　　　　　　　　　　　　　　BREL

Built: 1975–78 using Mark 2 bodyshell for outer-suburban services from London King's Cross and London Liverpool Street and in the West Midlands area. Gangwayed within set.
System: 25 kV AC overhead.
Original Formation: BDTSOL–MBSO–TSO–DTCOL.
Traction Motors: Four English Electric 546 of 201.5 kW.
Maximum Speed: 90 mph.

TSO	20.18 x 2.82 m	30.5 tonnes	–/98
DTCOL	20.18 x 2.82 m	33.0 tonnes	25/47 1T

71205	TSO	(ex-units 312 112–312 792)	Colne Valley Railway	York 1976
78037	DTCOL	(ex-units 312 112–312 792)	Colne Valley Railway	York 1976

CLASS 313/1　　　　　　　　　　　　　　　　　　　　　　　　　　　BREL

Built: 1976–77 for use on Moorgate–Welwyn/Hertford services. Gangwayed within set.
System: 25 kV AC overhead/750 V DC third rail.
Original Formation: DMS–PTS–BDMS.
Traction Motors: Four GEC G310AZ of 82.125 kW.
Maximum Speed: 75 mph.

DMS	20.33 x 2.82 m	36.0 tonnes	–/74
PTS	20.18 x 2.82 m	37.5 tonnes	–/74
BDMS	20.33 x 2.82 m	31.0 tonnes	–/83

62549	DMS	(ex-unit 313 021–313 121)	Fife Heritage Railway	York 1976
62613	BDMS	(ex-unit 313 021–313 121)	Fife Heritage Railway	York 1976
71233	PTS	(ex-unit 313 021–313 121)	Fife Heritage Railway	York 1976

Class 313/2. Details as Class 313/1 except 750 V DC only. Formation: DMS–TS–BDMS.

DMS	20.33 x 2.82 m	37.0 tonnes	–/64
TS	20.18 x 2.82 m	31.0 tonnes	–/64
BDMS	20.33 x 2.82 m	37.0 tonnes	–/64

62529	DMS	(ex-unit 313 001–313 201)	Arlington Fleet Services, Eastleigh Works	York 1976
62593	BDMS	(ex-unit 313 001–313 201)	Arlington Fleet Services, Eastleigh Works	York 1976
71213	TS	(ex-unit 313 001–313 201)	Arlington Fleet Services, Eastleigh Works	York 1976

CLASS 315　　　　　　　　　　　　　　　　　　　　　　　　　　　　BREL

Built: 1980–81 for use on London Liverpool Street–Shenfield services. Gangwayed within set.
System: 25 kV AC overhead.
Original Formation: DMS–TS–PTS–DMS.
Traction Motors: Four GEC G310AZ of 82.125 kW.
Maximum Speed: 75 mph.

DMS	20.18 x 2.82 m	38.2 tonnes	–/74
TS	20.18 x 2.82 m	27.4 tonnes	–/86
PTS	20.18 x 2.82 m	33.8 tonnes	–/75

64571	DMS	(ex-unit 315 856)	Llanelli & Mynydd Mawr Railway	York 1981
64572	DMS	(ex-unit 315 856)	Llanelli & Mynydd Mawr Railway	York 1981
71336	TS	(ex-unit 315 856)	Llanelli & Mynydd Mawr Railway	York 1981
71444	PTS	(ex-unit 315 856)	Llanelli & Mynydd Mawr Railway	York 1981

CLASS 317 — BREL

Built: 1981–87 using Mark 3 bodyshell for outer suburban services from London St Pancras and London King's Cross. Gangwayed throughout.
System: 25 kV AC overhead.
Traction Motors: Four GEC G315BZ of 247.5 kW.
Maximum Speed: 100 mph.

Class 317/1. Formation: DTS(A)–MS–TC–DTS(B).

TC	19.92 x 2.82 m	29.0 tonnes	22/46 2T	
DTS(B)	19.83 x 2.82 m	29.5 tonnes	–/71	
71621	TC	(ex-unit 317 345)	Oracle UK, Reading	Derby 1982
77092	DTS(B)	(ex-unit 317 345)	East Anglian Railway Museum	York 1982

CLASS 321 — BREL

Built: 1988–91 using Mark 3 bodyshell for outer-suburban services from London Liverpool Street and London Euston, and in West Yorkshire. Gangwayed within set.
System: 25 kV AC overhead.
Original Formation: DTC–MS–TS–DTS.
Traction Motors: Four Brush TM2141C of 268 KW.
Maximum Speed: 100 mph.

DTC	20.43 x 2.82 m	29.8 tonnes	16/52	
MS	20.18 x 2.82 m	51.6 tonnes	–/79	
TS	20.18 x 2.82 m	29.2 tonnes	–/74 2T	
DTS	20.43 x 2.82 m	29.8 tonnes	–/78	
63128	MS	(ex-unit 321 434)	Eastern Rail Services, Great Yarmouth	York 1989
72014	TS	(ex-unit 321 434)	Eastern Rail Services, Great Yarmouth	York 1989
78154	DTC	(ex-unit 321 434)	Eastern Rail Services, Great Yarmouth	York 1989
78303	DTS	(ex-unit 321 434)	Eastern Rail Services, Great Yarmouth	York 1989

CLASS 332 — HEATHROW EXPRESS — CAF/SIEMENS

Built: 1997–98 for use on express services between London Paddington and Heathrow Airport. Gangwayed within set.
System: 25 kV AC overhead.
Original Formation: DMF–TS–PTS–DMS.
Traction Motors: Two Siemens monomotors asynchronous of 350 KW.
Maximum Speed: 100 mph.

TS	23.35 x 2.75 m	38.4 tonnes	–/64	
PTS	23.35 x 2.75 m	47.6 tonnes	–/39 1T	
DMS	23.63 x 2.75 m	49.9 tonnes	–/43	
63400	PTS	(ex-unit 332 001)	Siemens Mobility, Goole	CAF 1997
72412	TS	(ex-unit 332 001)	Siemens Mobility, Goole	CAF 1998
78400	DMS	(ex-unit 332 001)	Siemens Mobility, Goole	CAF 1997

CLASS 365   NETWORKER EXPRESS   ABB YORK

Built: 1994–95 for Great Northern and South Eastern outer suburban and express services. Gangwayed within set.
System: 25 kV AC overhead but with 750 V DC third rail capability.
Original Formation: DMC(A)–TS–PTS–DMC(B).
Traction Motors: Four GEC-Alsthom G354CX asynchronous of 157 kW.
Maximum Speed: 100 mph.

DMC(A)	20.89 x 2.81 m	41.7 tonnes	12/56
TS	20.06 x 2.81 m	32.9 tonnes	–/58 1T
DMC(B)	20.89 x 2.81 m	41.7 tonnes	12/56

65917	DMC(A)	(ex-unit 365 524)	East Kent Railway	York 1995
65974	DMC(B)	(ex-unit 365 540)	East Kent Railway	York 1994
72287	TS	(ex-unit 365 524)	East Kent Railway	York 1995

CLASS 370 PROTOTYPE ADVANCED PASSENGER TRAIN (APT-P)

Built: 1978–80. Designed to run as pairs of 6-car articulated units with two power cars in the middle, these electric trains featured active hydraulic tilt and proved to be a maintenance nightmare. The power cars were reasonably successful and are partly the basis of the Class 91 electric locomotive.
System: 25 kV AC overhead.
Normal Formation of Trailer rake: DTSOL–TSOL–TSRBL–TUOL–TFOL–TBFOL.
Formation of Preserved Set: DTSOL–TBFOL–M–TRSBL–TBFOL–DTSOL.
Traction Motors: Four ASEA LJMA 410F body mounted.
Wheel Diameter: 853 mm.   **Maximum Speed:** 125 mph.

DTSOL	21.44 x 2.72 m	33.7 tonnes	–/52 1T
TBFOL	21.20 x 2.72 m	31.9 tonnes	25/– 1T
TRSBL	21.20 x 2.72 m	26.75 tonnes	–/28 1T
M	20.40 x 2.72 m	67.5 tonnes	–

48103	DTSOL	Crewe Heritage Centre	Derby 1978
48106	DTSOL	Crewe Heritage Centre	Derby 1979
48404	TRSBL	Crewe Heritage Centre	Derby 1979
48602	TBFOL	Crewe Heritage Centre	Derby 1978
48603	TBFOL	Crewe Heritage Centre	Derby 1978
49002	M	Crewe Heritage Centre	Derby 1979
49006	M	Crewe Heritage Centre	Derby 1980

CLASS 390   PENDOLINO   ALSTOM

Built: 2001–5 for use on express services over the newly upgraded West Coast Main Line from London Euston to the West Midlands, North-West of England and Glasgow. Through the use of active tilt and a design speed of 140 mph, these trains were intended to significantly reduce journey times, but not all of the infrastructure upgrades that were needed to support this were delivered, so they were unable to operate at any more than 125 mph. 390 001–034 entered service as 8-car sets (without the 688xx TS). They were lengthened to 9-cars during 2004–05. An extra 62 vehicles were built in 2010–12 to lengthen 31 sets to 11-cars. Gangwayed within set.
System: 25 kV AC overhead.
Original Formation: DMRFO–MFO–PTFO–MFO–TSO–MSO–PTSRMB–MSO–DMSO.
Traction Motors: Two Alstom ONIX 800 of 425 KW.
Maximum Speed: 125 mph.

DMRFO	24.80 x 2.73 m	55.6 tonnes	18/–
PTSRMB	23.90 x 2.75 m	52.0 tonnes	–/48
MSO	23.90 x 2.75 m	51.7 tonnes	–/64 1T

69133	DMRFO	(ex-unit 390 033)	Avanti West Coast Talent Academy, Crewe	Alstom 2003
69833	PTSRMB	(ex-unit 390 033)	Avanti West Coast Talent Academy, Crewe	Alstom 2003
69933	MSO	(ex-unit 390 033)	Cranfield Safety & Accident Investigation Centre	Alstom 2003

▲ Class 365 DMC(A) 65917 and TS 72287 (ex-unit 365524) and DMC(B) 65974 (ex-unit 365540) are seen on static display at Eythorne on the East Kent Railway on 8 April 2023. **Robert Pritchard**

▼ Making a rare trip out from Southall depot, Class 416/2 2EPB DMBSO 65373 and DTSso 77558 (unit 5759) stand at Alresford during a visit to the Mid Hants Railway on 15 July 2022. **Ian Beardsley**

CLASSES 410 & 411 (4 Bep & 4 Cep) — BR

Built: 1956–63 for Kent Coast electrification. Rebuilt 1979–84. Class 410 (4Bep) was later reclassified Class 412. Gangwayed throughout.
System: 750 V DC third rail.
Original Formation: DMBSO–TCK–TSK (4Cep) TRSB (4Bep)–DMBSO.
Formation as Rebuilt: DMSO–TBCK–TSOL (4Cep) TRSB (4Bep)–DMSO.
Traction Motors: Two English Electric EE507 of 185 kW.
Maximum Speed: 90 mph.

DMSO	20.34 x 2.82 m	49.0 tonnes	–/56
TSOL	20.18 x 2.82 m	36.0 tonnes	–/64 2T
TBCK	20.18 x 2.82 m	34.0 tonnes	24/8 2T
TRSB	20.18 x 2.82 m	35.5 tonnes	–/24

61229	DMSO	(ex-unit 7105–1537–2325)	Southall Depot, London	Eastleigh 1958
61230	DMSO	(ex-unit 7105–1537–2325)	Southall Depot, London	Eastleigh 1958
61736	DMSO	(ex-7175–2304–2314–1198)	Chinnor & Princes Risborough Railway	Eastleigh 1960
61737	DMSO	(ex-7175–2304–2314–1198)	Chinnor & Princes Risborough Railway	Eastleigh 1960
61798	DMSO	(ex-unit 7016–2305–2315)	Eden Valley Railway	Eastleigh 1961
61799	DMSO	(ex-unit 7016–2305–2315)	Eden Valley Railway	Eastleigh 1961
61804	DMSO	(ex-unit 7019–2301–2311)	Eden Valley Railway	Eastleigh 1961
61805	DMSO	(ex-unit 7019–2301–2311)	Eden Valley Railway	Eastleigh 1961
69013	TRSB	(ex-units 7014, 2305 & 2325)	Chinnor & Princes Risborough Railway	Eastleigh 1961
70229	TSOL	(ex-units 7105–1537 & 2315)	Eden Valley Railway	Eastleigh 1958
70235	TBCK	(ex-units 7105–1537–2325)	West Coast Railway Company, Carnforth	Eastleigh 1958
70262	TSOL	(ex-unit 7113–1524)	St Leonards Railway Engineering	Eastleigh 1958
70273	TSOL	(ex-units 7124–1530 & 1392)	East Kent Railway	Eastleigh 1958
70284	TSOL	(ex-unit 7135–1520)	Northamptonshire Ironstone Railway	Eastleigh 1959
70292	TSOL	(ex-units 7143–1554 & 1398)	Grantown-on-Spey East Station	Eastleigh 1959
70296	TSOL	(ex-unit 7147–1559)	Northamptonshire Ironstone Railway	Eastleigh 1959
70345	TBCK	(ex-units 7153–1500 & 1547)	Hydraulic House, Sutton Bridge	Eastleigh 1959
70354	TBCK	(ex-units 7011 & 2305–2315)	Eden Valley Railway	Eastleigh 1959
70510	TSOL	(ex-unit 7161–1597)	Northamptonshire Ironstone Railway	Eastleigh 1960
70527	TSOL	(ex-units 7178–1589 & 1393)	Whitwell & Reepham Station, Norfolk	Eastleigh 1960
70531	TSOL	(ex-units 7152–1610 & 1396)	Grantown-on-Spey East Station	Eastleigh 1961
70539	TSOL	(ex-units 7190–1568 & 2311)	Eden Valley Railway	Eastleigh 1961
70547	TSOL	(ex-unit 7198–1569)	Source Farm Shop, near Hungerford	Eastleigh 1961
70549	TSOL	(ex-unit 7200–1567)	East Lancashire Railway	Eastleigh 1961
70573	TBCK	(ex-7175–2304–2314–1198)	Chinnor & Princes Risborough Railway	Eastleigh 1960
70576	TBCK	(ex-unit 7178–1589)	Great Central Railway	Eastleigh 1960
70607	TBCK	(ex-unit 7019–2301–2311)	Eden Valley Railway	Eastleigh 1961

69013 also carried the number 69345 after rebuild as a TRSB.
70262 is currently formed in HASTINGS DEMU 1001 (see page 144).
70547 was latterly formed in DEMU 207 203 and 70549 was latterly formed in DEMU 207 202.

61229 is being rebuilt as a DMBSO.

CLASS 414 (2 Hap) — BR

Built: 1959 for the South Eastern Division of the former BR Southern Region. Non-gangwayed.
System: 750 V DC third rail.
Original Formation: DMBSO–DTCsoL.
Traction Motors: Two English Electric EE507 of 185 kW.
Maximum Speed: 90 mph.

DMBSO	20.44 x 2.82 m	42 tonnes	–/84
DTCsoL	20.44 x 2.82 m	32.5 tonnes	19/60 1T

61275	DMBSO	(ex-unit 6077–4308)	National Railway Museum, Shildon (N)	Eastleigh 1959
61287	DMBSO	(ex-unit 6089–4311)	Elliot Group, Port Elphinstone, Inverurie	Eastleigh 1959
75395	DTCsoL	(ex-unit 6077–4308)	National Railway Museum, Shildon (N)	Eastleigh 1959
75407	DTCsoL	(ex-unit 6089–4311)	Elliot Group, Port Elphinstone, Inverurie	Eastleigh 1959

CLASS 416/2 (2 EPB) BR

Built: 1954–56. 65373 & 77558 were built for the South Eastern Division of what was BR's Southern Region. 65321 and 77112 were former North Eastern Region vehicles originally used between Newcastle and South Shields but were transferred to join the rest of the class on the Southern Region when the South Tyneside line was de-electrified in 1963. Non-gangwayed.
System: 750 V DC third rail.
Original Formation: DMBSO–DTSso.
Traction Motors: Two English Electric EE507 of 185 kW.
Maximum Speed: 75 mph.

DMBSO	20.44 x 2.82 m	42.0 tonnes	–/82
DTSso	20.44 x 2.82 m	30.5 tonnes	–/102

65302–977874	DMBSO	(ex-units 5703–6203 & 930 204)	Nemesis Rail, Burton-on-Trent	Eastleigh 1954
65304–977875	DMBSO	(ex-units 5705–6205 & 930 204)	Nemesis Rail, Burton-on-Trent	Eastleigh 1954
65321–977505	DMBSO	(ex-unit 5791–6291–930 053)	Battlefield Line	Eastleigh 1955
65373	DMBSO	(ex-unit 5759–6259)	Southall Depot, London	Eastleigh 1956
65379–977925	DMBSO	(ex-units 5765–6265 & 930 206)	Reid Freight Services, Cockshute Sidings, Stoke-on-Trent	Eastleigh 1956
65382–977924	DMBSO	(ex-units 5768–6268 & 930 206)	Reid Freight Services, Cockshute Sidings, Stoke-on-Trent	Eastleigh 1956
77112–977508	DTSso	(ex-units 5793–6293 & 930 054)	Battlefield Line	Eastleigh 1955
77558	DTSso	(ex-unit 5759–6259)	Southall Depot, London	Eastleigh 1956

65373 and 77558 are currently under overhaul at Nemesis Rail, Burton-on-Trent.

CLASS 419 (MLV) BR

Built: 1959–61. Motor luggage vans for Kent Coast electrification. Fitted with traction batteries to allow operation on non-electrified lines. Non-gangwayed single cars with two driving cabs.
System: 750 V DC third rail.
Traction Motors: Two English Electric EE507 of 185 kW.
Maximum Speed: 90 mph.

Also fitted with vacuum brakes for hauling parcels trains.

DMLV	20.45 x 2.82 m	45.5 tonnes	

68001	(ex-units 9001–931 091)	Southall Depot, London	Eastleigh 1959
68002	(ex-units 9002–931 092)	Southall Depot, London	Eastleigh 1959
68003	(ex-units 9003–931 093)	Eden Valley Railway	Eastleigh 1961
68004	(ex-units 9004–931 094)	Mid Norfolk Railway	Eastleigh 1961
68005	(ex-units 9005–931 095)	Eden Valley Railway	Eastleigh 1961
68008	(ex-units 9008–931 098)	Southall Depot, London	Eastleigh 1961
68009	(ex-units 9009–931 099)	Southall Depot, London	Eastleigh 1961
68010	(ex-units 9010–931 090)	Eden Valley Railway	Eastleigh 1961

CLASS 420 & 421 (4 Big & 4 Cig) BR

Built: 1963–72 for the Central Division of BR Southern Region. Class 420 (4 Big) was later reclassified Class 422. Gangwayed throughout.
System: 750 V DC third rail.
Original Formation: DTCsoL–MBSO–TSO (4 Cig), TRSB (4 Big)–DTCsoL.
Traction Motors: Four English Electric EE507 of 185 kW.
Maximum Speed: 90 mph.

MBSO	20.18 x 2.82 m	49 tonnes	–/56
TSO	20.18 x 2.82 m	31.5 tonnes	–/72
DTCsoL	20.23 x 2.82 m	35 tonnes	24/28 2T
TRSB	20.18 x 2.82 m	35 tonnes	–/40

62043	MBSO	(ex-unit 7327–1127–1753)	Nemesis Rail, Burton-on-Trent	York 1965
62364	MBSO	(ex-unit 7376–1276–2251–1394–1499)	Barrow Hill Roundhouse	York 1971
62385	MBSO	(ex-unit 7397–1297–2256–1399)	East Kent Railway	York 1971
62402	MBSO	(ex-units 7414–1214–1883–1497)	Spa Valley Railway	York 1971
62411	MBSO	(ex-units 7423–1223–1888–1498)	Quirky Nights Glamping Village, Ireland	York 1972

▲ During a visit to the Mid Hants Railway on 15 July 2022, Class 419 MLV DMLV 68002 (unit 9002) pauses in-between duties at Alresford. **Ian Beardsley**

▼ Latterly used in unit 2002, Class 422 4 Big TRSB 69306 stands at Tunbridge Wells West on the Spa Valley Railway on 16 July 2022. **Ian Beardsley**

69302	TRSB	(ex-units 7032–2101 & 2251)	Neath Abbey Industrial Estate	York 1963
69304	TRSB	(ex-units 7034–2110 & 2260)	Northamptonshire Ironstone Railway	York 1963
69306	TRSB	(ex-units 7036–2104 & 2254–2002)	Spa Valley Railway	York 1963
69316	TRSB	(ex-units 7046–2108 & 2258)	Waverley Route Heritage Association, Whitrope	York 1963
69318	TRSB	(ex-units 7048–2109 & 2259–2004)	Last Moorings, Stickney	York 1963
69332	TRSB	(ex-units 7051–2203 & 2257–1407)	Swanage Railway	York 1969
69333	TRSB	(ex 7055–2207, 2112 & 2262–2001)	Lavender Line	York 1969
69335	TRSB	(ex-unit 7057–2209–1409)	Eden Valley Railway	York 1969
69337	TRSB	(ex-unit 7058–2210–1411)	St Leonards Railway Engineering	York 1969
69338	TRSB	(ex-unit 7054–2206–1404)	Station Restaurant, Gulf Corporation, Bahrain	York 1969
69339	TRSB	(ex-unit 7053–2205–1405)	Nemesis Rail, Burton-on-Trent	York 1969
70721	TSO	(ex-units 7327–1127–1753)	Nemesis Rail, Burton-on-Trent	York 1965
71041	TSO	(ex-units 7373–1273–1819–1306)	Hever Station, Kent	York 1971
71085	TSO	(ex-units 7417–1217–1884)	The Old Ambulance Station, Bexhill	York 1970
76048	DTCsoL	(ex-units 7327–1127–1753)	Nemesis Rail, Burton-on-Trent	York 1965
76102	DTCsoL	(ex-units 7327–1127–1753)	Nemesis Rail, Burton-on-Trent	York 1965
76747	DTCsoL	(ex-units 7397–1297–2256–1399)	East Kent Railway	York 1971
76762	DTCsoL	(ex-units 7412–1212–1881)	Barrow Hill Roundhouse	York 1971
76764	DTCsoL	(ex-units 7414–1214–1883–1497)	Spa Valley Railway	York 1971
76773	DTCsoL	(ex-units 7423–1223–1888–1498)	Quirky Nights Glamping Village, Ireland	York 1972
76835	DTCsoL	(ex-units 7414–1214–1883–1497)	Spa Valley Railway	York 1971
76844	DTCsoL	(ex-units 7423–1223–1888–1498)	Quirky Nights Glamping Village, Ireland	York 1972

62043 is named "Chris Green", 62402 is named Freshwater and 62411 is named Farringford.

69337 is currently formed in HASTINGS DEMU 1001 (see page 144).

CLASS 423 (4 Vep/4 Vop) BR

Built: 1967–74 for BR Southern Region. Gangwayed throughout.
System: 750 V DC third rail.
Original Formation (4 Vep): DTCsoL–MBSO–TSO–DTCsoL.
Amended Formation (4 Vop): DTSsoL–MBSO–TSO–DTSsoL.
Traction Motors: Four English Electric EE507 of 185 kW.
Maximum Speed: 90 mph.

DTCsoL	20.18 x 2.82 m		35.0 tonnes	18/46 1T
DTSsoL	20.18 x 2.82 m		35.0 tonnes	–70 1T
TSO	20.18 x 2.82 m		31.5 tonnes	–/98
MBSO	20.18 x 2.82 m		48.0 tonnes	–/76

62236	MBSO	(ex-units 7775–3075 & 3417)	Strawberry Hill Depot, London	York 1969
62266	MBSO	(ex-units 7805–3105 & 3463–3905)	Peak Rail	York 1969
62321	MBSO	(ex-units 7820–3120 & 3532–3918)	Barrow Hill Roundhouse	York 1970
70797	TSO	(ex-unit 7717–3017–3417)	Strawberry Hill Depot, London	Derby 1967
70904	TSO	(ex-unit 7753–3053–3463–3905)	East Kent Railway	York 1968
76262	DTCsoL	(ex-unit 7717–3017–3417)	Strawberry Hill Depot, London	York 1967
76263	DTCsoL	(ex-unit 7717–3017–3417)	Strawberry Hill Depot, London	York 1967
76397	DTSsoL	(ex-unit 7753–3053–3463–3905)	East Kent Railway	York 1968
76398	DTSsoL	(ex-unit 7753–3053–3463–3905)	East Kent Railway	York 1968
76527	DTSsoL	(ex 7799–7912–3099–3532–3918)	Allelys, Studley	York 1969
76528	DTSsoL	(ex 7799–7912–3099–3532–3918)	Allelys, Studley	York 1969
76875	DTCsoL	(ex-units 7861–3161–3545)	East Kent Railway	York 1973
76887	DTCsoL	(ex-units 7867–3167–3568)	Mizens Railway	York 1973

CLASS 442 (5 Wes)   WESSEX ELECTRICS   BREL DERBY

Built: 1988–89 using Mark 3 bodyshell for London Waterloo–Bournemouth–Weymouth services.
System: 750 V DC third rail.
Original Formation: DTFsoL–TSOL(A)–MBRSM–TSOL(B)–DTSOL.
Formation as Rebuilt: DTSO–TSO–MBC–TSO(W)–DTSO(B).
Traction Motors: Four EE546 of 300 kW recovered from Class 432 (4 Rep).
Maximum Speed: 100 mph.

DTSO(A)		23.15 x 2.74 m	38.5 tonnes	–/74 (built as DTFsoL 50/– 1T)
77382	DTSO(A)	(ex-unit 442401)	Arlington Fleet Services, Eastleigh Works	Derby 1988

CLASS 457 — BREL

Built: 1981 by BREL Derby Works using Mark 3 bodyshell as a prototype DEMU designated Class 210. Rebuilt as an EMU in 1988–89 to assess the three-phase traction equipment that was planned to be used on the Networker EMUs. Gangwayed throughout.
System: 750 V DC third rail.
Original formation: DMBSO–TSO–TSOL–DTSO.
Formation as rebuilt: DMSO–TSO–TSO–DMSO.
Traction Motors:
Maximum Speed: 75 mph.

DMSO	20.52 x 2.82 m	38.6 tonnes	–/74	
54000–60300–67300	DMSO	East Kent Railway		Derby 1981

Formerly part of units 210 001, 7001 and 316 999.

CLASS 483 — METRO-CAMMELL

Built: 1938–40 for London Passenger Transport Board. Converted 1989–90 for the Isle of Wight line. Former London Underground numbers are shown first. Non gangwayed.
System: 660 V DC third rail.
Original Formation: DMSO(A)–DMSO(B).
Traction Motors: Two Crompton Parkinson/GEC/BTH LT100 of 125 kW (170 hp).
Maximum Speed: 45 mph.

DMSO(A)	15.93 x 2.69 m	27.4 tons	–/42
DMSO(B)	15.93 x 2.69 m	27.4 tons	–/42

10205–124	DMSO(A)	(ex-unit 483 004)	House of Chilli, Branstone, Isle of Wight	MC 1939
10221–122	DMSO(A)	(ex-unit 483 002)	RSS, Rye Farm, Wishaw	MC 1939
10229–129	DMSO(A)	(ex-unit 483 009)	Apple Mount Retreat, Thorpe Morieux	MC 1940
10255–128	DMSO(A)	(ex-unit 483 008)	Llanelli & Mynydd Mawr Railway	MC 1940
10291–127	DMSO(A)	(ex-unit 483 007)	Isle of Wight Steam Railway	MC 1940
10297–126	DMSO(A)	(ex-unit 483 006)	Llanelli & Mynydd Mawr Railway	MC 1940
11142–225	DMSO(B)	(ex-unit 483 002)	RSS, Rye Farm, Wishaw	MC 1939
11205–224	DMSO(B)	(ex-unit 483 004)	House of Chilli, Branstone, Isle of Wight	MC 1939
11229–229	DMSO(B)	(ex-unit 483 009)	Reid Freight Services, Cockshute Sidings, Stoke-on-Trent	MC 1940
11255–228	DMSO(B)	(ex-unit 483 008)	Llanelli & Mynydd Mawr Railway	MC 1940
11297–226	DMSO(B)	(ex-unit 483 006)	Llanelli & Mynydd Mawr Railway	MC 1940
11291–227	DMSO(B)	(ex-unit 483 007)	Isle of Wight Steam Railway	MC 1940

10229–129 currently carries the number 10289.

10221–122 and 11142–225 carried the name RAPTOR, 10205–124 and 11205–224 carried the name T. REX and 10297–126 and 11297–226 carried the name TERRY.
10291–127 carries the name Jess Harper.

11205–224 was also used in 483 003.
11142–225 was also used in 483 003, 483 005 and 483 001.

CLASS 485 (4 Vec & 5 Vec) — LONDON ELECTRIC RAILWAY

Built: 1923–35 for London Electric Railway/London Passenger Transport Board. Converted 1967 for the Isle of Wight line. Former London Underground numbers are shown first. Non gangwayed.
System: 660 V DC third rail.
Original formation: DMBSO–TSO–TSO–DMBSO.
Amended formation: DMBSO–DTSO–TSO–DTSO–DMBSO.
Traction Motors: Two GEC WT54 of 112 kW (150 hp).
Maximum Speed: 45 mph.

DTSO	15.70 x 2.60 m	19 tons	–/38
TSO	15.17 x 2.60 m	17 tons	–/42

LER	LPTB	BR			
1789–5279	5279	27 DTSO	(ex-unit 485 041)	London Transport Museum Depot, Acton	MC 1925
846–7296	7296	49 TSO	(ex-unit 485 044)	London Transport Museum Depot, Acton	CL 1923

▲ Class 423 4Vep DTCsoL 76887 (ex-unit 3568) stands on static display at the Mizens Railway on 10 July 2022. **Ian Beardsley**

▼ With 33111 at the rear, Class 491 4TC DTSO 76297 (ex-unit 8015) leads the Swanage Railway's 10.39 Corfe Castle–Swanage away from Harmans Cross on 12 May 2023. **Tom McAtee**

CLASS 489 (GLV) BR

Rebuilt: 1979–84 from Class 414 (2 Hap) as Motor Luggage Vans for the London Victoria–Gatwick Airport "Gatwick Express" service. Seats removed.
System: 750 V DC third rail.
Traction Motors: Two English Electric EE507 of 185 kW.
Maximum Speed: 90 mph.

DMLV   20.04 x 2.82 m   45 tonnes

61269–68500	DMLV (ex-units 6071–9101)	Ecclesbourne Valley Railway	Eastleigh 1959
61277–68503	DMLV (ex-units 6079–9104)	Spa Valley Railway	Eastleigh 1959
61280–68509	DMLV (ex-units 6082–9110)	East Kent Railway	Eastleigh 1959
61292–68506	DMLV (ex-units 6094–9107)	Ecclesbourne Valley Railway	Eastleigh 1959

CLASS 491 (4 TC) BR/METRO-CAMMELL

Built: 1967 (* 1974). Unpowered units designed to work push-pull with Class 430 (4 Rep) tractor units and Class 33/1, 73 and 74 locomotives. Converted from locomotive-hauled coaching stock built 1952–57 (original numbers in brackets). Gangwayed throughout.
Original Formation: DTSO–TFK–TBSK–DTSO.
Maximum Speed: 90 mph.

DTSO	20.18 x 2.82 m		32 tonnes	–/64
TFK	20.18 x 2.82 m		33.5 tonnes	42/– 2T
TBSK	20.18 x 2.82 m		35.5 tonnes	–/32 1T

70823 (34970)	TBSK	(ex-unit 412–8012)	London Underground, Ruislip Depot	MC 1957
70824 (34984)	TBSK	(ex-unit 413–8013)	Swanage Railway	MC 1957
70826 (34980)	TBSK	(ex-unit 415–8015)	Station Railway Heritage Centre, Sandford	MC 1957
70855 (13018)	TFK	(ex-unit 412–8012)	Swanage Railway	Swindon 1952
70859 (13040)	TFK	(ex-unit 416–8016)	The Old Station Guest House, Stravithie Station	Swindon 1952
70860 (13019)	TFK	(ex-unit 417–8017)	Longstowe Station, near Bourn	Swindon 1952
71163* (13097)	TFK	(ex-unit 430–8030)	London Underground, Ruislip Depot	Swindon 1954
76275 (3929)	DTSO	(ex-unit 404–8004)	Swanage Railway	Eastleigh 1955
76277 (4005)	DTSO	(ex-unit 405–8005)	Independent Rail Engineering, Chesterfield	Swindon 1957
76297 (3938)	DTSO	(ex-unit 415–8015)	London Underground, Ruislip Depot	Eastleigh 1955
76298 (4004)	DTSO	(ex-unit 415–8015)	Swanage Railway	Eastleigh 1957
76301 (4375)	DTSO	(ex-unit 417–8017)	Swanage Railway	Swindon 1957
76302 (4382)	DTSO	(ex-unit 417–8017)	Swanage Railway	Swindon 1957
76322 (3936)	DTSO	(ex-unit 427–8027)	Swanage Railway	Eastleigh 1955
76324 (4009)	DTSO	(ex-unit 428–8028)	London Underground, Ruislip Depot	Eastleigh 1957

70823 was also used in 4 TC unit 8015.
70824 was also used in 4 TCT unit 2806–8106, 3 Rep unit 1902, 5 TC unit 8110 and 6 Rep unit 1901.
70826 was also used in 4 TC unit 8017.
70855 was also used in 4 TC unit 8015.
70859 was also used in 3 Rep unit 1902, 5 TC unit 8110 and 4 TC unit 8010.
71163 was also used in 4 Rep unit 1901 and 6 Rep units 1906 and 1901.
76275 was also used in 5 TCB 2808, 6 Rep 1903 and 1904 and 4 Vep 3473 and 3169–3582 for a time.
76277 was also numbered DB 977335 for a time when in departmental service.
76302 was also used in 4 TC unit 401 for a time.
76322 was also used in 6 Rep units 1906 and 1901 for a time.
76324 was also used in 6 Rep units 1903 and 1901 for a time.
Unit 430–8030 was originally 3 TC 302. 71163 was added in 1974 when it was augmented to become 4 TC set 430.

CLASS 501 — BR

Built: 1957 for Euston–Watford and North London lines. Non-gangwayed.
Original Formation: DMBSO–TSO (originally TS)–DTBSO.
System: 630 V DC third rail.
Traction Motors: Four GEC of 135 kW.
Maximum Speed: 60 mph.

DMBSO	18.47 x 2.82 m		47.8 tonnes	–/74
DTBSO	18.47 x 2.82 m		30.5 tonnes	–/74

BR	AD				
61183–DB 977349			DMBSO	D Site, Graven Hill, Ambrosden, Bicester	Eastleigh 1957
75186	WGP 8809		DTBSO	D Site, Graven Hill, Ambrosden, Bicester	Eastleigh 1957

CLASS 504 — BR

Built: 1959 for Manchester–Bury line. Non-gangwayed.
Original Formation: DMBSO–DTSO.
System: 1200 V DC protected side-contact third rail.
Maximum Speed: 65 mph.
Traction Motors: Four English Electric EE of 90 kW.

DMBSO	20.31 x 2.82 m		50 tonnes	–/84
DTSO	20.31 x 2.82 m		33 tonnes	–/94

65451		DMBSO	East Lancashire Railway	Wolverton 1959
77172		DTSO	East Lancashire Railway	Wolverton 1959

CLASS 508 — BREL

Built: 1979–80 for use on Merseyrail network. Entered service on former Southern Region as 4-car units but reduced to 3-cars before being moved to Merseyside. Gangwayed within set.
System: 750 V DC third rail.
Original Formation: DMSO–TSO–TSO–BDMSO.
Revised Formation: DMSO–TSO–BDMSO.
Traction Motors: Four GEC G310AZ of 82.125 KW.
Maximum Speed: 75 mph.

Class 508/2. Formation DMSO–TSO–BDMSO.

DMSO	20.18 x 2.82 m	36.0 tonnes	–/66
TSO	20.18 x 2.82 m	26.5 tonnes	–/79
BDMSO	20.18 x 2.82 m	36.5 tonnes	–/74

64649	DMSO	(ex-unit 508 101– 508 201)	Emergency Services Training Centre, Seacombe	York 1979
64681	DMSO	(ex-unit 508 133– 508 212)	The Fire Service College, Moreton-in-Marsh	York 1980
64712	BDMSO	(ex-unit 508 121– 508 209)	Emergency Services Training Centre, Seacombe	York 1980
64724	BDMSO	(ex-unit 508 133– 508 212)	The Fire Service College, Moreton-in-Marsh	York 1980
71511	TSO	(ex-unit 508 133– 508 212)	The Fire Service College, Moreton-in-Marsh	York 1980

BATTERY EMU — BR DERBY/COWLAIRS TWIN UNIT

Built: 1958. Normal formation. BDMBSO–BDTCOL. Gangwayed within unit.
Power: 216 lead-acid cells of 1070 Ah.
Traction Motors: Two 100 kW Siemens nose-suspended motors.
Maximum Speed: 70 mph.

Vacuum brakes.

BDMBSO	18.49 x 2.79 m	37.5 tonnes	–/52
BDTCOL	18.49 x 2.79 m	32.5 tonnes	12/53 1T

79998–DB 975003		BDMBSO	Royal Deeside Railway	Derby/Cowlairs 1958
79999–DB 975004		BDTCOL	Royal Deeside Railway	Derby/Cowlairs 1958

5.11. EUROSTAR UNITS

CLASS 373

Eurostar units were built for high-speed services between Great Britain and Continental Europe via the Channel Tunnel. UK sets were originally owned by European Passenger Services, the division of British Rail responsible for Eurostar operations, with the others being owned by French Railways (SNCF) and Belgian Railways (SNCB/NMBS). In 1996, ownership of the UK sets passed to London & Continental Railways following the privatisation of British Rail.

Built: 1992–93. Full-length Eurostars were built as two 10-car half sets, with driving cars at the outer ends, which were intended to operate as pairs. The Regional Eurostars were built as 8-car half sets, again with driving cars at the outer ends, which ran as 16-car trains. 3308 never turned a wheel in passenger service and was mainly used for static trials.
Builders: GEC-Alsthom/Brush/ANF/De Dietrich/BN/ACEC.
Systems: 25 kV AC 50 Hz overhead/3000 V DC overhead.
Continuous Rating: 12240 kW (25 kV AC); 5700 kW (1500 and 3000 V DC).
Maximum Speed: 186 mph.

DM	22.15 x 2.81 m	68.5 tonnes	–/–
TBFO	21.85 x 2.81 m	39.4 tonnes	25/– 1T

Class 373/0. 10-car sets. Built for services from London to Continental Europe via the Channel Tunnel.
Formation: DM–MSO–4TSO–RB–2TFO–TBFO. Gangwayed within pair of units. Individual vehicles in each set were allocated numbers 373xxx0 + 373xxx1 + 373xxx2 + 373xxx3 + 373xxx4 + 373xxx5 + 373xxx6 + 373xxx7+ 373xxx8 + 373xxx9, but only DM vehicles carry numbers.

3101	DM	National College for Advanced Transport & Infrastructure, Doncaster	GEC-Alsthom 1993
3102	DM	HNRC, Worksop	GEC-Alsthom 1993
3106	DM	Haine Saint Pierre depot, Belgium	GEC-Alsthom 1993
3106-9	TBFO	Haine Saint Pierre depot, Belgium	GEC-Alsthom 1993

Class 373/2. 8-car sets. Built for Regional Eurostar services.
Formation: DM–MSO–3TSO–RB–TFO–TBFO. Gangwayed within pair of units. Individual vehicles in each set were allocated numbers 373xxx0 + 373xxx1 + 373xxx2 + 373xxx3 + 373xxx4 + 373xxx5 + 373xxx6 + 373xxx7 + 373xxx9, but only DM vehicles carry numbers.

3304	DM	Locomotive Storage, Margate	GEC-Alsthom 1996
3304-9	TBFO	Locomotive Storage, Margate	GEC-Alsthom 1996
3308	DM	National Railway Museum, York (N)	GEC-Alsthom 1996
3314	DM	Temple Mills Depot, London	GEC-Alsthom 1995

3314 carries the name ENTENTE CORDIALE.

6. GRIMSBY & IMMINGHAM LIGHT RAILWAY TRAMWAY CARS

The trams listed in this section saw service on the Grimsby & Immingham Light Railway, which was built by the Great Central Railway primarily to transport workers to the docks at Immingham.

GREAT CENTRAL RAILWAY LIGHT RAILWAY TRAM

Built: 1915 by GCR Dukinfield.
Type: Single deck tram.
Motors: 2 x Dick Kerr DK9 of 37 kW (50 hp).
Bogies: Brush.
Seats: 64 + 8 tip-up.

14	Crich Tramway Village	GCR Dukinfield 1915

GATESHEAD & DISTRICT TRAMWAYS COMPANY LIGHT RAILWAY TRAM

Built: 1925 and 1927. Built for Gateshead & District Tramways Company. Sold to British Railways in 1951 for use on Grimsby & Immingham Light Railway.
Type: Single deck tram.
Motors: 2 x Dick Kerr 31A of 18 kW (25 hp) (* 26 kW (35 hp)).
Bogies: Brill 39E.
Seats: 48.

BR	Gateshead		
20	5	Crich Tramway Village	Gateshead & District Tramways Co. 1927
26 *	10	Beamish: The Living Museum of the North	Gateshead & District Tramways Co. 1925

APPENDIX I. LIST OF LOCATIONS

The following is a list of preservation sites and operating railways in Great Britain where locomotives and multiple units included in this book can be found, together with Ordnance Survey grid references. At certain locations locomotives and rolling stock may be dispersed at several sites, in such cases the principal location where locomotives can normally be found is given. Enquiries at this location will normally reveal the whereabouts of other locomotives or rolling stock, but this is not guaranteed.

§ denotes a site not generally open to the public.

	OS GRID REF
Airedale General Hospital, Skipton Road, Steeton, Keighley, West Yorkshire.	SE 025444
Allelys Heavy Haulage, The Slough, Studley, Warwickshire.§	SP 057637
Aln Valley Railway, Lloyds Field, Lionheart Industrial Estate, Alnwick, Northumberland.	NU 200122
Andrew Briddon Locomotives, Station Goods Yard, Darley Dale, Derbyshire.§	SK 273627
Apple Mount Retreat, Thorpe Morieux, Suffolk.	TL 923520
Appleby-Frodingham RPS, British Steel, Appleby-Frodingham Works, Scunthorpe, Lincolnshire.	SE 913109
Arlington Fleet Services, Eastleigh Works, Campbell Road, Eastleigh, Hampshire.§	SU 457185
Avanti West Coast Talent Academy, Tatton House, Crewe Business Park, Westmere Drive, Crewe, Cheshire.§	SJ 719549
Avon Valley Railway, Bitton Station, Bitton, Gloucestershire.	ST 670705
Aysgarth Station, Carperby, North Yorkshire.§	SE 012889
Balbuthie Farm, Kilconquhar, Leven, Fife.§	NO 502019
Barrow Hill Roundhouse, Campbell Drive, Staveley, Chesterfield, Derbyshire.	SK 414755
Barry Tourist Railway, Station Approach Road, Barry Island, Vale of Glamorgan.§	ST 118667
Battlefield Line, Shackerstone Station, Shackerstone, Leicestershire.	SK 379066
Beamish: The Living Museum of the North, Beamish Hall, Beamish, County Durham.	NZ 217547
Bluebell Railway, Sheffield Park, near Uckfield, East Sussex.	TQ 403238
Bo'ness & Kinneil Railway, Bo'ness Station, Union Street, Bo'ness, Falkirk.	NT 003817
Bodmin Railway, Bodmin General Station, Harleigh Road, Bodmin, Cornwall.	SX 074664
Bressingham Steam Museum, Bressingham Hall, near Diss, Norfolk.	TM 080806
Buckinghamshire Railway Centre, Quainton Road Station, Aylesbury, Buckinghamshire.	SP 736189
Caledonian Railway, Brechin Station, Brechin, near Montrose, Angus.	NO 603603
Cambi UK, Radnor Park Industrial Estate, Congleton, Cheshire.§	SJ 847637
Cambrian Heritage Railways, Llynclys Station, Llynclys, near Oswestry, Shropshire.	SJ 284239
Cambrian Heritage Railways, Oswestry Station Yard, Oswestry, Shropshire.	SJ 294297
Carriages of Cambridge, Capability Barns, Huntingdon Road, Fen Drayton, Cambridgeshire.	TL 327679
Cefn Coed Colliery Museum, Old Blaenant Colliery, Cryant, Neath, Port Talbot.	SN 786034
Chasewater Railway, Chasewater Pleasure Park, Brownhills, Staffordshire.	SK 034070
Chinnor & Princes Risborough Railway, Chinnor Station, Chinnor, Oxfordshire.	SP 756002
Cholsey & Wallingford Railway, St John's Road, Wallingford, Oxfordshire.	SU 600891
Chrysalis Rail, Landore Depot, Plasmarl, Swansea.§	SS 658952
Churnet Valley Railway, Cheddleton Station, Cheddleton, Leek, Staffordshire.	SJ 983519
Class G5 Locomotive Company, Unit 8S, Hackworth Industrial Park, Shildon.	NZ 223255
Colne Valley Railway, Castle Hedingham Station, Halstead, Essex.	TL 774362
Corby & District Model Railway Society, Quarry Close, off Kelvin Grove, Corby.§	SP 891893
Cranfield Safety & Accident Investigation Centre, University Way, Cranfield Technology Park, Cranfield, Bedfordshire.§	SP 938422
Crewe Heritage Centre, Vernon Way, Crewe, Cheshire.	SJ 708552
Crich Tramway Village, Crich, near Matlock, Derbyshire.	SK 345549
CTL Seal, Butterthwaite Lane, Ecclesfield, Sheffield, South Yorkshire.§	SK 364940
Danum Gallery, Library & Museum, Waterdale, Doncaster, South Yorkshire.	SE 577030
Darlington Locomotive Works, Bonomi Way, Darlington, County Durham.	NZ 288158
Dartmoor Railway, Okehampton Station, Station Road, Okehampton, Devon.	SX 592944
Dartmouth Steam Railway, Queen's Park Station, Paignton, Devon.	SX 889606
Dean Forest Railway, Norchard, near Lydney, Gloucestershire.	SO 629044
Denbigh & Mold Junction Railway, Sodom, near Bodfari, Denbighshire, Wales.§	SJ 103711
Derwent Valley Light Railway, Yorkshire Museum of Farming, Murton, York, N Yorks.	SE 650524
Didcot Railway Centre (Great Western Society), Didcot, Oxfordshire.	SU 524906
D Site, Graven Hill, Ambrosden, Bicester.§	SP 585198
East Anglian Railway Museum, Chappel & Wakes Colne Station, Essex.	TL 898289

East Kent Railway, Shepherdswell, Kent.	TR 258483
East Lancashire Railway, Bolton Street Station, Bury, Greater Manchester.	SD 803109
East Somerset Railway, Cranmore Station, Shepton Mallet, Somerset.	ST 664429
Eastern Rail Services, Yarmouth Vauxhall Carriage Sidings, Acle New Road, Great Yarmouth, Norfolk.§	TG 516087
Ecclesbourne Valley Railway, Wirksworth Station, Wirksworth, Derbyshire.	SK 289542
Eden Valley Railway, Warcop Station, Warcop, Cumbria.	NY 753156
Elliott Group, Inverurie Mills, Port Elphinstone, Inverurie.§	NJ 780192
Embsay & Bolton Abbey Railway, Embsay Station, Embsay, Skipton, North Yorks.	SE 007533
Emergency Services Training Centre, East Street, Seacombe, Birkenhead, Merseyside.§	SJ 324904
Epping Ongar Railway, Ongar Station, Station Road, Chipping Ongar, Essex.	TL 552035
Fagley Primary School, Falsgrave Avenue, Fagley, Bradford, West Yorkshire.§	SE 186348
Fawley Hill Railway, Fawley Green, near Henley-on-Thames, Buckinghamshire.§	SU 755861
Flour Mill Workshop, Bream, Forest of Dean, Gloucestershire.§	SO 604067
Foxfield Railway, Blythe Bridge, Stoke-on-Trent, Staffordshire.	SJ 976446
Garw Valley Railway, Pontycymer Locomotive Works, Old Station Yard, Pontycymer, Bridgend, Mid Glamorgan.	SS 904914
Glasgow Riverside Museum, Pointhouse Quay, Yorkshill, Glasgow.	NS 557661
Gloucestershire Warwickshire Railway, Toddington Station, Gloucestershire.	SP 049321
Grantown-on-Spey East Station, Grantown-on-Spey, Highland.	NJ 037262
Great Central Railway, Loughborough Central Station, Loughborough, Leicestershire.	SK 543194
Great Central Railway (Nottingham), Mere Way, Ruddington, Nottinghamshire.	SK 575322
Gwendraeth Valley Railway, former Coed Bach Washery, Kidwelly, Carmarthenshire.§	SE 025444
Gwili Railway, Bronwydd Arms Station, Carmarthen, Carmarthenshire.	SN 417236
Harry Needle Railroad Company, Worskop Traincare Depot, Nottinghamshire.§	SK 580799
Head of Steam, Darlington Railway Museum, North Road Station, Hopetown, Darlington, County Durham.	NZ 289157
Helston Railway, Prospidnick, near Helston, Cornwall.	SW 645313
Hever Station, Hever, Kent.§	TQ 465445
Hitachi Rail Europe, Newton Aycliffe, County Durham.§	NZ 267220
Honeybourne Airfield Industrial Estate, Honeybourne, near Evesham, Worcestershire.§	SP 115422
Hope Farm, Sellindge, near Ashford, Kent.§	TR 119388
House of Chilli, Holliers Farm, Branstone, near Sandown, Isle of Wight.	SZ 554836
Hydraulic House, West Bank, Sutton Bridge, near Spalding, Lincolnshire.§	TF 479209
Hydrus Group, Brechin Business Park, Brechin, Angus.§	NO 582604
Independent Rail Engineering, Stagecoach Chesterfield Depot, Stonegravels Lane, Chesterfield, Derbyshire.§	SK 383721
Isle of Wight Steam Railway, Havenstreet Station, Isle of Wight.	SZ 556898
Keighley & Worth Valley Railway, Haworth, near Keighley, West Yorkshire.	SE 034371
Keith & Dufftown Railway, Dufftown, Moray.	NJ 323414
Kent & East Sussex Railway, Tenterden Town Station, Tenterden, Kent.	TQ 882336
Kirk Merrington Primary School, South View, Kirk Merrington, Spennymoor, County Durham.§	NZ 262310
Knottingley Depot, Spawd Bone Lane, Knottingley, West Yorkshire.§	SE 493235
Lakeside & Haverthwaite Railway, Haverthwaite, Cumbria.	SD 349843
Last Moorings, East Fen Lane, Stickney, Boston, Lincolnshire.§	TF 352566
Lavender Line, Isfield Station, Station Road, Isfield, East Sussex.	TQ 452171
Leaky Finders, Station Road, Hele, nr Exeter, Devon.§	SS 997020
Leicestershire County Museum store, former Snibston Colliery, Coalville, Leics.§	SK 420144
Lincolnshire Wolds Railway, Ludborough Station, Ludborough, Lincolnshire.	TF 309960
Llanelli & Mynydd Mawr Railway, Cynheidre, near Llanelli, Carmarthenshire.	SN 495071
Llanelli Railway Goods Shed Trust, Llanelli Station, Carmarthenshire.	SS 510993
Llangollen & Corwen Railway, Llangollen Station, Llangollen, Denbighshire.	SJ 211423
Locomotive Maintenance Services, Bakewell Road, Loughborough, Leicestershire.§	SK 526214
Locomotive Storage, Old Hornby Factory, Westwood, Margate, Kent.§	TR 362685
London & North Western Railway Heritage Company, Crewe, Cheshire.§	SJ 712543
London Transport Depot Museum, Gunnersby Lane, Acton, Greater London.	TQ 194799
London Underground, Ruislip Depot, Ruislip, London.§	TQ 094862
Longstowe Station, near Bourn, Cambridgeshire.§	TL 315546
Mangapps Railway Museum, Southminster Road, Burnham-on-Crouch, Essex.	TQ 944980
McArthurGlen Designer Outlet Swindon, Kemble Drive, Swindon, Wiltshire.	SU 142849
Metropolitan Police Specialist Training Centre, Mark Lane, Gravesend, Kent.§	TQ 672740
Merseyside Transport Trust, Osprey Place, Guys Industrial Estate North, Burscough, Lancashire.§	SD 428108

Mid Hants Railway, Ropley Station, Ropley, Hampshire.	SU 629324
Mid Norfolk Railway, Dereham Station, East Dereham, Norfolk.	TF 994131
Mid Suffolk Light Railway, Brockford Green, Wetheringsett, near Stowmarket, Suffolk	TM 128659
Middleton Railway, Tunstall Road, Hunslet, Leeds, West Yorkshire.	SE 305310
Midland Railway-Butterley, Butterley Station, near Ripley, Derbyshire.	SK 403520
Mizens Railway, Barrs Lane, Knaphill, Woking, Surrey.	TQ 966595
Moreton Park Railway, Moreton-on-Lugg, near Hereford, Herefordshire.§	SO 503467
Mountsorrel & Rothley Community Heritage Centre, Swithland Lane, Mountsorrel, Leicestershire.	SK 571140
Museum of Liverpool, Pier Head, Liverpool, Merseyside.	SJ 339900
Museum of Liverpool Store, Juniper Street, Bootle, Merseyside.§	SJ 343935
National College for Advanced Transport & Infrastructure, Carolina Way, Doncaster, South Yorkshire.§	SE 593012
National Railway Museum, Leeman Road, York, North Yorkshire.	SE 594519
National Railway Museum, Shildon, County Durham.	NZ 238256
NELPG, 1861 Shed, Whessoe Road, Darlington, County Durham.§	NZ 288157
Neath Port Talbot Youth Justice Service, BASE 15, Neath Abbey Industrial Estate, Neath Abbey, Port Talbot.§	SS 734973
Nemesis Rail, Old Wagon Works, Burton-on-Trent, Staffordshire.§	SK 251245
Nene Valley Railway, Wansford Station, Peterborough, Cambridgeshire.	TL 093979
NL Engineering (North West), c/o Advance Scaffolding, Blackrod Industrial Estate, Scot Lane, Blackrod, near Bolton, Greater Manchester.§	SD 623089
North Dorset Railway Trust, St Patricks Industrial Estate, Station Road, Shillingstone, Blandford Forum, Dorset.	ST 824117
North Norfolk Railway, Sheringham Station, Norfolk.	TG 156430
North Side Works, Malton Road, Leavening, near Malton, North Yorkshire.§	SE 784637
North Yorkshire Moors Railway, Grosmont Station, North Yorkshire.	NZ 828049
Northampton & Lamport Railway, Pitsford, Northamptonshire.	SP 736666
Northamptonshire Ironstone Railway, Hunsbury Hill, Northampton, Northamptonshire.	SP 735584
Northern Steam Engineering, Ross Road, Lonsdale House, Stockton-on-Tees.§	NZ 457200
Oaklands, Toprow, Norfolk.§	TM 170978
Oracle UK, Oracle Parkway, Thames Valley Park, Reading, Berkshire.§	SU 738739
Peak Rail, Rowsley South Station, near Matlock, Derbyshire.	SK 262642
Platform 1, Huddersfield Station, St George's Square, Huddersfield.§	SE 142168
Plym Valley Railway, Marsh Mills, Plymouth, Devon.	SX 520571
Pontypool & Blaenavon Railway, Furnace Sidings, Garn Yr Erw, Blaenavon, Torfaen.	SO 237093
Poulton & Wyre Railway, Hillhouse Business Park, Thornton, Lancashire.§	SD 342437
Railway Support Services, Rye Farm, Ryefield Lane, Wishaw, Sutton Coldfield, Warwickshire.§	SP 180944
Railway Technical Centre, RTC Business Park, London Road, Derby.§	SK 366347
Reid Freight Services, Cinderhill Industrial Estate, Stoke-on-Trent.§	SJ 925435
Reid Freight Services, Cockshute Sidings, Shelton New Road, Stoke-on-Trent.§	SJ 871464
Ribble Steam Railway, off Chain Caul Road, Riversway, Preston, Lancashire.	SD 504295
Riley & Son (Electromec), Premier Locomotive Works, Sefton Street, Heywood, Greater Manchester.§	SE 865103
Rother Valley Railway, Robertsbridge Station Yard, Robertsbridge, East Sussex.	TQ 734236
Royal Deeside Railway, Milton, Crathes, Banchory, Aberdeenshire.	NO 743962
Rushden Transport Museum & Railway, Rectory Road, Rushden, Northamptonshire.	SP 957672
Science & Industry Museum, Liverpool Road, Castlefield, Greater Manchester.	SJ 831978
Science Museum, Imperial Institute Road, South Kensington, London.	TQ 268793
Science Museum Store, Wroughton, near Swindon, Wiltshire.§	SU 131790
Scolton Manor Park, Scolton Manor, Haverfordwest, Pembrokeshire.	SM 991222
Severn Valley Railway, Bridgnorth Station, Shropshire.	SO 715926
Siemens Mobility, Tom Pudding Way, Goole, East Riding of Yorkshire.§	SE 731232
Somerset & Dorset Railway Heritage Trust, Midsomer Norton Station, Silver Street, Midsomer Norton, Somerset.	ST 664937
Somerset & Dorset Steam, c/o John Weavers Yard, The Hailey Centre, Holton Road, Holton Heath Trading Park, Poole.§	SY 948905
Sonic Rail Services, Springfield Industrial Estate, Burnham-on-Crouch, Essex.§	TQ 942964
Source Farm Shop, Hungerford Park, Hungerford, Berkshire.§	SU 350676
South Devon Railway, Buckfastleigh, Devon.	SX 747663
South Wales Police Training Centre, Waterton Road, Bridgend, Mid Glamorgan.§	SS 920785
Southall Depot, Southall, Greater London.§	TQ 133798
Spa Valley Railway, Tunbridge Wells West Station, Tunbridge Wells, Kent.	TQ 578385

St Leonards Railway Engineering, West Marina Depot, Bridge Way, St Leonards, East Sussex.§	TQ 778086
Stainmore Railway, Kirkby Stephen East Station, Kirkby Stephen, Cumbria.	NY 769075
Statfold Engineering, The Sidings, Statfold Barn Farm, Ashby Road, Tamworth.	SK 239064
Station Railway Heritage Centre, Station Road, Sandford, Winscombe, Somerset.	ST 416595
Station Yard, The Causeway, Stow Bridge, King's Lynn, Norfolk.§	TF 606070
STEAM – Museum of the Great Western Railway, Old No. 20 Shop, Old Swindon Works, Kemble Drive, Swindon, Wiltshire.	SU 143849
Stephenson Steam Railway, Middle Engine Lane, West Chirton, Tyne & Wear.	NZ 323693
Stewarts Lane Depot, Dickens Street, Nine Elms, Greater London.§	TQ 288766
Strathspey Railway, Aviemore Station, Dalfaber Road, Highland.	NH 898131
Strawberry Hill Depot, Twickenham, Greater London.§	TQ 154720
Summerlee Museum of Scottish Industrial Life, West Canal Street, Coatbridge, North Lanarkshire.	NS 728655
Sussex Police Training Centre, Kingstanding, Maresfield, near Crowborough, East Sussex.§	TQ 476291
Swanage Railway, Swanage Station, Swanage, Dorset.	SZ 028789
Swindon & Cricklade Railway, Blunsden Road Station, Swindon, Wiltshire.	SU 110897
Tanat Valley Light Railway, Nantmawr, near Llanyblodwel, Shropshire.	SJ 253243
Tanfield Railway, Marley Hill Engine Shed, Sunniside, Tyne & Wear.	NZ 207573
Tarka Valley Railway, Torrington Station, Great Torrington, Devon.	SS 480197
Telford Steam Railway, Bridge Road, Horsehay, Telford, Shropshire.	SJ 675073
Temple Mills Depot (Eurostar), Leyton, Greater London.§	TQ 371864
The Dales School – Blythedale, Cowpen Road, Blyth, Northumberland.§	NZ 287816
The Fire Service College, London Road, Moreton-in-Marsh, Gloucestershire.§	SP 222323
The Old Ambulance Station, Bexhill, East Sussex.	TQ 737078
The Old Station Guest House, Stravithie Station, Stravithie, near St Andrews, Fife.	NO 533134
The Old Station Hub, Station Road, Talybont-on-Usk, Powys.	SO 117228
The Shires Removal Group, The Depository, Hoyle Mill Road, Kinsley, Pontefract.§	SE 422145
Thinktank Birmingham Science Museum, Millennium Point, Curzon Street, Birmingham.	SP 079873
Thomas Muir (Rosyth), Port of Rosyth, Dunfermline, Scotland.§	NT 100822
Tiverton Museum, St Andrew's Street, Tiverton, Devon.	SS 955124
Tyseley Locomotive Works, Warwick Road, Tyseley, Birmingham.§	SP 105841
UK Rail Leasing, Leicester TMD, Beal Street, Leicester.§	SK 597044
UK Rail Leasing, Gordon Road, Loughborough, Leicestershire.§	SK 541210
Vale of Berkeley Railway, The Engine Shed, Dock Road, Sharpness, Gloucestershire.§	SO 667023
Vale of Rheidol Railway, Aberystwyth, Ceredigion.	SN 587812
Vincent Engineering, Styles Farm Workshop, Henstridge, Somerset.§	ST 749203
Warner Brothers Studio Tour, Studio Tour Drive, Leavesden, Hertfordshire.	TL 095005
Waverley Route Heritage Association, Whitrope, near Hawick, Scottish Borders.	NT 527005
Weardale Railway, Wolsingham, County Durham.	NZ 081370
Wensleydale Railway, Leeming Bar Station, Leeming Bar, North Yorkshire.	SE 286900
West Coast Railway Company, Warton Road, Carnforth, Lancashire.§	SD 496708
West Somerset Railway, Minehead Station, Minehead, Somerset.	SS 975463
Whistlestop Valley Railway, *(previously the Kirklees Light Railway)*, Clayton West, near Huddersfield, West Yorkshire.	SE 258112
Whitstable Community Museum & Gallery, Oxford Street, Whitstable, Kent.	TR 107662
Whitwell & Reepham Station, near Alysham, Norfolk.	TG 091217
Yeovil Railway Centre, Yeovil Junction, near Yeovil, Somerset.	ST 571141

PLATFORM 5 MAIL ORDER
www.platform5.com

WATERLOO TO THE ATLANTIC COAST DURING THE DIESEL ERA
Part 1: Waterloo to Exeter Central

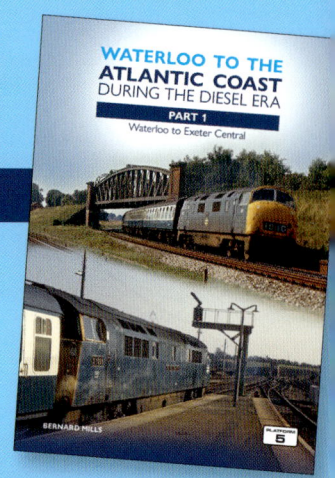

A wonderful selection of colour images dating back as far as the mid-1960s. Features Warship, Hymek and Western classes, plus plenty of diesel-electric classes including some rare visitors. Very detailed captions and personal anecdotes outline the history of the route with a focus on the time when diesel-hauled trains were the order of the day.

RAILWAYS OF CORNWALL: A Decade of Change
Part 1: The Cornish Main Line: Saltash to Penzance

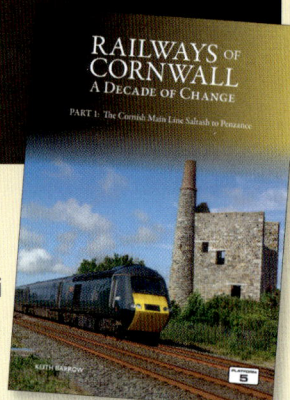

Keith Barrow records the picturesque Cornish Mail Line during a time of great transition, capturing classic and modern traction types in a breathtaking railway landscape. Features BR era rolling stock, mechanical signalling, and the unique china clay operations, as well as modern Hitachi IET trains and bulk freight operations. Contains over 150 top quality images, all with extended captions telling the story of Cornwall's Main Line and its trains.

Both books contain 96 pages, A4 size, published 2024.
Cover Prices £21.95 each. Mail Order Prices £19.95 each plus P&P.
If ordering from www.platform5.com use the promotion codes **WACDE** and **RCDC** at the basket.

ORDER BY POST, TELEPHONE OR AT www.platform5.com

POSTAGE & PACKING: 10% UK; 30% Europe; 50% Rest of World. Cheques payable to Platform 5 Publishing Ltd.

Mail Order Department (PL), Platform 5 Publishing Ltd,
52 Broadfield Road, SHEFFIELD, S8 0XJ, ENGLAND. Tel: 0114 255 8000

APPENDIX II. ABBREVIATIONS USED

AD	Alexandra Docks & Railway Company
AD	Army Department of the Ministry of Defence
BP	BP (formerly British Petroleum)
BPGVR	Burry Port & Gwendraeth Valley Railway
BR	British Railways
BTH	British Thomson Houston
CARR	Cardiff Railway
CFD	Compagnie de Chemin de Fer Départementaux
CR	Caledonian Railway
DEMU	Diesel Electric Multiple Unit
DMU	Diesel Multiple Unit
EKR	East Kent Railway
EMU	Electric Multiple Unit
FR	Furness Railway
FS	Ferrovie dello Stato (Italian State Railways)
GCR	Great Central Railway
GER	Great Eastern Railway
GJR	Grand Junction Railway
GNR	Great Northern Railway
GNSR	Great North of Scotland Railway
GSWR	Glasgow & South Western Railway
GVR	Gwendraeth Valley Railway
GWR	Great Western Railway
H&B	Hull & Barnsley Railway
HNRC	Harry Needle Railroad Company
HR	Highland Railway
HSDT	High Speed Diesel Train
HST	High Speed Train
L&MR	Liverpool & Manchester Railway
L&Y	Lancashire & Yorkshire Railway
LBSCR	London, Brighton & South Coast Railway
LCDR	London, Chatham & Dover Railway
LER	London Electric Railway
LMS	London Midland & Scottish Railway
LNER	London & North Eastern Railway
LNWR	London & North Western Railway
LPTB	London Passenger Transport Board
LSWR	London & South Western Railway
LTE	London Transport Executive
LTSR	London Tilbury & Southend Railway
MAV	Hungarian Railways
MoD	Ministry of Defence
MR	Midland Railway
MS&LR	Manchester, Sheffield & Lincolnshire Railway
MSJ&A	Manchester South Junction & Altrincham Railway
MT	Mixed Traffic
(N)	Locomotive or multiple unit vehicle that forms part of the National Collection.
NBR	North British Railway
NER	North Eastern Railway
NLR	North London Railway
NMBS	Belgian State Railways
NP&FR	North Pembroke & Fishguard Railway
NS	Nederlandse Spoorwegen (Netherlands Railways)
NSR	North Staffordshire Railway
P&M	Powlesland & Mason
PKP	Polish Railways
PTR	Port Talbot Railway
RA	Route Availability
ROD	Railway Operating Department
SBB	Swiss Federal Railways
SDJR	Somerset & Dorset Joint Railway
SDR	South Devon Railway
SECR	South Eastern & Chatham Railway
SER	South Eastern Railway
SJ	Swedish State Railways
SNCB	Belgian State Railways
SNCF	French State Railways
SPR	Sandy & Potton Railway
SR	Southern Railway
TCDD	Türkiye Cumhuryeti Devlet Demiryollan (Turkish Railways)
TVR	Taff Vale Railway
UIC	International Union of Railways
USATC	United States Army Transportation Corps
WD	War Department
WR	British Railways Western Region
WT	Wantage Tramway

APPENDIX III. WEIGHTS & MEASUREMENTS

The following abbreviations are used to denote units of measurement throughout this book.

AC	Alternating current
DC	Direct current
hp	Horse power
Hz	Hertz
kN	Kilonewtons
km/h	Kilometres per hour
kW	Kilowatts
lbf	Pounds force
lbf/sq in.	Pounds force per square inch
m	Metres
mm	Millimetres
mph	Miles per hour
rpm	Revolutions per minute
V	Volts

APPENDIX IV. DMU, DEMU & EMU TYPE CODES

The former BR operating departments used a series of Type Codes to describe the various types of multiple unit in service. Type Codes used to describe the various types of diesel, diesel-electric and electric multiple unit vehicles are listed here. These have been used in Sections 5.5–5.11.

Brake vehicles contain luggage space and a guard's/conductor's compartment.

Second is now known as Standard and before 1956 was referred to as Third.

BDMBSO	Battery Driving Motor Brake Second Open
BDMS	Battery Driving Motor Standard
BDMSO	Battery Driving Motor Standard Open
BDTBS	Battery Driving Trailer Brake Second (non-gangwayed)
BDTBSO	Battery Driving Trailer Brake Second Open
BDTCOL	Battery Driving Trailer Composite Open with Lavatory
BDTCsoL	Battery Driving Trailer Composite semi-open with Lavatory
BDTSO	Battery Driving Trailer Second Open
BDTSOL	Battery Driving Trailer Second Open with Lavatory
DM	Driving Motor
DMBC	Driving Motor Brake Composite
DMBS	Driving Motor Brake Second
DMBSK	Driving Motor Brake Second side corridor with Lavatory
DMBSL	Driving Motor Brake Second with Lavatory
DMBSO	Driving Motor Brake Second Open
DMC	Driving Motor Composite
DMCL	Driving Motor Composite with Lavatory
DMLV	Driving Motor Luggage Van
DMPBSOL	Driving Motor Pullman Brake Second Open with Lavatory
DMPMV	Driving Motor Parcels & Miscellaneous Van
DMRFO	Driving Motor First Open
DMS	Driving Motor Second
DMSL	Driving Motor Second with Lavatory
DMSO	Driving Motor Second Open
DTBSO	Driving Trailer Brake Second Open
DTC	Driving Trailer Composite
DTCK	Driving Trailer Composite side corridor
DTCL	Driving Trailer Composite with Lavatory
DTCO	Driving Trailer Composite Open
DTCOL	Driving Trailer Composite Open with Lavatory
DTCsoL	Driving Trailer Composite semi-open with Lavatory
DTPMV	Driving Trailer Parcels & Miscellaneous Van
DTS	Driving Trailer Second
DTSL	Driving Trailer Second with Lavatory
DTSO	Driving Trailer Second Open
DTSOL	Driving Trailer Second Open with Lavatory
DTSso	Driving Trailer Second semi-open
DTSsoL	Driving Trailer Second semi-open with Lavatory
M	Motor
MBS	Motor Brake Second
MBSK	Motor Brake Second side corridor with Lavatory
MBSO	Motor Brake Second Open
MBSOL	Motor Brake Second Open with Lavatory
MS	Motor Second (non-gangwayed)
MSO	Motor Second Open
PTS	Pantograph Trailer Standard
PTSRMB	Pantograph Trailer Standard Buffet
TBCK	Trailer Brake Composite side corridor with Lavatory
TBFOL	Trailer Brake First Open with Lavatory
TBSK	Trailer Brake Second side corridor with Lavatory

TBSL	Trailer Brake Second with Lavatory
TBSO	Trailer Brake Second Open
TC	Trailer Composite
TCK	Trailer Composite side corridor with Lavatory
TCL	Trailer Composite with Lavatory
TCO	Trailer Composite Open
TCsoL	Trailer Composite semi-open with Lavatory
TFK	Trailer First side corridor with Lavatory
TFOL	Trailer First Open with Lavatory
TPCK	Trailer Pullman Composite side corridor with Lavatory
TPFKOL	Trailer Pullman First Kitchen open with Lavatory
TPSOL	Trailer Pullman Second open with Lavatory
TRCBL	Trailer Composite with Buffet and Lavatory
TRCsoBL	Trailer semi-open Composite with Buffet and Lavatory
TRSB	Trailer Second Buffet
TRSBL	Trailer Second Buffet with Lavatory
TRSKB	Trailer Second with Kitchen and Buffet
TRUB	Trailer Unclassified Buffet
TS	Trailer Second
TSK	Trailer Second side corridor with Lavatory (seating in compartments)
TSL	Trailer Second with Lavatory
TSO	Trailer Second Open
TSOL	Trailer Second open with Lavatory
TSso	Trailer semi-open Second
TUOL	Trailer Unclassified Open with Lavatory

APPENDIX V. PRIVATE MANUFACTURER CODES

The following codes are used to denote private locomotive manufacturers. These are followed by the works number and build year, eg AW 1360/1937 – built by Armstrong-Whitworth and Company, works number 1360, year 1937. Unless otherwise shown, locations are in England.

AB	Andrew Barclay, Sons & Company, Caledonia Works, Kilmarnock, Scotland.
ABB	ASEA Brown Boveri
AC	AC Cars, Thames Ditton, Surrey.
AE	Avonside Engine Company, Bristol, Avon.
AEC	Associated Equipment Company, Southall, Berkshire.
AL	American Locomotive Company, USA.
Alan Keef	Alan Keef, Ross-on-Wye, Herefordshire.
AW	Armstrong-Whitworth & Company, Newcastle, Tyne & Wear.
BBC	Brown-Boveri et Cie, Switzerland.
BCK	Bury, Curtis & Kennedy, Liverpool, Merseyside.
BE	Brush Electrical Engineering Company, Loughborough, Leicestershire.
Bluebell Railway	Bluebell Railway, Sheffield Park, East Sussex.
BLW	Baldwin Locomotive Works, Philadelphia, Pennsylvania, USA.
BMR	Brecon Mountain Railway Company, Pant, Merthyr Tydfil, Wales.
BP	Beyer Peacock and Company, Gorton, Manchester.
BRCW	Birmingham Railway Carriage & Wagon Company, Smethwick, Birmingham.
BREL	British Rail Engineering Ltd (later BREL, then ABB, now Alstom).
BTH	British Thomson-Houston Company, Rugby, Warwickshire.
BUT	British United Traction
CAF	Construcciones y Auxiliar de Ferrocarriles, Zaragoza, Spain.
CE	Clayton Equipment Company, Hatton, Derbyshire.
Cravens	Cravens, Darnall, Sheffield, South Yorkshire.
Darlington Hope Street	A1 Steam Trust, Darlington Hope Street, Darlington, County Durham.
Didcot	Great Western Society, Didcot Railway Centre, Didcot, Oxfordshire.

DC	Drewry Car Company, London.
DK	Dick Kerr & Company, Preston, Lancashire.
Dodman	Alfred Dodman & Company, Highgate Works, Kings Lynn, Norfolk.
EE	English Electric Company, Bradford and Preston.
Embsay	Embsay & Bolton Abbey Railway, Embsay, Skipton, North Yorkshire.
EP	Electroputere, Craiova, Romania.
FW	Fox, Walker & Company, Atlas Engine Works, Bristol.
Gateshead & District Tramways Co	Sunderland Road Works, Gateshead, Tyne & Wear.
GCR Dukinfield	Great Central Railway Carriage & Wagon Works, Dukinfield, Tameside, Greater Manchester.
GE	George England & Company, Hatcham Ironworks, London.
GEC-Alsthom	GEC-Alsthom, Saltley, Birmingham.
GRCW	Gloucester Railway Carriage & Wagon Company, Gloucester, Glous.
Hack	Timothy Hackworth, Soho Works, Shildon, County Durham.
HC	Hudswell-Clarke & Company, Hunslet, Leeds, West Yorkshire.
HE	Hunslet Engine Company, Hunslet, Leeds, West Yorkshire.
HL	R&W Hawthorn, Leslie & Company, Forth Bank Works, Newcastle upon-Tyne.
K	Kitson & Company, Airedale Foundry, Hunslet, Leeds, West Yorks.
Kitching	A Kitching, Hope Town Foundry, Darlington, County Durham.
KS	Kerr Stuart & Company, California Works, Stoke-on-Trent, Staffs.
Leyland	British Leyland Lillyhall Works, Workington, Cumbria.
Lima	Lima Locomotive Works, Lima, Ohio, USA.
Llangollen	Llangollen Railway (now Llangollen & Corwen Railway), Llangollen, Clwyd, Wales.
Loco Ent	Locomotion Enterprises (1975), Bowes Railway, Springwell, Gateshead, Tyne & Wear.
Manchester	Museum of Science & Industry, Liverpool Road, Manchester.
MC	Metropolitan-Cammell Carriage & Wagon Company, Birmingham (Metro-Cammell).
MV	Metropolitan-Vickers, Trafford Park, Manchester.
N	Neilson & Son, Springburn Locomotive Works, Glasgow, Scotland.
NBL	North British Locomotive Company, Glasgow, Scotland.
NR	Neilson Reid & Company, Springburn Works, Glasgow, Scotland.
PR	Park Royal Vehicles, Park Royal, London.
PS	Pressed Steel, Swindon, Wiltshire.
Resco	Resco (Railways), Erith, London.
RH	Ruston & Hornsby, Lincoln.
RS	Robert Stephenson & Company, Newcastle-upon-Tyne, Tyne & Wear.
RSH	Robert Stephenson & Hawthorns, Darlington, County Durham.
RTC	Railway Technical Centre, Derby, Derbyshire.
S	Sentinel (Shrewsbury), Battlefield, Shrewsbury, Shropshire.
Sara	Sara & Company, Penryn, Cornwall.
Science Museum	Science Museum, South Kensington, London
Shildon	BREL Shildon Wagon Works, Shildon, County Durham.
SM	Siemens, London.
SS	Sharp Stewart & Sons, Manchester and then (1888) Glasgow, Scotland.
TKL	Todd, Kitson and Laird, Leeds, West Yorkshire.
Tyseley Locomotive Works	Tyseley Locomotive Works, Tyseley, Birmingham.
VF	Vulcan Foundry, Newton-le-Willows, Lancashire.
VIW	Vulcan Iron Works, Wilkes-Barre, Philadelphia, Pennsylvania, USA.
WB	WG Bagnall, Castle Engine Works, Stafford, Staffordshire.
Wkm	D Wickham & Company, Ware, Hertfordshire.
WMD	Waggon und Maschienenbau GmbH, Donauworth, Germany.
WSR	West Somerset Railway, Minehead, Somerset.
YE	Yorkshire Engine Company, Meadowhall, Sheffield, South Yorkshire.